THE I TATTI
RENAISSANCE LIBRARY

James Hankins, General Editor

PONTANO

BAIAE

ITRL 22

GIOVANNI GIOVIANO PONTANO
✦ ✦ ✦
BAIAE

TRANSLATED BY

RODNEY G. DENNIS

THE I TATTI RENAISSANCE LIBRARY

HARVARD UNIVERSITY PRESS

CAMBRIDGE, MASSACHUSETTS

LONDON, ENGLAND

2006

Series design by Dean Bornstein

Library of Congress Cataloging-in-Publication Data

Pontano, Giovanni Gioviano, 1426–1503.
[Baiae. English and Latin]
Baiae / Giovanni Gioviano Pontano ; translated by Rodney G. Dennis.
p. cm. — (The I Tatti Renaissance library ; 22)
Includes bibliographical references and index.
ISBN 0-674-02197-5 (cloth : alk. paper)
I. Dennis, Rodney G.   II. Title.   III. Series.
PA8570.P5 B35 2006
871'.04—dc22   2005056709

Contents

❧❧❧

Introduction

༅༅༅

In Umbria, in the town of Ceretto, some twenty-five miles south of Assisi, Giovanni Pontano was born, probably in 1429, although tradition places the date in 1426. He lived until 1503, having completed a life that was as manifold as it was consistent and astonishing, both in regard to achievement and to personality and character.[1] Over this lifetime he devoted himself to the affairs of the Kingdom of Naples, serving in important offices under five kings and managing to stay afloat during a French invasion. He was the foremost humanistic scholar-poet in a great age of humanism and he was an important scientist. He combined a deep devotion to his wife and family with the liveliest interest in large numbers of romantic alliances. He was never touched by scandal. He was friendly and humorous, utterly without rancor and universally trusted. His genius found its most definitive home in the production of short poems.

The seventy-one poems presented here, the *Two Books of Hendecasyllables or Baiae*, were composed during the last thirty years of his life, and they touch on all of the subjects mentioned and several more. They are about his friends, his royal patrons, his family and his girls, both serious and casual. They are about antiquity and the ancient writings he and his friends talked about and imitated. They deal in a great variety of ways with friendship and old age. Loss is dealt with generally through adumbration. Fulfillment is emphasized, the present, and pleasure. Most concern the great Neapolitan pleasure resort, Baiae. They are all written in the eleven-syllable meter known as Phalaecium, exemplified in English by Tennyson's poem *Hendecasyllabics*: "All composed in a metre of Catullus." The *Baiae* poems were published in 1505, two years after Pontano's death, both in Venice by Aldus and in Naples by

Pontano's great friend Pietro Summonte. In that book they have the title *Hendecasyllaborum seu Baiarum libri duo*.

In all the world there is the Bay of Naples, and on that bay is a shore "where shining Baiae pleases."[2] There are thermal springs and views of volcanoes; Cumae and Avernus provide alternate entrances to the Underworld. Cicero had a villa in Cumae. Vergil is buried nearby in Posillipo. In antiquity, wealthy Romans crowded the shore with their villas to the point, as Horace, remarked, that the sea was encroached upon.[3] Pleasure was available and stylish people misbehaved. Cicero upbraided Clodia Pulcher, Catullus's Lesbia, not just for her dinner parties and adulteries, but for her trips to Baiae.[4] This is the "myrtled shore" that Pontano and his friends frequented, powerfully aware that their pleasures were traditional and rooted in classical times.

The fact that the women who provided these pleasures were prostitutes, combined with the need to call them, if not Goddesses, at least Nymphs and Graces, lends a kind of social uncertainty to the arrangements. The men gave them names like Greciana, Thelesina and Venerilla, which seem casual and descriptive. Sometimes, however, the relationships are not casual. Pietro Summonte's girlfriend, Neera, appears three times in these poems and once in Pontano's long work *Eridanus*. In *De tumulis*, a collection of poems about graves, Summonte is seen as mourning at Neera's tomb.[5] Constantia (II.10) is not a prostitute. She is Constanza d'Avalos, of a noble family, and described elsewhere as a "Heliconian Goddess." Furthermore Baiae is not mentioned in that poem. Nevertheless, the reader cannot detect her rank from the way she is addressed. The poem to Alfonso, Duke of Calabria (I.16) describes making love to his Drusula with an unprecedented specificity. But Drusula is, almost certainly, Trusia Gazzella, who was the Duke's mistress and the mother of his son Alfonso. Again, it is easy to overlook the fact that Baiae is not mentioned in that poem either. Finally, there are instances of serious and lasting relationships which grew out of commercial liaisons. Fannia was important to Pontano. Stella, a courtesan Pontano met in Ferrara, was a major figure in his life and bore him a child. Focilla is mysterious. We shall return to this.

Of the seventy-one poems, forty are addressed to Pontano's male friends. Most of these friends were members of the celebrated literary society that came to be known as the Accademia Pontaniana in honor of its most important member. But Pontano was not its founder. That was Antonio Beccadelli, known in the society as "Panormita," the one from Palermo—they gave each other classicizing names—who started it under the auspices of King Alfonso I, the Magnanimous, shortly after Alfonso's final entry into Naples in 1442. The leadership of the Academy passed to Pontano in 1471 at Panormita's death. It was an informal conversation group of literati and friends. Pontano, who had acquired a classical middle name, Gioviano, described and embellished their conversations in his prose *Dialogues*. The dialogue *Antonius*, named for Beccadelli, takes place outdoors at the Portico Antoniano and starts out with a description of the leader: "Who is jollier when things go well and more graceful when times are difficult? And what an incredible power of language is his!"[6] The members were bound to each other by humor and good will as well as by learning, and these were traits that came to imbue Pontano's later hendecasyllabic poems. Two early members of the Academy were particularly important: Marino Tomacelli, to whom both books were dedicated, and Pietro Golino, known as Petrus Compater, who may have been Pontano's closest friend. Poem 28 of Book II celebrates 54 years of friendship, six times nine years for the three of them, tripled drinks and tripled love affairs. The poem has been dated 1501, the year of Compater's death, so their friendship in the Academy must have gone back to 1447.[7]

Of the friends mentioned in the *Libri hendecasyllaborum* (Beccadelli is not mentioned), none has been identified as being older than Pontano. Tomacelli was the same age, if we take 1429 as the date of Pontano's birth. Of the fifteen in Book I, eight were born on or before 1440. In Book II, of the additional men mentioned, none seems to have been older than Manlius Rallus who was born in 1447. Pontano was older than his friends, with the exception of Tomacelli; Compater was two years younger. But he addresses them almost always as though they were all old men together. He got along with the young. He jokes with them all, and he jokes with the nobility whom we have not yet mentioned. His intimacy with Alfonso, Duke of Calabria, who became king in 1495, is remarkable, not just because of the sexual detail he goes into in I.16, but far more for the way he makes fun of the Duke's little presents in I.32. Goethe, for all of his skill and adroitness, never addressed his Grossherzog in tones of such familiarity. The Duke's physician, called Galateo, almost twenty years Pontano's junior, is subjected to terrible ridicule for cutting a sorry figure in the baths — a poem closely modeled on Martial — but then he is allowed to take revenge.[8]

The jokes can really be compliments in disguise. Manilio Cabacio Rallo, called Manlius Rallus, born in Sparta, came to Italy in 1466 in flight from the Turks. The perfection of his Latin astonished everyone. Poliziano commented on it, and Gravina wrote a poem about it. Pontano dedicates a long poem to Rallus. He mentions Rallus's mistress, he speaks of his good Latin, referring to Rallus's poems and to his love for Propertius, and then he commends him to Venus's seven handmaidens, citing the traditional Graces, but adding four more with fanciful Greek names just bordering on the humorous. The result is flattery, but he sails, as he often does, quite close to the wind. And Rallus, a newcomer to the Academy, was almost twenty years his junior.[9]

Amid all the discussions of friendship, sexuality, old age and pleasure, the poet reveals himself as a family man, a husband and a father. He is, in fact, one of the greatest of all poets of married love, not that there are all that many of them. His earlier collection, *De amore coniugali* (*On married love*), deals exhaustively and amazingly with his wife, Ariane Sassone, whom he married in 1461, his three daughters and his son, Lucio, who was born last in 1469. The collection of *Neniae* or lullabies to Lucio, often in Latin baby talk, is simply unlike anything else. Ariane died in 1490, and Lucio died, at 29, in 1498. Pontano's devotion to them all seems consistent, and there appears to have been no secrecy or difficulties attending his sexual relations with the ladies at the baths. However, in 1483, in Ferrara on a diplomatic mission, Pontano encountered a very young woman who, as he later recalled, was standing on the banks of the river Po. He observed that when she turned her glance towards the river it burst into flames.[10] He called her Stella. She was apparently a courtesan, to use the polite word. He fell in love. The large collection of poems *Eridanus*, the Po, deals with Stella and with light and the brilliance of her eyes.

She appears only once in the hendecasyllabic poems. In I.28, her brilliance eclipses the sun, and her effect on Pontano is to cause his innards to melt, drop by drop, and the passage clearly echoes Catullus's lines (51.9–11):

> lingua sed torpet tenuis sub artus
>   flamma demanat, sonitu suopte
>   tintinant aures . . .

> but my words got jumbled and little flames went
> through my arms and legs, my ears began ringing . . .

This may be the first poem Catullus wrote to Lesbia, itself a translation from Sappho. Cicero, we recall, who did not intend to flatter, in speaking about Clodia Pulcher alludes to her *flagrantia oculorum*, her blazing eyes.[11]

xi

In respect to our text, Stella gives rise to certain problems. *Eridanus* II begins with a poem about Ariane's death. Pontano looks forward to joining her in the fields of Elysium, and, in fact, the last poem of our collection, which must be very late, expresses a happy confidence in this reunion. In *Eridanus* II, however, he states that in the meantime, in the interval between Ariane's death and his own, Stella will console him with her light and brilliance. Towards the end of our collection, II.29, "Ad Uxorem" ("To his Wife"), he berates his addressee with considerable bitterness for leaving him.

> Oblita es thalami torique nostri,
> o fallax senii mei levamen,
> connubii immemor immemorque amorum.

> Unmindful of our bedroom and our bed,
> Of my old age deceitful consolation,
> Forgetful of our promises and loves.

His language, as it often does, brings classical authority before us with great vividness, here Catullus 64 (lines 135, 139): "immemor . . . at non haec quondam blanda promissa dedisti?" ("Unmindful . . . But did you not give sweet vows once?"). Also the lines in *Aeneid* IV that doubtless derive from Catullus. It is a tone Pontano does not use elsewhere with his wife, and it is significant, perhaps, that the broken marriages in Catullus and Vergil were not real marriages but rather misinterpreted understandings. We recall that Dido mistakenly called her love a "marriage" (*Aeneid* IV, 172). Despite the use of the word "wife" it seems possible that the poem is addressed to Stella and that the subject is not death but infidelity. Had the poem been to Ariane, one could have dated it securely as after the death of Lucio, which is mentioned, in 1498. As it is, the date is uncertain.

Stella, then, was important. So, too, apparently, was Focilla, but she is much harder to pin down. She is almost completely absent from Pontano's other poetry, and she does not appear in Book I of our collection. Book II contains ten poems to her. The first, II.4, concerns her eyes, as do most of the others. Amor uses her glances as arrows. He should be careful lest he himself is damaged. The arrows are familiar. In *Eridanus* I.21, Amor is consoled for losing his arrows: "Stella's eyes provide a thousand arrows." Our Focilla poems are interrupted by a poem to Giovanni Pardo. Pardo also receives a poem in *Eridanus* I.31. It is about Stella's eyes: "Go softly, beauty, turn those fearsome arrows." Poem II.17 of our collection deals again with Focilla's eyes.

> et vittum remove et reclude ocellos
> quis lucem simul et diem ministras
> et lucem pariter diemque redde.

> Let fall the cloth and disclose your eyes,
> That minister both light and day,
> Bring back the light, bring back the day!

This recalls our poem I.28, and it recalls *Eridanus* I.10.

> In medio, mea Stella, die sub sole nitescis
> Clarior et per te solque diesque venit.

> My Stella, you gleam in the midday sun.
> Through you both the sun and the day shine brighter.

And the parallels between Stella, the star, and Focilla, the little hearth, increase and multiply. Focilla appears late in Pontano's life to dominate Book II. It is true that he uses this kind of language elsewhere, but nowhere does he do so as obsessively. And she does seem to have really lived. In *De tumulis* II.44, crowded between the grave-poems of two unknown girls, is a distich to Focilla: "no one will bring a branch to this extinct fireplace (*foco*)." It is also true that these are poems that show Pontano at his most brilliant and effective. Still, it seems most likely that Focilla was for Pontano a substitute for Stella, and it serves to remind the reader that behind all this splendid language there were real experiences.

The dating of the poems is, for the most part, very uncertain. The relative ages of the addressees in the two books, mentioned earlier, show that Book I is fairly early and Book II is quite late. Only three poems seem to have secure dates. II.27 states that Lucio is four years old, and that puts it around 1473, the earliest dated poem. I.10, dedicated to Franceschello Marchese on his return from Rome, should be from 1476 or 1477. Marchese had put out an edition of Horace in Rome in 1475 and returned to Naples in 1476. Pontano's poem is based on Horace's *Ode* II.7, in which the poet welcomes his friend Pompeius Varus home from a trip. Elizio Calenzio, who is also mentioned, returned from France in 1476. Poem II.28, as mentioned already, is datable at 1501, the date of Compater's death after 54 years of friendship. Beyond this, some dates are probable or approximate. Poem I.17, an invitation to a drinking party on November 11, St. Martin's Day, seems to suggest a raid on the wine cellar of Giovanni Antonio Petrucci. It dates from the years of their friendship. On that date in the year 1486, Petrucci was writing sonnets in prison and awaiting his beheading, which took place on December 11.[12] Poem I.31, dedicated to Masius Aquosa, should be 1495 or later, the year Tommaso Aquosa was named Magnificus Masius Aquosa by the Academy.[13] The poems to Federigo, II.31 and 32, can be placed between 1496, when Federigo became king, and 1501, when he was exiled. The poems to Alfonso as Duke of Calabria, I.16 and I.32, date from 1495 or before. And the poems to Batilla seem early, including II.33, which, like II.27, about Lucio, seem like early poems placed late, perhaps to balance the collection. As stated, the poems to Focilla seem late, perhaps quite late in the 1490s.

The collection consists of two books of 32 and 39 poems respectively, all composed in one meter associated through the ages with Catullus. In Summonte's edition of 1505, after the title, the editor adds, "He invokes the Muse of Catullus and addresses the hendecasyllables." Catullus himself begins his poem 42 "Adeste, hendecasyllabi, quot estis" ("Come, hendecasyllables, however many you are"). Pontano's line 10 of his first poem, "Huc, huc, hendecasyllabi, frequentes" ("Here, here, you thronging verses"), shows how close Pontano can come to Catullus without simply quoting him. Line 5 mentions the waters of Sirmio, Catullus's much loved country house on Lake Garda, and references to Sirmio, placed at the beginning of Book I and at the beginning and ending of Book II (assuming that II.37 is the real end of the collection and II.38 is a postlude) gives structure to the whole. In fact, Sirmio, in each case, is closely associated with Baiae, a place of pleasure. This association is telling.

Julia Haig Gaisser has, in a more than satisfactory manner, developed the story of Catullus's reception, describing in particular detail how he was read in the Renaissance.[14] One considers that Catullus, despite the brevity of his life and surviving works, was a poet of enormous range and that the word his contemporaries used to describe him was *doctus* or learned. Since antiquity, although his fame and popularity remain undiminished, his image has undergone a considerable narrowing. Catullus has become a poet not of passion, but of sexuality. The essential event took place about one hundred years after his death when Martial wrote "donabo tibi passerem Catulli" ("I shall give you Catullus's sparrow") and changed, for all time, the charming little bird into the *membrum virile*. Subsequent generations accepted Martial's reading of Catullus's sparrow poems. Pontano is certainly alluding to Martial in I.29:

Orando est mihi blanda Septimilla
Ut pro caseolis velit referre

centum basiola et Catulliana,
centum suaviola atque Lesbiana.

I'm going to beg sweet Septimilla
To make good the gift of cheeses
With a hundred kisses, Catullan ones,
And another hundred like Lesbia's.

Here the Catullan kisses are Martial's, "da nunc basia, sed Catul-
liana," from the same poem quoted above. Later, Poliziano con-
curred with Martial about the sparrow, and the case was settled.
Gaisser, reviewing all the facts, concludes that Martial's case
is "not proven."[15] The present writer (for full disclosure) feels
strongly that a *double entendre* of the kind imputed by Martial is
not consistent with Catullus's style or personality, and that the
glory of Catullus's sparrow is that it is a sparrow.

In considering the poems at hand, it is important to recall that,
with perhaps one minor exception, Catullus only becomes sexually
explicit in invective, never when he is amorous. In the exception,
poem 32 to Ipsitilla, he uses the vulgar word to describe his inten-
tion. There are no details. Pontano's poems, and those of numer-
ous Neo-Latin poets after him, are full of details, and a question
arises as to their origin. Walter Ludwig has discussed the love
making in I.16, between Duke Alfonso and Drusula, particularly
the transmission of souls in a kiss.[16] He recalls the pseudo-Pla-
tonic distich reported by Aulus Gellius, a Greek poem recited
to Gellius in Athens by a young man "not utterly without re-
finement" and the young man's translation of it into Latin iambic
verse. In the act of kissing, the young man's soul enters his part-
ner; he dies in himself but lives on in the other.[17] Ludwig demon-
strates that this is Pontano's source and that of his imitators,
Joannes Secundus and Joachim du Bellay. There are other ele-
ments to the kiss as well. The first, here and often throughout, is
ambrosia. In I.30 "stillatim ambrosiae liquebat humor" ("Am-

brosian essence dropwise liquefied"). When Catullus (99.2) stole his kiss from Juventius it was "sweeter than ambrosia." That is certainly Pontano's source, but it is the only element of the kiss that does go back to Catullus. And it is the only love fluid in Catullus. As for the tongue and the teeth, frequent in Pontano, they are not in Catullus at all. One has to go forward to the elegiac poets, to Tibullus, for that sort of thing.[18]

One reason it is useful to be precise about all this concerns the supposed influence of Catullus on later poets in the vernacular language. When one reads about "dewy lips" in Robert Herrick, one may be right in presuming that the source is Catullus 99. But when one encounters Herrick's "And when I shall meet / Thy silv'y feet, / My soule Ile poure into thee" ("The Night-piece, to Julia"), or Donne's "Since thou and I sigh one anothers breath, / Who e'r sighes most, is cruelest, and hasts the others death" ("A Valediction of Weeping"), we have no recourse but to look later in the tradition, and we shall probably find that our source is Pontano or another Renaissance Latin poet who had read Pontano. It may even be well to think of Stella and of Focilla when Shakespeare complains in Sonnet 130, "My mistress' eyes are nothing like the sun."[19]

To return now to Sirmio, Pontano would have us believe that Sirmio to Catullus was like Baiae to himself and his friends. What we know of Catullus's Sirmio is that he went there when he came back to Italy from service in Asia Minor and from visiting his brother's grave and that he was exhausted and happy to be at home in the "longed-for bed."[20] The transmutation of Sirmio into a pleasure resort with girls is an extreme one, and this transmutation may stand for the changing idea of Catullus across the centuries. Ludwig is certainly correct that "Pontano sees himself as Catullus's successor, that is to say, on the path inaugurated by Catullus."[21] It has been a long journey. Professor Gaisser concludes "henceforth Catullan poetry would speak in the language of Martial but with the Renaissance voice and accent of Pontano."[22] A more recent study by Bruce W. Swann seems to hold that Martial's view of Catullus has become so standard as to have acquired permanent legitimacy.[23] And the Catullus Martial praised was witty, sexy, epigrammatic and brief. Bearing all this in mind, one must not overlook how much of the real and original Catullus is present in these poems.

Catullus 45, the poem about Acme and Septimius, provides, as Ludwig remarks,[24] the basic three-part structure of our poem I.16 about Alfonso and Drusula. In Catullus, Acme, who is sitting on Septimius's lap, turns and kisses his eyes. Pontano develops this into a whole night of love at the end of which the poet asks, "Don't the gods envy you alone?" a line that surely comes from Catullus 51: "Ille, si fas est, superare divos" ("He's higher than the gods, if that is permitted"). I.13, the long poem to Pontano's wife Ariane, derived much of its material from Catullus's marriage poems 61 and 62. Some of the strength of Pontano's poem comes from the fact that he is celebrating his very old marriage in the language Catullus used for very new ones. II.22, an invitation to boys and girls to listen to the Graces, receives its form from Catullus 62: eight (Catullus) or nine (Pontano) sections ending with a refrain. The first lines: "Vesper adest: iuvenes, consurgite! Vesper Olympo" and "Ad myrtum, iuvenes, venite, myrti" echo each other exactly. Catullus is inviting the boys and girls to marry; Pontano is inviting them to take pleasure. Catullus does not avert his eyes from the painful aspects of the arrangement he is offering; Pontano is fixed on pleasure.

In II.31, King Federigo approaches the baths, and the question is posed "Progne et lugubrioribus querulis?" ("Isn't Procne [singing] even gloomier than usual?"). The lines come to mind, "qualia sub densis ramorum concinit umbras / Daulias absumpti fata gemens Itali" ("as the Daulian [Procne] sings deep in the woods' thick shade about Itys, about her own son's death"), from Catullus

(65.13–14). But that may seem rather a large echo to assume merely from one word, and that one a synonym: "the Daulian" for "Procne." However, when Pontano copied out the Corpus Tibullianum in his beautiful hand, he added at the end Ovid's *Heroides* XV, known as the "Sapphic Epistle." There in the facsimile edition, in line 154, is the Daulian bird, and in the margin, in Pontano's hand, are the two Catullan lines mentioned above.[25] Keeping in mind the allusion to Ariadne's complaint in Catullus 64 mentioned in connection with Pontano's complaint to his wife (or perhaps to Stella), these poems of Pontano show influences both major and minor of Catullus 61, 62, 64 and 65, all classed with the "longer poems" of Catullus, none witty, none epigrammatic and none vulnerable to the kind of influence from Martial discussed above. This does not, of course, dismiss the charge. Echoes here from the polymetric poems are numerous and they are witty, as is partly revealed in the appended Notes to the Translation. But Pontano's interest in Catullus was not limited to only one kind of poem.

Allusions, quotations, references, *loci classici*: they are everywhere — the Notes to the Translation in this volume only scratch the surface — and their function and purpose vary from poem to poem and defy classification. Perhaps the simplest type is the ancient poem that reappears in modern dress to suit a contemporary purpose. II.20 to the physician Antonius Galateus has been mentioned. It is lifted almost entirely out of Martial (XII.83): Fabianus, whose hernia makes him a laughingstock in the baths, is a doctor, and he revenges himself by prescribing terrible emetics for his tormentors. It is really a question of manners. No one can say that Pontano is being unkind because Martial did it first. And furthermore Galateus is allowed to win.

Something a little more subtle happens in I.20, "A Dark Girl Talks." There is a dark-skinned girl. The poem's program is revealed at the beginning of line 3, "quid tum?" ("and what of it?").

The signal is to Vergil's *Eclogues* (X.38): "quid tum, si fuscus Amyntas" ("What then if Amyntas is dark?"). Pontano does not need to say that "violets are black and hyacinths are black." The reader knows that. The poem that ensues is a brief variation or riff on the "quid tum?", and although its contents are strictly sexual, it is nevertheless imbued with a certain sympathy and affection that derive from the original reference.

References that compliment the addressee have also been mentioned. Francescello Marchese is complimented by a reference to Horace, whom he edited, Manlius Rallus by a mention of Propertius, whom he loved. Perhaps the most complex set of allusions are in I.11, dedicated to Actius Sincerus, the name given by Pontano to the poet Jacopo Sannazaro. The poem is an invitation to come to Baiae and have fun with the girls, but it begins by listing things that are to be renounced as useless, and, at first glance, the reader is overwhelmed with Vergilian references, appropriate to Sannazaro, who loved Vergil, lectured about him and composed the famous *Piscatory Eclogues*. The first line, "Quid cantus Siculae iuvant avenae?" ("Songs of the Sicilian [oaten] pipe, what good are they?"), conflates the openings of Vergil's *Eclogues* I and IV: "You meditate the rustic muse with slender oat" and "Sicilian Muses, we sing of something greater," respectively. Then he speaks of Meliseus — what good is he? and then the Vergilian tamarisk, using for Vergil the name Parthenas, which was, according to Servius, Vergil's nickname. Then there are little goats, white stippled, golden apples, the Menalian grove and Amaryllises. Mount Maenalus in Arcadia goes back to *Eclogue* VIII and Amaryllis brings us forward to *Eclogue* I: "Tu, Tityre, lentus in umbra / formosam resonare doces Amaryllida silvas" ("Tityrus, soft in the shade, you teach the woods to sing of beautiful Amaryllis"). This leaves Meliseus, the goat and the golden apples. At this point Pontano is not alluding to Vergil (although all three are in the *Eclogues*) but to himself referring to Vergil.

Meliseus is Pontano's youthful name for himself as a rustic shepherd. In his early eclogue *Acon*, the shepherd Meliseus sings "dulce in pratis dum gramina tondant / cernere capreolos variato tergere, pictis / distinctos maculis" ("sweet to watch while they clip the grass, the little goats with different coats, distinct with their colored spots").[26] The golden apples refer to Pontano's earlier *De hortis hesperidum*, a poem about citrus trees.

These braided allusions, on a simple level, mean: let us put aside our scholarly pursuits and enjoy ourselves, but of course Pontano is talking about his youth. One of the few early girl friends to make her way into this collection is Fannia. She appears in I.19, and in II.2. At the end of his life, he gave her a place of honor towards the conclusion of his long work *Urania*: "resonat virides Formosa per umbras Fannia" ("Beautiful Fannia sounds through the green shades"). So Fannia, over the years, became Amaryllis and took her place among those things Pontano had to set aside in his realistic pursuit of an old man's pleasure.

The longest poem in the collection, II.37, is the last but one, that last being a sort of postlude, and it carries the technique of allusion to a new level. It is dedicated to Pontano's friend Suardo Suardino, to whom in 1502 he sent several of his works to be delivered for publication to Aldus in Venice. Suardino had in 1499 published a work *In metamorphosim Ovidii praelectio*, apparently a public lecture — the work is of a defeating rarity.[27] Pontano's poem is crammed with Ovidian references, but the compliment does not end there, for the entire poem, or most of it, is in itself an Ovidian metamorphosis. And it is a virtuoso performance. The pace, the tone, the swift transitions: everything sounds very like Ovid. And the plot is new: Amor tries to shoot Athena, is paralyzed by the Gorgon's head, wanders disconsolate with his useless bows until his mother consults Apollo who tells her of the health-giving powers of Baiae's waters, and so forth. At the end, the talk returns to Sirmio, and the ending of the book is prepared.

The last poem is a farewell. Ariane is gone and so is Stella. He bids farewell to his hendecasyllables and to the baths and to both salt and wit. He wants to see his wife in Elysium and to dance with her. The tone is conciliatory, and he gives advice to those who are to come after. It is an expanded tomb inscription in the manner of Tibullus.

> Let bitterness be absent from your loving.
> Let everything be sweetness. Thus in loving
> You'll while away the nighttimes and the daytimes
> With Pleasure at your side as your companion.

Ludwig remarked that the essential element in these poems is Pleasure, *Voluptas*, and the word appears everywhere.[28] In II.1, the line "quae mentes hominum regit Voluptas" ("Pleasure wielding power over the hearts of men") immediately recalls Vergil's "trahit sua quemque voluptas" ("each is drawn by his own pleasure") in *Eclogues* II.65, but while Vergil's line is not without a certain ruefulness, Pontano's is simply factual, and in this collection he gives Pleasure quite literally the last word.

> assistat lateri et comes Voluptas.

> With Pleasure at your side as your companion.

Rosalie Prosser and Barbara Boltz were of enormous help in preparing this edition. Ariane Schwartz transferred the Latin text of Monti Sabia to electronic form. My friend Michael Putnam and my friend and General Editor James Hankins corrected, revised and polished the entire text. The resulting work is offered to my wife Christie.

NOTES

1. For details about Pontano's life see Carol Kidwell, *Pontano, Poet and Prime Minister* (London, 1991).

2. Horace, *Odes* III.4, 24.

3. Horace, *Odes* II.18, 17–22.

4. Cicero, *Pro Caelio* 15, 35.

5. For more detailed references see Notes to the Translation, I.24.

6. *Antonius* 22 ff., in Previtera, ed., Pontano, *I Dialoghi*. See the Bibliography for full citations of the works of Pontano consulted.

7. Walter Ludwig, "Catullus Renatus," in *Litterae Neolatinae, Schriften zur neulateinischen Literatur* (Munich, 1989), p. 183, n. 39.

8. See Notes II.20.

9. See Notes II.24.

10. See Notes I.28.

11. Cicero, *Pro Caelio* 20, 49.

12. On Pontano's friendship with Petrucci, see Kidwell p. 94.

13. Camillo Minieri Riccio, *Biografie degli Accademici Alfonsini* (Bologna, n.d.), p. 218.

14. Julia Haig Gaisser, *Catullus and His Renaissance Readers* (Oxford, 1993).

15. Ibid., p. 241. Gaisser's discussion "Kisses and Sparrows," pp. 233 ff., is thorough.

16. Ludwig, "Catullus Renatus," p. 183 ff. See also Gaisser, *Catullus*, p. 249 ff.

17. Gellius, *Noctes Atticae*, 19, 11.

18. See Notes I.16.

19. Ludwig, "Catullus Renatus," p. 194, commends this subject for future scholarship.

20. Catullus 31 and 101.

21. Ludwig, "Catullus Renatus," p. 183.

22. Gaisser, *Catullus*, p. 228.

23. Bruce W. Swann, *Martial's Catullus: The Reception of an Epigrammatic Rival* (Hildesheim, 1994).

24. Ludwig, "Catullus Renatus," p. 183 ff.

25. *Tibulli carmina, Sapphus Epistula Ovidiana, Codex Guelferbytanus 82.6 Aug.* (facsimile edition), preface by Friedrich Leo (Leiden, 1910).

26. Acon, *Ecloga Quarta*, 75–77 (in *Pontani Opera. Urania*).

27. Minieri Riccio, *Biografie*, p. 172.

28. Ludwig, "Catullus Renatus," p. 186.

HENDECASYLLABORUM SIVE BAIARUM LIBRI DUO

TWO BOOKS OF HENDECASYLLABLES, OR BAIAE

LIBER PRIMUS

: I :

Musam alloquitur

Nigris, Pieri, quae places ocellis
et cantum colis et colis choreas,
nigris, Pieri, grata dis capillis,
formosae quibus invident Napeae,
5   dum gratos prope Syrmionis amnes
et crinem lavis et comam repectis,
ne tu, Pieri, ne benigna desis,
dum laetis salibus sonante plectro
alterno et pede balneas adimus.
10   Huc huc, hendecasyllabi, frequentes,
huc vos quicquid habetis et leporum,
iocorum simul et facetiarum,
huc deferte, minutuli citique.
Quod vos en pretium, aut manet voluptas?
15   Inter lacteolas simul puellas,
inter molliculos simul maritos
ludetis simul atque prurietis.
Dum tractat tumidas puer papillas,
contrectat tenerum femur puella,
20   tractat delitias suas maritus,
tentat delitium suum puella
et ludunt simul et simul foventur
lassi languidulique fessulique,
tunc vos, hendecasyllabi beati,
25   quot, quot oscula morsiunculasque,
quot, quot enumerabitis duella!

BOOK I

He Addresses the Muse

Dark-eyed Muse, giving pleasure,
Good at singing, good at dancing,
Dark-haired, pleasing to the gods,
Envied by the lovely nymphs,
When by Sirmio's pleasant waters   5
You wash your hair and comb your tresses,
Don't, kind Muse, don't leave off
When, with happy leaps and strumming
Dancing, we approach the baths.
    Here, here, you thronging verses,   10
Bring here what you may possess
Of charm and humor and of wit.
Bring it over, swift and subtle.
Look, will price or pleasure keep you?
Both among the milky girls   15
And among their tender mates
You'll play your games and get excited.
A boy strokes her swelling nipples,
The girl strokes his tender thigh,
The man fondles his delights,   20
The girl touches his delight,
And they make sport, excite each other,
Lazy, languid, tired out.
And then you, my blessed verses,
How many kisses, little nibbles,   25
How many battles will you count!

3

Quot suspiria, murmura et cachinnos,
cum furtim liceat, sorpore in ipso,
contrectare papillulas sinumque,
30   occultam et femori admovere dextram!
    Hos tu sed comites, Marine, vita,
Baianis quotiens aquis lavaris,
tuas ne veneres libidinesque
et lusus referant salaciores,
35   sis et fabula, quod senex salaxque,
et thermas quoque balneas et ipsas
infames, nimio supinus usu.
Hanc laudem potius tuo relinque
Compatri. Chorus hunc puellularum
40   incanum sequitur, colunt sed illae
non annos vetuli, senis sed aurum.

How many sighs, whispers, giggles,
Secretly, while they're drowsing,
And they're squeezing breast and mound,
Touching thigh with stealthy hand!   30
　　Best Marinus, you often bathe
These, your friends, in Baian waters
Lest they call your sport and games
Uncustomarily salacious
And you, a by-word, old and raunchy,   35
Prostrated from excessive use,
Disgraceful even to the baths.
Better let your friend Compater
Reap this praise. The swarming girls
Will chase him, not because he's old,   40
But because they want his money.

: 2 :

Puellas alloquitur
admonens quid servare in balneis debeant

Quae dulces modo balneas petistis
et corpus calidis aquis fovetis,
inepte facitis nimis, puellae,
inepte nimium parumque recte,
5   quod solae sine amantibus lavatis,
quod corpus sine amantibus fovetis.
Quare consilium senis probati
et rectum capite et probum bonumque:
gaudet blanditiis Amor iocisque,
10   amplexus petit, osculis fovetur;
res est mutua: mutuus Cupido
odit tristia solitudinemque.
Quid solae sine amantibus lavatis?
Quid corpus sine amantibus fovetis?
15   Curas pellite solitudinemque,
ite in gaudia, mutuos fovete
amplexus: sine amante mutuum nil.
Quare nec sine amantibus lavate,
nec corpus sine amantibus fovete.
20   Intratis calidas? Vocate amantes.
Intrastis calidas? Fovete amantes.
Sint et mutua, sed nec ipsa muta.
Amplexus cupidi loquantur ipsi,
iniectaeque manus loquantur ipsae
25   et dens blandulus ebriique ocelli,
sonent oscula, personent cachinni,

6

: 2 :

He Speaks to Girls,
Telling Them How to Behave in the Baths

Now you sought out the sweetest baths
And heated your limbs in waters warm,
But, girls, you act too foolishly,
Imprudently and foolishly,
Because you're bathing without lovers,   5
Warming your limbs without your lovers.
So listen to a fine old man:
Seize the right, the fine, the good.
Love delights in charm and wit,
He likes a hug, he's warmed by kisses;   10
It's a shared thing: sharing Cupid
Detests sadness and solitude.
Why wash alone without your lovers?
Why heat your limbs without your lovers?
Cast off care and solitude.   15
Seek out gladness. Foster shared
Embraces. Unshared love is nothing.
So don't go bathing without lovers
Nor warm yourselves without your lovers.
Going into hot water? Call the lovers.   20
Was it hot? Warm up your lovers.
Let it be mutual but not mute.
Eager embraces themselves speak out;
The touch of hands itself speaks out,
Flashing teeth, drunken eyes.   25
Kisses echo, laughter roars,

vincant murmura Cyprias columbas.
Hanc legem statuit Venusque Amorque,
hanc legem sibi balneae edidere:
30 'Ne solae sine amantibus lavate,
ne corpus sine amantibus fovete.'

Whispers drown out the Cyprian dove.
Venus and Amor established this law,
Published by the baths themselves:
"Don't bathe alone without your lovers, 30
Nor warm yourselves without your lovers."

: 3 :

De Batilla puella in balneis

Baianas petiit Batilla thermas
dumque illi tener it comes Cupido
atque una lavat et fovetur una,
dum molli simul in toro quiescit
5   ac ludos facit improbasque rixas,
sopito pueroque lassuloque
arcum surripuit Batilla ridens,
mox picta latus instruit pharetra
et molles iacit huc et huc sagittas.
10   Nil, o nil reliquum, miselli amantes,
nil his impenetrabile est sagittis:
heu, cladem iuvenum senumque, Baias!

: 3 :

Batilla in the Baths

Batilla sought out the Baian waters,
And tender Cupid went along.
Then they wash and warm themselves,
Take soft ease in bed a while,
Play some games, start a brawl, 5
And from the lazy, sleepy boy
Batilla, laughing, steals the bow,
Arms her flank with painted quiver
And shoots soft arrows here and there.
Oh, poor lovers, no one's spared: 10
Those arrows can pierce anything.
Oh Baiae, ruin of young and old!

: 4 :

Ad Hermionen
ut papillas contegat

Praedico, tege candidas papillas
nec quaeras rabiem ciere amantum.
Me, quem frigida congelat senecta,
irritas male calfacisque: quare,
5   praedico, tege candidas papillas
et pectus strophio tegente vela.
Nam quid lacteolos sinus et ipsas
prae te fers sine linteo papillas?
An vis dicere: 'Basia papillas
10   et pectus nitidum suaviare?'
Vis num dicere: 'Tange, tange, tracta?'
Tene incedere nudulis papillis?
Nudo pectore tene deambulare?
Hoc est dicere: 'Posce, posce, trado,'
15   hoe est ad venerem vocare amantes.
Quare, aut contege candidas papillas
et pectus strophio decente vesti,
aut, senex licet, involabo in illas,
ut possim iuvenis tibi videri.
20   Tithonum, Hermione, tuae papillae
possunt ad iuvenis vocare munus.

: 4 :

To Hermione,
to Cover Her Breasts

I'm telling you to clothe those shining breasts,
Desist from stirring the insanity of lovers.
Me, congealed already by cold age,
You're heating up unpleasantly. And so
I'm telling you to clothe those shining breasts   5
And veil your bosom with a decent halter.
Those milky breasts, why carry them about,
Those very nipples, naked and exposed?
Are you really saying "Kiss these breasts,
Caress these glowing breasts." Is that your meaning?   10
Are you saying "Touch them, touch them, stroke them?"
Do you go out with bosoms all exposed?
Do you stroll around with naked breasts?
I think you're saying "Only ask. They're yours."
Which simply is an invitation to have sex.   15
And so you'll either clothe those shining nipples
And cover yourself with a decent halter,
Or, though an old man, I'll sweep down on them,
In such a way that I'll seem young to you.
Hermione, those breasts could make Tithonus   20
Cry out for the remembered tasks of youth.

: 5 :

Ad Marinum Tomacellum
de lege balneorum virginibus dedicatorum

'His virguncula thermulis lavetur,
nullam quae venerem integella sensit;
his se balneolis lavet puella,
nullum quae tetigit viri cubile;
5   hoc se fonticulo eluat sacerdos,
nullae quam recreent amoris aurae.
Quod si quae laticis sacri pudorem
et castum temerarit ausa fontem,
iratae timeat deae flagellum.'
10   Haec lex est tabulae deae dicatae,
vis haec thermuleae dicationis.
Squalent hinc latices, Marine, sacri
et serpunt hederae deae sacello,
nullae his virgineis aquis lavantur,
15   nec casta est quoniam, nec integella
seu virguncula, seu puella, sive
custos Romulei foci sacerdos.

: 5 :

To Marinus Tomacellus
Concerning the Rules Governing Baths Dedicated to Virgins

"A little maid may wash in these warm waters
Who, untouched, never gave a thought to sex;
A young girl may make use of these hot baths
Who's never occupied a lover' s bed;
A priestess may bathe in this little fountain   5
To whom Love's breath has never brought relief.
But if a girl, daring to use this fountain,
Profanes the sacred water's chastity,
Let her beware the angry goddess's whip."
This the goddess' s written proclamation,   10
Such is this thermal proclamation's force.
Hence holy streams, Marinus, have turned foul;
Now twining ivy cloaks the goddess' shrine.
No one washes in these virgin streams,
Because no one is chaste, no one untouched,   15
Not even a young girl, a little maiden,
Not even a priestess guarding Romulus' hearth.

: 6 :

Ad Marinum Tomacellum

Salaces refugis, Marine, Baias
et fontes nimium libidinosos.
Quid mirum? Senibus nocet libido.
An non, o Tomacelle, vina prosunt
5   et prodest senibus liquor Falernus
et prosunt latices Thyoniani?
An non et senibus, Marine, somnus
et prodest requies soporque prodest?
Baiis somniculosius quid ipsis?
10   Quid thermae nisi lene, molle, mite,
rorantis cyathos merumque poscunt,
senum delicias, iocos seniles?
Senex ad calices iocatur, idem
ludit ad cyathos: senile vinum,
15   senilis sopor et quies senilis.
Huc huc en propera, Marine. Verum
huc ipsis sine testibus venito
et lumbis sine: nam quies senile est,
libido iuvenile. Siccitasque
20   et tecum veniat Sitis, fidelis
et senum comes atque balneorum.
Pergrate accipiere: Siccitasque
atque una Sitis accubabit, ipse
miscebo tibi poculis minutis
25   idemque e vario frequens Liaeo.
Hoc aetas iubet utraque et sodalis,
hoc et balnea sicculaeque arenae.

: 6 :

To Marinus Tomacellus

Marinus, you shun the debauches of Baiae,
Its all too libidinous fountains you shun.
Well, of course. Lust is bad for the elderly,
But oh, Marinus, isn't wine good,
And Falernian draughts and Thyonian drink, 5
Aren't they good for the elderly?
Rest and drowsing, aren't they good?
And what is more sleepy than Baiae herself?
What do these waters want but wine,
Soft, mild and gentle with foaming lather, 10
Delights and mirth for elderly people?
An old man jokes in his cups, and he also
Takes pleasure in ladles: elderly wine,
Elderly sleep, elderly quiet.
Hurry on over, Marinus. Come 15
Here, leaving your balls behind
And your member, too. Rest's for the old,
Lust for the youthful. Let Dryness come
Along with you and Thirst, faithful
Friend of the elderly and the baths. 20
You will be well received. And Dryness
And Thirst recline together well.
I shall mix tiny cups for you,
Busy with Bacchus of various flavors.
Our age and comradeship demand it. 25
The baths and the thirsty sands demand it.

: 7 :

Balneae loquuntur

'Nostrum si titulum, puella, nescis,
hic est: "Praegravida recedet alvo,
quae venit vacua." Hoc habet tabella;
quod vero officium tuum meumque,
5   quae partes, moneam. Virum ipsa tecum
adducas validum, ioci peritum,
cui telum viride et virens iuventa;
nec tu defueris comes iocanti,
aut ore, aut femore, aut manu iocisve:
10   namque et balnea mutuum requirunt.
Nunc ad me venio meumque munus
quod sit, subiciam. Tibi senex vir
si sit, nec validus, nec ore gratus,
nec aptus thalamis torive rebus,
15   qui rursus iuvenis decens valensque
iam sit, substituam, salaciorque
verno passere, martiis columbis,
cui rubro caput horreat cucullo.
Haec vis est tabulae vigorque fontis.'
20   Quare, si sapies, Marine, cum sis
effetus, fugies repente Baias,
vites balnea myrteumque litus,
elumbis, tremulus, macer senexque:
setosum Hectora balneae requirunt.

: 7 :

The Baths Speak

"Perhaps, my girl, you do not know our motto.
It's this: 'Who enters with an empty belly
Leaves with a full one.' That is what is written.
Now as to what's your part and what is mine,
Give heed. You are to bring along a man   5
Stout and capable of fun,
Flowering in youth and strong of tool.
Nor will you fail him as a pleasant comrade
In face, in leg, in touch or laughter:
The baths insist on mutuality.   10
Now I'll get to myself, and I'll reveal
The gifts I offer. If your man is old,
Neither stout nor fair of face,
Neither good in bedroom nor in bed,
I'll give you one who's fine and young and strong,   15
Randier than a sparrow in the spring
Or than combative doves whose heads
Bristle with crimson crowns. This is
The force of this motto, the strength of this fountain."
   So if you're smart, Marinus, you'll leave Baiae   20
Right away, since you are past your prime.
Shun these baths and this myrtled shore,
Weak in the loin, shaky, thin and old.
A bristling Hector is what these baths require.

: 8 :

Ad Deianiram puellam

Cur, o Deianira, cur moraris
auroram cupidis referre terris?
Cur non lumina poetulosque ocellos
in lucem exeris ac diem reducis?
5   Pellit sol radiis suis tenebras
et lucem pariter diemque reddit;
tu, lucem referens tuis ocellis,
pellas tristitiam et gravis dolores
et curas abigas benigna amantum
10   et quod sol radiis, id ipsa ocellis
praesta, Deianira, amantibusque
et lucem pariter diemque redde.

: 8 :

To Young Deianira

Why wait, Deianira, to bring the dawn
Back once more to this yearning earth?
Why not turn those glancing little eyes,
Toward the light and welcome back the day?
The sun exiles shadows with its rays   5
And brings the day together with the light.
You, who bring back light with your eyes,
Exile melancholy, banish gloom,
And, kind, drive off your lover's painful cares.
So, Deianira, what the sun with its rays bestows,   10
Give with your eyes and to your lovers bring
Back their light together with the day.

: 9 :

Ad Petrum Compatrem Neapolitanum

Quod cani tibi, Compater, capilli
et toto capite albicant pruinae,
amplexus fugiunt tuos puellae,
iunxisse et femori femur recusant
5   (quod nec carminibus suis Apollo,
nec blandis redimet iocis Thalia).
Quaenam, quae tibi, Compater miselle,
quae vita, aut quis erit modus querenti?
Hic est, quem tenerae timent puellae,
10   quem cultae fugiunt nurus, amorque
omnis — undique et undecunque et usque,
usque et undique et undecunque et usque —
omnis horret amor venusque hymenque.
    Sed nil sit tibi, Compater, molesti,
15   nec canos, celerem aut time senectam,
sed tristis animo repelle curas:
quod nec carminibus suis Apollo,
nec blandis numeris dabit Thalia,
id numus dabit aureus petenti,
20   vel te ut lacteolae petant puellae.
Quae tum, quae tibi, Compater beate,
quae vita, aut quis erit modus iocanti?
Hic est, quem roseae volunt puellae,
quem cultae cupiunt nurus, amorque
25   omnis — undique et undecunque et usque,

22

: 9 :

To Petrus Compater, the Neapolitan

Because your hair is grey, Compater,
Your head utterly white with frost,
Maidens flee from your embrace,
Decline to meet you thigh to thigh
(Which not Apollo with his songs   5
Makes good nor Thalia with her fun).
Poor Compater, what a life!
Will nothing limit your complaints?
Here's the one whom the soft girls shun
The smart young brides, and all   10
Love — here, there, and everywhere,
Here, everywhere and there and here —
All love and sex and marriage shun.
    But don't let it bother you, Compater.
Don't fear grey hairs or swift old age.   15
Expel the sorrow from your heart.
What Apollo with his songs
And Thalia's rhythms will not give
One golden coin will yield:
Then the milky girls will seek you out.   20
Now, blessed Compater, what a life!
Will nothing limit your happiness?
Here's the one rosy maids all want
And the smart young brides, and all
Love — here, there and everywhere,   25

usque et undique et undecunque et usque—
omnis ambit amor venusque hymenque.
　　Felix canities, senecta felix,
cui canae nitet aureus capillus,
30　　cui flavae riget aureus Priapus!

Here, everywhere and there and here—
All love and sex and marriage want.
    Happy grey hair, happy old age
Where gold hair shines upon the grey,
Where gold Priapus rises amid the glow!   30

: 10 :

Laetatur de reditu Francisci Aelii

E Roma meus Aelius revisit
dulcem Parthenopen, lares paternos:
o lucem niveam diemque faustum!
Antiquum video et bonum sodalem
5   et caram teneo manum fruorque
gratis colloquiis, fruor cachinnis
et laetis salibus facetiisque:
o vere niveum diemque faustum!
Quid non pro reduci libens amico
10   persolvam? Puer, i, voca sodales
Albinum Elisiumque Compatremque
et dulcem Altilium, bonum Marullum:
ad coenam veniant, bibamus uncti,
uncti, permadidi atque lippientes.
15   Albinus numerum novem sororum,
at monstra Herculea ebibat Marullus,
bis septem volo Compater puellas
Iunonis, volo quot deae marinae
cinxerunt niveae latus ministrae,
20   cum Troiam peteret misella mater;
ductet Altilius ciens coronam,
saltans Elisius bibat quot olim
Didonis famulae penum struebant,
dum coenam profugo parat marito.
25   Me tot pocula totque totque totque,
tot me pocula iuverint bibentem,
tot carchesia laverint madentem,

: IO :

He Rejoices at the Return of Franciscus Aelius

My Aelius is back again from Rome
To see sweet Naples, his paternal Lares.
O light as white as snow, o lucky day!
I have my good and ancient friend once more
And hold his dear hand and rejoice   5
In his welcome talk, in his laughter,
In his wit and in his funny stories:
Truly the day is white as it is lucky!
Now what would I not spend at the return
Of such a friend? Boy, go bid the comrades,   10
Elisius, Albinus and Compater
And sweet Altilius and good Marullus
To come to dinner. Perfumed we shall drink,
Perfumed, soaked through and bleary-eyed.
Albinus may drink nine for the Sisters,   15
Marullus as many as Hercules's labors,
Compater twice seven for Juno's maidens
I want as many as the snowy servants
Escorting the Goddess of the Sea,
A grieving mother as she sought out Troy.   20
Let Altilius lead, urging the onlookers,
Let Elisius, dancing, drain as many as
Dido's servants bringing in the food
When she laid out the feast for her runaway lover:
I want cup upon cup upon cup,   25
So many goblets for myself imbibing,
So many beakers moistening me

quotquot di simul et deae biberunt
ad mensam Oceani patris vocati,
30 aut quot, dum illa canit, senex Homerus
siccavit calices, relevit obbas.
Dulce est ob reducem madere amicum.

As all the gods and goddesses drank together
Called to the feast by father Oceanus,
Or as many as, singing the while, old Homer   30
Chalices drank dry and flagons drained.
When a friend comes home it's sweet to get good and soused.

Ad Actium Sincerum

Quid cantus Siculae iuvant avenae?
Quid cantor Meliseus aut amanti
prosunt Partheniae tibi myricae?
Aut quid capreoli decemve mala,
albo capreoli liti colore,
aureo mala tibi, quid o quid, Acti,
prosunt? aut gemitus tibi columbae?
aut quid sibila murmurantis austri?
Quare, o, Menalium nemus relinque
atque istas Amarillidas, Tevennae
cultrices gelidae, aridi et Tanagri,
et Baias pete myrteumque litus
et litus cole myrteasque Baias.
Hic fas est iuveni, hic licet puellae
certatim teneros inire lusus,
hic et basia morsiunculasque
surreptim dare, mutuos fovere
amplexus licet, et licet iocari
impune ad cyathos, choros, lucernas.
Baianae hoc statuunt lavationes.
Hic seni liceat mihi duella
et rixas iuvenum et puellularum
ad pacem lepidam et iocum vocare,
miscere et lacrimis iocos iocisque
rursus lacrimulas. Queretur Agnes
demorsam sibi lingulam? Licebit
Agneti tenerum proci labellum
insignisse nota. Dolebit Aulus

: II :

To Actius Sincerus

Songs of the Sicilian pipe,
Melisean singers, Parthenean tamarisk,
What good are these to a lover?
Or the little goats, the apples ten,
Little goats stippled all over with white,   5
Apples of gold, what good are they, Actius,
The moaning of the doves,
Whispering of the Southern Wind?
Therefore, oh, leave the Menalian grove,
Those Amaryllises who haunt   10
Cold Tevenna, barren Tanagra.
Seek Baiae and the myrtled shore,
Dwell on that shore and myrtled Baiae.
Here it's permitted to boys and girls
To engage in tender combat   15
And steathily give kisses and bites.
They're allowed to fondle each other;
They may sport and play unpunished
With wine and lanterns and choral dance.
The Baian baths established this.   20
I'm old and allowed the settle the fights
And quarrels of the boys and girls,
Making peace with jokes and wit,
Mingling jokes with tears and then
Tearlets with jokes. Does Agnes complain   25
Her tongue got bitten? She's allowed
To make a mark on her boyfriend's
Delicate lip. Is Aulus sad

negatum sibi basium? Licebit
30   triplex basiolum dedisse amicae.
Irata est quotiens Lyco Lycella,
possum compositas novare leges,
possum foederibus ligare amantes,
ut coenent pariter, laventur una
35   atque uno simul ut toro quiescant,
coniuncto et simul ore suavientur
et somnos agitent quiete ut una.
Has et delicias et hos lepores
praestarint tibi balneae salubres,
40   Baiani dederint tibi recessus,
ut dicas: 'Siculae valete avenae,
umbroso valeat Tevenna monte:
meme balneolae beent beatae,
nam Baias homines colunt deique.'

He's denied a kiss? He's permitted
To give his girl three little kisses.   30
When Lycella's mad at Lycus
I can adjust the established rules,
Join lovers in agreements,
To eat together, bathe together,
And rest together in one bed   35
And sweetly kiss each other's faces
And quietly go off to sleep.
These the delights, these the charms
That our healthy baths afford you,
That Baian haunts bestow on you.   40
So you'll say, "Sicilian pipes, farewell;
Farewell, Tevenna's shady peak;
I'm gladdened by these blessed baths.
Men and gods dwell in Baiae!"

: 12 :

Uxorem ac liberos invitat
ad diem natalem celebrandum

    Dulces filiolae, paterni ocelli,
    dulcis nate, patris tui voluptas,
    et coniux, requies senis mariti,
    mecum templa piis adite votis:
5   natalis meus est, deos rogate
    atque hunc atque alios agamus annos
    fausto sidere, candidis lapillis,
    dum caros mihi redditis nepotes,
    qui—blanda oscula balbulasque voces—
10   incompto simul ore blandiantur,
    inculto simul ore suavientur.
    Mox convivia villula propinqua
    securis animis, dolore pulso
    nocturnas ineamus ad lucernas.
15   Hic patri liceat seni Falernum
    diffusum cyatho minutiore
    roratim ingeminare ter quaterque,
    dum lassos oculos sopor reclinet.
    At vos, quis pudor eripit Liaeum
20   nativaque sitis levatur unda,
    dulci intingite melle cinnamoque:
    haec sunt pocula virginis Dianae,
    siquando ad superum dapes vocatur.
    Tu myrtum foribus rosamque mensae
25   appone et violis humum colora,
    resperge et Cyprio domum liquore,
    nec desit lyra eburneusque pecten,

: 12 :

He Invites His Wife and Children
to Celebrate His Birthday

Sweet daughters, apples of your father's eye,
My sweet son, who gives your father pleasure
And wife, who are an old husband's repose,
Come to the temple now with earnest prayer:
Today's my birthday; let us call the gods,   5
And let us live this year and other years,
Under a lucky star and with white stones,
While you present me with dear grandchildren
Who — kisses sweet, baby-talking sounds —
Please me with untidy faces,   10
And kiss me with their unkempt faces.
Then let us repair to the lamps of evening,
A party now in a neighboring villa,
With carefree hearts, sorrow cast away.
For the old father some Falernian   15
Served out with rather tiny ladles
May be repeated three times, four times,
Till sleep makes his tired eyelids droop.
But you whose modesty forbids Lyaeus,
The native water can relieve your thirst.   20
Flavor it with sweet honey and cinnamon:
These are virginal Diana's cups
When she is called to the feasts of the gods.
And you, deck the gates with myrtle,
Place a rose on the table, strew the ground with violets,   25
And sprinkle the whole house with Cyprian scent.
Don't forget the lyre, the ivory plectrum

qui gratas Genio citet choreas:
et dulces Genium decent choreae.
30   Hunc vos, hunc hilares rogate, mentem
det recti cupidam simulque honesti
permittatque alia a deis regenda.

That stirs up dances pleasing to Genius.
Sweet dances are acceptable to Genius.
Oh happy ones, ask that he grant a heart   30
That longs at once for justice and for honor;
And may he let the rest be ruled by gods.

: 13 :

Ad Ariadnam uxorem

Uxor, deliciae senis mariti
et casti thalami fides amorque,
per te vel viridis mihi senecta est,
quem curae fugiunt senem seniles,
5   qui seram supero senex senectam
et canus iuvenum cano furores;
sed tanquam redeat calor iuventae
et sis cura recens amorque primus
et primus furor impetusque saevus,
10   antiquas volo suscitare flammas.
    Qualis floridulo nitens in horto
nondum puniceas comas reclusit,
et iam puniceas comas recludit
ac rarum decus explicare quaerit
15   quae laeto rosa ramulo refulget,
talis purpureis genis et ore,
ut quae non tenerum capit maritum,
sed iam iam tenerum cupit maritum,
cui prima oscula dedicet suumque
20   florem virginei dicet pudoris
suspirans viduo puella lecto,
fulgebas mihi primulosque amores
spirabas oculis sinuque blando
afflabas Arabum suos odores,
25   fundebas Charitum suos honores
et laetum Gnidiae deae nitorem.
    Qualis fulgidulo renidet ore
quae cano vehitur decora cygno,

: 13 :

To His Wife, Ariane

Wife, your elderly husband's delight,
Love and trust of our chaste bed,
You who keep my old age fresh,
Who set an old man's cares to flight,
And help me triumph over old age,   5
A grey head singing of youthful passion;
But, as if fires of youth return
And you were at once first love and new,
First passion, headlong rush,
I want to fan those ancient flames.   10
    As shining in a bed of flowers,
Not revealing its red petals,
Now revealing its red petals,
Unfolding hidden comeliness,
A rose gleams on its lustrous stem,   15
So blushing now in face and cheek
As would not take a loving husband
But now, now! wants a loving husband
To offer her first kisses,
Her flower of virgin modesty,   20
A girl sighs in an empty bed,
You gleam at me and from your eyes
Emit love's dawning rays
And from your soft, sweet breasts
Exhale Arabian fragrances.   25
The Graces' beauty streams from you,
The happy shimmer of Cnidos' goddess.
    As shining in her glowing face,

cum compsit caput et coma repexa
30   procedit thalamo novosque amores
et novas parat excitare flammas:
spirant omnia, qua comam reflectit,
splendent omnia, qua reflectit ora;
talis, qua niveos pedes ferebas,
35   et qua splendidulos moves ocellos
et qua per vacuum reflectis ora,
spirabas Cyprios tuosque odores,
stillabas Syrium et tuum liquorem,
omnisque ambrosiam refragat aura.
40   Qualis de croceo toro resurgens
mane Aurora nigras repellit umbras,
cum lucem simul et diem reportans
irrorat teneros benigna flores
et spargit varios humi colores:
45   rident prata canuntque concinuntque
et frondes siluaeque ramulique;
tails de thalamo vocata quando
ad mollis thyasos venis canisque,
pellis tristitias, metus, dolores,
50   rixas, murmura, turbidos tumultus,
irrorans animis quietem, amores,
ludos, laetitias, iocos, lepores,
lusus, gaudia candidamque pacem
et spargis veneres cupidinesque:
55   rident omnia et aerem serenas
et qui te iuvenis videt senexque
et quae femina seu videt puella
optatum cupiunt tibi maritum,
felices tibi nuptias precantur.
60   Tunc, ut de tenui solet favilla
crescens igniculus focum repente

40

Lovely, drawn by a snow-white swan,
When, with hair arranged and combed,   30
She enters the chamber and prepares
To stir to life new loves and flames —
All things breathe when she turns her head,
All things shine where she turns her face —
So where walk your snowy feet,   35
Where you turn those splendid eyes,
Turn your face through the empty air,
You breath your Cyprian fragrances,
Drip your Syrian dew,
Redolence of ambrosia.   40
   As, rising from her saffron couch,
Aurora drives away black shades
Bringing light, bringing day,
Kind, she waters the tender flowers,
Scatters colors on the earth —   45
And the fields laugh, sing and shout
The leaves and branches of the woods —
So, when called from the bridal chamber
To gentle rites, you come and sing,
You drive off sadness, fear and sorrow,   50
Grumbling, conflict, disagreement,
Sprinkling the heart with quiet,
Loves, games, mirth, jokes and charm,
Laughter, joy and shining peace,
You scatter love and hot desire;   55
All things laugh, you clear the air,
Whoever sees you, young or old,
Every woman, every girl
Desires for you the longed-for husband,
Prays for you a happy marriage.   60
   Then, as when a tiny spark

41

flammis corripere, aridisque lignis
quodcunque adicies edit voratque,
sic me de tenui levis favilla
65   conceptus calor et nigris ocellis
imas corripuit vorans medullas:
urebat roseus per ora fulgor,
urebat niveus per ora candor,
urebat coma, myrreus capillus
70   urebat tumidis latens papillis,
mox cursans Amor huc et huc et illuc
et per guttura, per genas manusque
et per collaque lucidamque frontem,
et per pectora candidosque dentis,
75   ut iam non Amor is, sed ignis esset,
qui seram quoque calfacit senectam.

Ignites a flame and suddenly
Bursts into fire and devours
The seasoned wood you heap on it,
So for me, heat ignited   65
By the spark of your dark eyes,
Greedy, devours my deepest marrow.
Your face's rosy radiance burned,
Your face's snowy whiteness burned,
Your hair burned, those perfumed tresses   70
Covering your swelling nipples burned.
Presently Love ran here and here,
Over your throat and cheeks and hands,
Over your neck and lucid brow,
Over your shining teeth, your breast,   75
Till it wasn't Love, but fire
Warming my declining years.

: 14 :

Ad Batillam
de amaraco colenda

Et mollem cole amaracon, Batilla,
et multo madidam fove liquore,
et sparsas digitis comas repone
atque illas patulam reflecte in umbram,
5   lusum et delitias tuae fenestrae
et rarum cupidi senis levamen.
Dum te prospicit hortulos colentem
tondentemque comas simulque ramos
in conum docili manu prementem,
10   miratur digitos stupetque ocellos
et totus miser haeret in papillis
frigensque aestuat aestuansque friget,
infelix simul et simul beatus.
Felices sed apes, nemus beatum
15   quae circumvolitant leguntque flores
et rorem simul et tuos labores
in tectis relinunt liquantque nectar!
    O qui Mesopii liquoris auram
Hyblae et quaeritis, et valere Hymetum
20   Hyblam et dicite, mel Batillianum
ipsi quaerite. Sordet Hybla, sordet
vertex Atticus et liquor Panhormi:
ite et quaerite mel Batillianum.

: 14 :

To Batilla Cultivating Marjoram

Tend your marjoram, Batilla
And water it abundantly.
Gather the scattered leaves by hand
And arrange them in the ample shade,
The play and pleasure of your window   5
A treat for elderly desire.
When he sees you gardening,
Shearing off the leaves and shoots,
Shaping a cone with a skillful hand,
Her hands astonish, her eyes amaze,   10
Helpless, he adores her breasts,
And freezing burns and burning freezes,
And wretched is and blessed at once.
But the bees are happy. They fly about
The blessed grove, sipping flowers and dew,   15
They reseal your labors in their honeycombs
And clarify the honey!
   O you, who seek the fragrances
Of Hybla, of Mopsopius,
Call Hybla and Hymettus rich: 20
Seek out Batilla's honey.
Hybla's honey is muck, and so's
Palermo's and the Attic peak's.
Go and find Batilla's honey.

: 15 :

Ad Batillam

Cum rides, mihi basium negasti,
cum ploras, mihi basium dedisti;
una in tristitia libens benigna es,
una in laetitia volens severa es.
5   Nata est de lacrimis mihi voluptas,
de risu dolor. O miselli amantes,
sperate simul omnia et timete!

: 15 :

To Batilla

Laughing, you refused to kiss me,
Weeping, you bestowed a kiss;
Only kind when you are sad,
Only harsh when you are happy.
All my pleasure comes from tears,   5
Grief from laughter. My poor lovers,
Hopes and fears are joined together!

: 16 :

Ad Alfonsum ducem Calabriae

Carae mollia Drusulae labella
cum, dux magne, tuis premis labellis,
uno cum geminas in ore linguas
includis simul et simul recludis
5 educisque animae beatus auram,
quam flat Drusula pectore ex anhelo,
cui cedunt Arabi Syrique odores
et quas Idaliae deae capilli
spirant ambrosiae, cum amantis ipsa
10 in mollis thalamos parat venire,
dic, dux maxime, dic, beate amator,
non felix tibi, non beatus esse,
non vel sorte frui deum videris?
 Idem cum tenero in sinu recumbis
15 et iungis lateri latus genisque
componisque genas manusque levi
haeret altera collo et altera illas
quas partis pudor abdidit retractas,
mox, post murmura mutuosque questus,
20 post suspiria et osculationes,
imis cum resolutus a medullis
defluxit calor et iacetis ambo
lassi languidulique fessulique,
ignorasque tuaene Drusulaene
25 tuus pectore spiritus pererret,
tuo an spiritus illius recurset,
uterque an simul erret hic et illic,
dic, dux maxime, dic, beate amator,

48

: 16 :

To Alfonsus, Duke of Calabria

When, great Duke, you place your lips
Upon Drusula's tender mouth,
When two tongues meet and separate
Both within one single mouth
And, blessed, you breathe in the soul's breath   5
Drusula gave from her panting heart —
A scent sweeter than Syriac
Or Arab scents, ambrosia
From the Idalian goddess's tress —
When she enters her lover's delicate chamber,   10
Tell, greatest Duke, tell, blessed lover,
Are you not happy, are you not blessed?
Have you not the luck of the gods?
    And when you recline on her tender breast
And you're side by side, placing your cheek   15
By her cheek, one hand
Touching her smooth neck, the other
Stroking those parts that shame conceals,
Soon, after murmurs and mutual cries,
After sighing, after kissing,   20
Out of your very deepest marrow
The heat subsides, and you lie together,
Spent, languid, quite exhausted,
Don't you know that your spirit roams
In the heart of your Drusula?   25
That her spirit runs to yours,
That in both hearts they roam together?
Tell, greatest Duke, tell, blessed lover,

non sordent tibi regna, sordet aurum,
30   non unus tibi coelitum videris?
    Et cum lacteolo sinu quiescens
fessus languidulum capis soporem,
carpis dulciculum, beate, somnum,
non fallor, tibi, credo, dormienti
35   occurrit Charitum nitens figura,
occurrit Veneris decora imago:
miraris faciem, genas, capillum,
dentis, oscula, candidamque frontem,
nigra et lumina, poetulos ocellos,
40   colla et candida, vesculas papillas;
at cum te placidus sopor reliquit,
reliquit Charitum nitens figura,
reliquit Veneris decora imago,
sola et Drusula lectulo remansit,
45   quas somnus Veneremque Gratiasque
ostendit tibi, quas quies sopora,
nonne his Drusula par tibi videtur,
unamque has tibi Drusulam referre?
Dic, dux maxime, dic, beate amator,
50   non credis simul et deas dolere,
atque uni tibi et invidere divos?

Are not gold and kingdoms cheap?
Are you not one of the gods?   30
    And when upon that milky breast
You sleep a little languidly,
Blessed, you take a sweet little nap,
Unless I'm wrong, I think you see
The shining shapes of Graces,   35
The lovely form of Venus.
You see her face, her tresses, cheeks,
Her teeth, mouth, shining brow
And dark eyes, slanting eyes,
White throat and delicate breasts;   40
But when this quiet sleep departs,
The shining shapes of Graces leave,
The lovely form of Venus leaves
And Drusula remains alone in bed,
And Venus and the Graces   45
That sleep and peaceful dreams revealed:
Is Drusula not their equal?
Didn't they remind you only of Drusula?
Tell, great Duke, tell, blessed lover,
Don't you think that even goddesses resent you?   50
Don't even the gods envy you alone?

: 17 :

Sodales invitat ad Martinalia

Martini sacer est dies. Abite
curae pervigiles; venite, somni;
quicquid sollicitum recedat a me,
dulces undique perstrepant cachinni:
5   hac nil luce bibacius sit unquam,
nil his somniculosius tenebris.
Sed somnos pater excitet Liaeus:
festina, puer, i, Petrutianas
cellas ictibus usque verberato
10   (illas nam pater incolit Liaeus),
illinc promito, quas volo, quietes.
Cretensis fluat hinc et inde Bacchus,
hinc illinc liquor aureus Falerni;
certent Massica Cecubis racemis,
15   et lenis Chios ac severa Lesbos
ac Vernacia Brutiis diotis;
fundat regia Moroan Panhormus,
sed nec Corsica Barolumque, gratae
Bacchi deliciae, aut madens Tarentum
20   non dulces mihi funditent lagenas;
mite et Melfia, Clariana mite
muscatum mihi mittat haec et illa:
raros postulat haec dies liquores,
nardo non sine Cypriaque myrra.
25   Tu Scalam pete, non novum sodalem;
dic e scriniolo sinuque amatae
uxoris mihi Cyprios odores,
zebethi quoque proferat liquores.

: 17 :

He Invites Friends to the Martinalia

Martin's holy day is here. Be gone,
Wakeful worrying. Dreams, come here;
May all kinds of cares depart from me.
Let sweet laughter peal out everywhere.
Nothing was ever more bibulous than this day,   5
Nothing more somniferous than these shadows.
But father Liaeus casts off sleep:
Hurry, my boy. Go and batter hard
Upon the cellars of Petrucianus
(For Father Liaeus dwells inside.)   10
Fetch me thence the quiet I desire,
Let Cretan wine flow everywhere,
Everywhere golden liquor of Falernum.
Let Massic grapes contend with Caecuban,
And soft Chios, Lesbos the dry,   15
May Vernacia vie with Bruttian flagons.
Let royal Palermo pour out its Moroan
But not Corsica or Barolo, those
Pleasures dear to Bacchus, nor drunken
Tarento pour its sweet flagons my way;   20
But let Melfi and Clariana
Send their gentle muscat to me.
This day has need of special vintages,
Not without nard and Cyprian myrrh.
So go find Scala, my old friend.   25
Take from his little chest or from the breast
Of his dear wife some Cyprian smells for me,
And see if he will give Zebethan liquors.

Heu, quod frigida me gravat senecta:
30   non, non haec sine vinula puella
abiret mihi nox. Adest Liaeus,
adest letitiae pater: valete
tristes excubiae; sopor venito.
35   Misce nunc cyathos, puer, repostos:
sic somni pater imperat Liaeus.

Alas, cold old age presses on me now.
Let not this night depart from me without   30
A tipsy little girl. Liaeus come!
Come, father of happiness! Farewell
To you, nocturnal vigils. Drowsiness, come.
Boy, fill the bowls up once again.
Thus orders Liaeus, the father of sleep.   35

: 18 :

De nuptiis Ioannis Brancati et Maritellae

Brancato Maritella copulatur.
Dulcis coniugii bonum sit omen,
sit felix simul et viro et puellae
et natis pariter nepotibusque;
nascatur similis puer parenti,
nascatur similis puella matri,
gratus Castaliae puer choreae,
grata et Dulichiae puella divae:
haec nos coniugibus bene ominemur.
Nunc qualis tibi sit futura pugna,
Brancate, accipias, novus maritus
cum sis et nova cum tibi sit uxor.
Intras cum thalamum quiete prima,
ne statim venias ad arma dico,
sed blandis precibus iocisque blandis
pertentes aditum cachinnulisque;
misce his oscula, nunc petita blande,
nunc furtim tibi rapta, nunc negata,
quae per vim capias, nec erubescas
mox ad lacteolas manum papillas
tractans inicere ac subinde collo
impressum tenero notare dentem,
nec non et tumidum femur latusque
tractabis niveum manuque laevi
ad dulcem venerem viam parabis,
nam dulcis veneris manus ministra est.
Post blanda oscula garrulasque voces
dulcisque illecebras iocosque molles,

: 18 :

The Marriage of Joannes Brancatus and Maritella

Maritella is joined to Brancatus.
May the marriage be a sweet one;
Good luck, both to the man and the girl
And joy to their children and children's children.
May the son resemble his father,   5
May the daughter resemble her mother,
The boy loved by the Castalian throng,
The girl by Dulichium's goddess.
We presage good things for this marriage.
    Now as for the battle that lies in store,   10
Brancatus, listen, since it's the case
That you're a new husband and she's a new wife.
First, you're to enter the chamber quietly,
Don't take up arms too fast.
Make an entrance with soft imploring,   15
With soft jokes and little chuckles,
And add some kisses, some asked for sweetly,
Some stolen slyly, some denied,
Which call for force. Now don't blush
To seize and stroke those milky breasts,   20
Then to leave behind the mark
Of your teeth upon her tender throat.
And you will stroke her swelling thigh,
Her snowy flank, and your other hand
Will ready the way to her sweet sex,   25
For the hand is sweet sex's servant.
After sweet kisses, chatter and talk,
Sweeter charms, little jokes,

post tactus teneros levesque rixas,
30 cum sese ad cupidos resolvit illa
complexus simul et timet cupitque
tunc signum cane, tunc licebit arma
totis expedias, amice, castris,
telum comminus hinc et inde vibrans,
35 dum vulnus ferus inferas amatum.

Tender touching, playful struggles,
When she resolves herself to love,   30
Fearing but wishing to be clasped,
Then sound the trumpet. Now, my friend,
You may empty the camps of all your troops
And hand to hand, brandish your weapon
As, fierce, you inflict the wound of love.   35

: 19 :

De Fanniae labellis

Si quaeris Venerem Cupidinemque,
dulcis Fanniolae labella quaeras:
hic sedes posuit suas Cupido
hic laetas agitat Venus choreas.

: 19 :

Fannia's Lips

If you are looking for Venus and Cupid,
Look for sweet little Fannia's lips.
Cupid makes her home here;
Here Venus leads her joyful dance.

: 20 :

Loquitur puella fuscula

Quod sim fuscula, quod nigella, et ipsae
fusco in pectore nigricent papillae,
quid tum? Nox nigra, fusculae tenebrae;
nocturnis colitur Venus tenebris,
5   optat nox Venerem, Venus tenebras,
et noctes Venerem tenebricosae
delectant, pueri in sinu locata
lusus dum facit improbasque rixas.
Ergo his in tenebris latebricosis,
10   his nos in latebris tenebricosis,
lecto compositi, quiete in una
ductemus Venerem, toroque vincti
condamus tenebras, sopore ab ipso
dum solis Venus excitet sub ortum.

: 20 :

A Dusky Girl Talks

I'm dusky, a little black girl, and my nipples
Glint darkly on my dusky breasts.
And what of it? Night's black, shadows dusky,
Venus is worshiped in the shadowy nighttime.
The night wants Venus, who wants the shadows,   5
And in the shadiest night Venus is
Pleasured, folded in a young man's arms
While she sports, conducts unseemly struggles.
And so within these hidden shady places,
Within these very shady hidden places,   10
Settled in bed, together, quiet,
We'll have our sex and bound in bed,
We'll lay the shadows to rest until
Venus at sunrise shakes us out of sleep.

: 21 :

Mortem sibi imprecatur ob zelotipiam

Quis haec, me miserum, labella suxit?
Quis has, me miserum, genas momordit?
Quis collo, ah miserum, notas reliquit?
Quis, ah, quis teneras sacer papillas
5   tractavit digitis manuque pressit?
Quis candentia gutture ex eburno
accepit spolia ore, dente, labris?
Quis felix animam, beatus udo
quis de pectore rettulit salivam?
10   Quis o caetera? Sed quis, ah quis, ehu,
(meme iam miserum iuvat perire!),
quis stricto pugione pectus haurit?
Hic, hic est dolor ense finiendus!

: 21 :

Suffering from Jealousy He Prays for Death

Woe is me, who sucks those lips?
Pitiful me, who bites that cheek,
Leaves, ah pitiful, marks on that throat?
Strokes with his fingers, oh what wretch
Presses with his hand those tender breasts?   5
Who from that ivory throat receives
Shining spoils with tooth and lip?
Who steals her breath, what blissful man
Licks moisture from a glistening breast?
And all the rest! But who, alas! —   10
For it's better to die now in my misery —
Gouges his breast with naked dagger?
This torment must be ended by the sword!

: 22 :

Turtures alloquitur
sciscitans eas de amoris natura

Quae ramo geminae sedetis una
atque una canitis, vagae volucres,
una et gutture luditis canoro,
cum vobis amor unus, una cura,
5   unum sit studium fidele amoris
(nostri nam variant subinde amores),
vos, blandae volucres, amoris instar,
exemplum fidei iugalis unum,
quae vis, obsecro, dicite, est amoris
10   tam constans male dissidensque secum?
Nam, si pascitur e calore et igni,
cur, o cur miseri subinde amantes
frigescunt simul et tremunt geluque
toto pectore sanguis obrigescit?
15   Sin est frigida vis geluque ab ipso
horrescit simul omnibus medullis,
cur, o cur miseri subinde amantes
uruntur tacito calore et igni,
toto et pectore sanguis ustilatur?
20   Quaen haec tam varians subinde vis, ut
alternis calor imperet geluque?
Vos o dicite, blandulae volucres,
exemplum fidei atque amoris unum.

: 22 :

He Speaks to Turtle-Doves
Inquiring about the Nature of Love

You passing birds, perching side by side
Upon a branch, singing side by side
As if you two shared one melodious throat,
As if you were united in one love,
One thought, eager and constant in your love   5
(Our loves from time to time are changeable)
You charming birds, of love the very image,
Of yoked fidelity the prime example,
Tell, I pray, what is this force of love,
So seldom constant and so prone to difference?   10
For if it should be fed on heat and fire,
Why then, oh why, do poor lovers sometimes
Freeze and tremble together in the frost
As through their whole bodies the blood congeals?
But if that force freezes and sends   15
Shivers from that ice to every marrow
Why then, oh why, do poor lovers sometimes
Burn within from flames and silent heat
As through their whole bodies the blood is scorched?
What is this sometimes variable force   20
That alternately rules by heat and frost?
Tell us then, oh charming birds, who are
Of trust the prime example and of love.

: 23 :

De fulgentissimis Lucillae papillis

Cum mollis digitos acumque miror,
miror artifices manus opusque,
inter fasciolas papillulasque
obliquis oculis repente vidi . . .
5   Quid vidi? Video, an videre credo?
Sed certe video: en videtis ipsi
pulcro e pectore, gemmeis papillis
Lucillae radium refulse solis.
Nox est conscia, quae repente luxit,
10   quaeque expalluit illico lucerna,
ad quam tum digitos movebat ipsa.
Quod ni fasciolis papillulisque
admosset teneram manum repente,
fulsisset roseus dies repente,
15   fulsissent mediam diem tenebrae.
Fert Lucilla diem sinu corusco et
splendet pectore candicante solem.

: 23 :

Lucilla's Dazzling Breasts

I was admiring her supple fingers and the needle,
Admiring her clever hands about their tasks,
And in between her halter and her breasts,
Out of the corner of my eyes, I suddenly saw . . .
What did I see? I see. Did I really see it?   5
Yes. I saw it. You'd have seen it too.
From that pretty breast, those jeweled buds,
The sunshine of radiant Lucilla.
The nighttime saw it, how it suddenly brightened,
This lamp, by how it grew dim right where   10
She had just now been working with her hands.
And if over her halter and her breasts
She had not swiftly moved her tender hand,
A rosy day would then have burst forth swiftly,
Shadows shining forth in the broad noon.   20
Lucilla bears the day on her glittering breast,
And with her incandescent breast outshines the sun.

: 24 :

Ad Petrum Summontium

Baianas petiit Neera thermas,
Neeram sequitur Venus, Cupido
it matri comes, it Iocusque Amorque,
succedunt Charites, praeit Neera.
5   Haec acris oculis iacit sagittas,
incensas Venus excutit favillas,
at suspiria suscitat Cupido,
cit curas teneras Iocus levesque
et risus movet et serit lepores;
10 torquet spicula, tendit acer arcum
innitens Amor hucque et huc et illuc
spargit vulnera, funditat venenum,
at blandae Charites canunt levantque
curas sollicitas linuntque plagas,
15 miscent et lacrimis iocos. Neera
ipsa inter Veneres Cupidinesque
incedit dominans regitque euntis
et legem statuit diis deabusque.
    O felix (mihi crede) Petre, felix,
20 cui formosa Neera, cui Cupido
et Cypris favet et favent Amores,
cui blandae Charites parant choreas
et motus numeris modosque miscent!
O felix iterum et quater beate
25 Summonti: tibi lacteae puellae
praetendunt teneros sinus, Neera
praefert oscula, mordicat labella!

: 24 :

To Petrus Summontius

Neera goes to take the Baian baths,
Venus follows Neera, Cupid goes
Along for company, then Jest and Love.
The Graces follow Neera, who takes the lead.
She's hurling sharpened arrows with her eyes,   5
Venus scatters flaming sparks about,
But Cupid goes on stimulating sighs,
Jest rouses tender thoughts, and he rouses
Light laughter, sowing wit and grace.
Love hurls spears and, eager, draws his bow   10
And leaning, here and there and over there
He scatters wounds, pouring out his poisons.
But the winsome Graces sing, lightening
Burdensome concerns. They soften blows
And mingle jokes with tears, while Neera   15
Herself, among the Venuses and Cupids,
Steps forth leading, ruling the whole train,
Setting up laws for goddesses and gods.
   Oh happy Petrus (trust me), happy you
On whom lovely Neera, on whom Cupid   20
And Venus smile, on whom Loves smile,
He for whom the winsome Graces dance,
Blending modes and motions all in measure!
Oh happy once again and four-times blessed
Summontius! Girls white as milk thrust towards you   25
Their tender breasts, and Neera
Offers you her kisses, bites your lips!

: 25 :

De Altilio

Comptis Altilius placet puellis,
incomptae Altilio placent puellae,
iratam quia fecerit Dionen.
Cano candidior puella cygno,
5   quam totis Amor insidens medullis
fulgentis pueri usserat calore,
oblatum sibi dum suaviari,
dum laevi cupit hinc et inde collo
utraque et simul implicare palma,
10   hic trux Altilius reflectit ora
et dextra cupidas manus repellit
ac verbis ferus improbis minatur.
Tunc illa in miseros abit dolores
et largus cadit imber ex ocellis;
15   torpent pectora mensque corculumque,
semi et mortua lectulo recumbit,
ultricem in puerum imprecata divam.
Incomptae Altilio hinc placent puellae.

: 25 :

Altilius

Altilius pleases elegant girls;
Inelegant girls please Altilius,
Because he's made Dione angry,
A girl yet whiter than the whitest swan,
In whose deep marrow Love residing,   5
Burned with the fire of that brilliant boy.
When she wanted to kiss, when
She desired around that reluctant neck,
To encircle both her hands,
This cruel Altilius turned his face,   10
Struck away her hungry hands
And berated her with angry words.
She then dissolved in grief,
Great tears poured from her little eyes,
Dead her little heart and mind and breast   15
She lay, half-dead upon her bed
Begging the goddess for vengeance.
So inelegant girls please Altilius.

: 26 :

De Marulli amoribus

'Musae, quas adamet meus Marullus,
aut si quae redament meum Marullum,
Musae, dicite, nanque amare certum est.'
'Nosti delitias puellularum,
5   nosti, quae veneres cupidinesque
argutis iaculatur ex ocellis,
quae spirat casiamque cinnamumque,
ministrat pharetram facesque Amori,
pulcro pectore dia Septimilla:
10   haec illa est, quam adamat tuus Marullus,
quae contra redamat suum Marullum,
felix copula, mutui calores!'

: 26 :

Marullus's Loves

"Tell, Muses, which girls my Marullus loves,
Or if any girls love my Marullus back.
Tell me, for he's sure to be in love."
"You know what pleasures little girls can give,
You know about the Venuses and Cupids   5
That come forth darting from her eloquent eyes.
Who breathes the scents of cinnamon and cassia,
Who wields the quiver and the torch of Love?
Goddess Septimilla, fair of form,
She's the one whom your Marullus loves,   10
She's the one who loves him in return.
A happy union! Each burns hot as the other."

: 27 :

De amoribus Francisci Caracioli

Quid Caraciolus meus sodalis,
quid Franciscus agit meus? Caletne?
Quidni, cui tener ignis usque et usque,
usque et mollibus ardet in medullis,
usque et fulgidulis micat favillis?
Crudelis pueri impias sagittas,
immanem pharetram dei minacis!
Absens uritur hic amans misellus,
absenti rapitur misellus igni,
ardenti miser ustilatur aura;
at trux Harmosine faces ministrat
et ridet simul et dolet querentem,
promittit simul et negat roganti:
o quam difficiles gravesque amores!
Sed tu, si sapies, meus sodalis,
contemne Harmosinas Myrosinasque
et dulcis tibi quaere Postumillas,
ad quas tu venias meridiator,
et nocturnus eas, eas diurnus,
cum quis in socio toro quiescas,
in quarum tenero sinu recumbas.
optatos capiens simul sopores
post gratam venerem levesque rixas,
cum sese improbulus remisit ardor,
languent corpora succiduntque ocelli,
e colloque graves cadunt lacerti

: 27 :

Franciscus Caraciolus's Loves

My comrade, Caraciolus, what's he up to?
My friend Franciscus, is he burning now?
Why wouldn't he? Deep and deep the tender fire
Burns in his soft marrow, deep and deep,
Shining with its sparkling little flames.   5
Impious the arrows of the cruel boy,
Vast is the quiver of the menacing god!
He burns, loving, wretched and absent,
Wretched, tortured by the absent flame,
Wretched, scorched by an ardent wind.   10
But cruel Harmosine wields her torches,
Both mocks and hurts the plaintive man,
Promises and refuses to do his bidding:
O loves, how difficult, how grave!
    But you, if you have any brains, my friend,   15
Give up the Harmosines, Myrosines,
And go and find the darling Postumillas
Whom you may visit for a little nap,
Showing up by day as well as night,
Getting a little rest in their friendly bed,   20
Reclining on their tender breasts a while
And snatching a little sleep while you're at it,
After pleasant sex and gentle tussles
When your wicked little fires have abated,
Your bodies languish and your eyes succumb   25
And tired arms untangle from each other

et mutae reticent in ore linguae.
Tum felix (mihi crede), tum beatus,
tum luces tibi fulserint serenae,
30   tum noctes tibi luxerint beatae:
quaerunt ludere, non dolere amores!

And tongues return silent to each mouth.
Then happy (now believe me), then blessed,
Then calm, bright days will shine upon you,
Then blessed nights will gleam for you.   30
Love is a game, not a time for grief!

: 28 :

Ad Stellam puellam

Dum furtim mihi connives ocello,
flectis mox aciem simulque rides,
post hinc et variat color per ora
et suspiria lassa sentiuntur,
5   stillatim mihi corda deliquescunt
sudor tempora frigidus pererrat
et passim tremor ossibus vagatur,
ut sensus animum repente linquant,
ut fiam miser et beatus una.
10   Sed iam plus solito nitescit aer,
iam lux candidior diem serenat;
cur ah, cur tenebrae repente nobis,
cur nox exoritur, nigrescit aura?
An sentis, miser, an, miselle, sentis?
15   Stella est ad speculam, refulsit in te:
solem lumina victa pertimescunt.
O claras medio die tenebras,
o lucem sine nube nigricantem!

: 28 :

To Stella

You're looking at me sidewise, secretly,
And suddenly you turn and face me laughing.
Then everything before me changes color
And I seem to hear a soft sighing.
Now drop by drop my innards melt away,   5
A cold sweat appears on my forehead,
And a trembling goes through all my bones
As suddenly I think I may be fainting,
As if, at once, I were both blessed and wretched.
But the air shines with unaccustomed brightness,   10
A whiter light clarifies the day.
And what's the meaning of this sudden shadow?
Why is it night? Does the air grow dark?
Ah, what do you feel, poor man, poor little man?
Stella's at her mirror. She shines on you.   15
Your dazzled eyes take terror at the Sun.
Oh brilliant darkness in the midst of day!
Oh daylight dimming in a cloudless sky!

: 29 :

De Marulli munusculis

Misit caesolos mihi Marullus
cumque his versiculos venustiores,
quales Menaliae canunt puellae,
una cum gelido lavantur amne,
5   quales Aoniae canunt sorores,
cum laetas agitant simul choreas.
Par est versiculis referre versus:
quid pro caseolis referre par est?
Oranda est mihi blanda Septimilla,
10   ut pro caseolis velit referre
centum basiola et Catulliana
centum suaviola atque Lesbiana.

: 29 :

Little Gifts from Marullus

Marullus sent me some little cheeses
Along with some nice little poems
Such as sing the Menalian girls
When they wash in the icy stream,
Such as sing the Aonian sisters   5
When aroused to the joyful dance.
You can send back a poem for a poem,
But what can you send back for cheeses?
I'm going to beg sweet Septimilla
To make good the gift of cheeses   10
With a hundred kisses, Catullan ones,
And another hundred like Lesbia's.

: 30 :

Ad Chariteum

Sunt gratae in tenebris faces, in aestu
afflatus levior recentis aurae,
defessis sopor, instrepentis undae
languenti sonitus sitique pressis
5 stillans e patera fluente lympha,
est grata et senibus quies merumque;
nec aegro iuveni sopor, nec aura,
nec rivus strepitans, quies merumve
aufert tristitiam aut levat dolores,
10 sed risus tenerae procax puellae
poetisque ex oculis remissa flamma,
afflat quae veneremque gratiamque,
sed dulces recreant leporis aurae
et molles choreae et modi canori.
15   Felix Endimion suopte somno!
Non curae vigiles amoris illum
torquent, sollicitudo nec diurna,
non suspiria garrulive questus,
quem coelo dea dum petit relicto,
20 dum Lamon petit et suos amores,
sopitum placido toro titillat,
sopito illecebras facit iocosque,
sopiti immoritur labris genisque,
parcit sed placidae tamen quieti.
25   At te balneolae tuae bearunt,
beavit Veneris sopora myrtus,
bearunt Charites deae ministrae,
e quis, o Charitee, nomen hauris.

: 30 :

To Chariteus

Welcome torches light the dark, a soft
Breath of fresh air relieves the heat,
Sleep for the tired, the sound of crashing waves
For those who rest, and for those who thirst,
Drink, dripping from a brimming bowl,   5
Quiet for the elderly, and wine.
For a troubled youth, not sleep nor breezes,
Not splashing streams, quiet, wine
Carry off the sadness, lift the cares,
But a little girl's seductive laugh,   10
Fire provening from slanting eyes
Which kindle sex, kindle pleasure;
It is charm's soft breezes that refresh,
Gentle dancing to melodious tunes.
    Endymion, happy in his own sleep!   15
He is untormented by the wakeful
Cares of love, the worries of the daytime,
By sighing or by chattering complaints,
He whom the goddess seeks forsaking
Heaven, seeking Latmus and her loves.   20
Asleep, she stirs him in his quiet bed,
Flirts with the sleeping one, teases him,
Places slow kisses on his cheeks and mouth,
Preserving the whole time his quiet rest.
    But those baths of yours, they blessed you,   25
The sleepy myrtle Venus loves blessed you,
The Charites, handmaids of the goddess, blessed you.
You got your name from them, Chariteus.

Hae, dum balneolis frequens lavaris,
30   dum myrtos canis et canis Dionen
et Lunae revocas per ora nomen,
illam composito toro locarunt
et laetam gelida stetere in umbra.
Effulsitque novo decore Luna
35   ac nudis iubar extulit papillis,
cuius roridulo e sinu beatae
spirabant rosei liquoris aurae,
cuius de teneris fluens labellis
stillatim ambrosiae liquebat humor,
40   quo myrtos ubi lectulumque et ipsum
afflavit zephyrumque ab ore civit,
in te delicias suas refudit,
refudit Cyprium et Syrum liquorem
ac tecum viridi iocosa in umbra
45   tecumque Assyrio beata lecto
ludit Idaliae iocos palestrae
et tecum placida cubat quiete.
    Felix balneolum lavante Luna
felicesque dea iocante myrti,
50   felix lectule lusitante diva,
felices Charitee amante Baiae!

They, on your frequent visits to the baths,
While you sang of myrtle and Dione,   30
Summoning Luna before you by name,
Would place her down in a tidy bed,
Happy in the cool shade, they placed her.
And Luna shone forth with a new splendor,
And a radiance streamed from her naked breasts;   35
Out of the blessed one's dewy parts
A redolence of rosy liquor breathed,
And flowing down from her tender lips
Ambrosian essence dropwise liquefied.
Where she stirs the myrtle and the little bed   40
She breaths a little zephyr from her mouth,
Pours back upon you all her pleasures,
Syrian scent and Cyprian she pours.
And playful with you in the verdant shade,
Blessed with you in the Assyrian bed,   45
Wrestles in the manner of Idalia,
Sleeps with you then, quietly and sound.
    Happy the baths where Luna bathed
And happy myrtles where the goddess sports,
O happy bed whereon the goddess plays,   50
Happy Baiae while Chariteus loves!

: 31 :

Ad Masium Aquosam

Ne tu, ne pete balneas, Aquosa,
quin molles iubeas valere Baias
et litus madidum ebriosque fontis:
nil illis petulantius lacunis,
5   infractum magis impudentiusque.
O iam iam pete balneas, Aquosa,
et litus tepidum et lacus salubres:
nil Baiis moderatius severis,
ad quas Palladius chorus migravit,
10   migravit studium pudoris omne,
migrarunt simul Attici lepores
atque artes itidem bonae migrarunt,
his postquam Hippolyte lavavit undis,
quam Musae erudiere, Comitasque
15   fovit Cecropio sinu, Decorque
atque una Pudor arte temperarunt,
et Virtus, numeros suos per omnes
exornans, solio suo locavit
reddentem populo patrique iura.
20   Hinc mores dominae sequuntur undae,
ut nil sit mage balneis severum,
nil Baiis moderatius sit ipsis.
Quocirca cole balneas, Aquosa,
et litus medicum atque aquas salubres,
25   quas et Pierides colunt puellae,
quis et se Cicero Maroque lavit,
dum hic Anchisiaden canit vagantem,
illic Socraticos refert libellos.

: 31 :

To Masius Aquosa

Stay away from the baths, Aquosa,
No, bid lanquid Baiae farewell,
Its soaking shore and drunken fountains.
Nothing is saucier than these pools,
More effete, more impudent.   5
But seek, Aquosa, now those baths,
The mild shore and the healthy lake.
Nothing's more measured than the austere Baiae
To which Athena's worshipers came
All earnest modesty as well   10
Together with Attic charm.
And the liberal arts came as well
After Hippolyta washed in these waves,
Whom the Muses taught, and Companionship
Warmed in the Cecropian breast, where Grace   15
And Modesty mingled together in tune,
And Virtue, adorned in every part,
Placed upon his throne the one who
Granted laws to his people and country.
The waves here follow the goddess's laws;   20
There's nothing more austere than these baths,
More temperate than this Baiae.
Therefore, Aquosa, cultivate
The medicinal shore and the healthy waters
Where the Muses' young daughters also dwell,   25
Where Cicero and Maro bathed.
One sang of Anchises' wandering son;
The other brought back the Socratic books.

: 32 :

De Albini munusculis

Nolo caseolos ducis tenacis:
vani caseoli ducis, valete!
Ducis caseolos nihil moramur:
ducis caseoli valete, abite!
5   Albini volo dona liberalis:
Albinus mihi carduos Sicanos,
Albinus mihi salsulas olivas,
Albinus mihi mella succarumque,
quin et fasciculos dedit rosarum,
10   promisit quoque Cyprios odores,
missurus quoque myrteos liquores.
Vani caseoli ducis, valete!
Nil iam caseolos ducis moramur:
Albini volo dona liberalis.
15   Albinum faciles ament puellae,
Albino faveat Venusque Amorque.
Alfonsum tetricae doment puellae,
Alfonso noceat Venusque Amorque,
sint et Drusula Drusulaeque ocelli
20   irati nimis atque sevientes
et caepas simul haliumque ructet,
siquando ad thalamum vocabit illum,
professus dare qui mihi recusat
paucos caseolos, inane donum.

: 32 :

Albinus's Little Gifts

I don't want the Duke's little cheeses;
Duke's parsimonious cheeses, farewell!
The Duke's little cheeses don't interest me.
Farewell, be gone with you, Duke's little cheeses!
I like Albinus' s generous gifts.   5
He gave me Sicilian thistles, Albinus,
He gave me pickled olives.
Albinus, he gave me honey and sugar,
Albinus, even bundles of roses,
And he promised to send me Cyprian scents   10
And juices pressed from myrtle.
Farewell to you, Duke's little cheeses.
The Duke's little cheeses don't interest me.
I like Albinus's generous gifts.
Let tractable girls love Albinus,   15
And Venus and Amor too;
May fierce girls subdue Alfonsus;
May Venus and Amor punish him,
And may Drusula with her eyes
Savage and altogether wild   20
Belch odors of onions and garlic whenever
She calls him into her bedroom—
Him, who having promised, refused
A few little cheeses, ridiculous gift!

LIBER SECUNDUS

Ad Marinum Tomacellum

Et fontis calidos amant Camenae
et Musae calidis aquis lavantur
et Musae placidos colunt recessus
et dulcis numeros amant Camenae
5   et Musae choreis, choris Camenae
traducunt rapidos per antra soles,
et soles rapidi tepent per antra,
dum Musae placidas agunt choreas,
dum mollis agitant choros Camenae.
10   Nobis tristitiae gravesque curae
mulcendae numeris, Marine, et inter
ludendum cyathos. Bene ominemur:
pax est Italiae futura, pacem
et vina et choreae et Venus sequuntur,
15   hac et balnea lege sunt colenda.
Assitis, Charites, seni iocanti,
assis, Syrmio, o insularum ocelle,
assitis, cineres Catulliani,
cantu dum senium levo molestum.
20   Ne tu, ne calidas, Marine, thermas
intres cum tenera senex puella:
nil habet socium senex puellae,
a sene omnimodis puella differt.
Pro thermis paterae et merum, lagena
25   assit pro tenera tibi puella,
assit Melphiaci cadus Liaei:

BOOK II

To Marinus Tomacellus

Camenae love the warming fountains,
Muses bathe in warming waters,
Muses haunt the quiet nooks,
Camenae favor pleasant song,
Muses dance, Camenae dance,   5
Scorn hot suns throughout the grottos,
Grottos warmed by scorching suns,
And Muses do a quiet dance,
Camenae lead a gentle dance.
And our grief and heavy cares   10
Songs soften, and we, Marinus,
Play in our cups and prophesy
Peace for Italy succeeded
By wine and dancing and by Venus:
This is the law that rules the baths.   15
Graces, come to this blithe old fellow;
Jewel of islands, Sirmio,
Come, and come Catullan ashes
While I sooth harsh age with song.
But you, Marinus, do not enter   20
Warm baths with a tender girl,
Not an old man's fit companion,
Girls are different from old men.
Cups and wine instead of baths,
Jugs not little girls for you,   25
Melphiacan wine in flagons.

93

thermae nam iuvenes decent, tabernae
Leneae invalidos senes. Is ipse es,
arens, frigidulus minutulusque
30   cui pendet cucumis rigentque venae,
quae Bacchum sitiant madentiorem.
Amabo, puer, hos minutiores
irrora calices. Marine, sume:
nam quotquot calices tibi propinas,
35   tot divos tibi feceris propinquos,
et quotquot cyathos tibi litabis,
tot aras statues diis benignis.
Hae sunt deliciae, haec senurn voluptas.

Baths are for the boys, wine taverns
Suit decrepit men. And you,
Dried up, frigid, minuscule,
Hung with just a little pickle,   30
Your stiff veins want a wetter Bacchus.
If you please, lad, moisten these
Tinier cups. Marinus, lift one,
For every chalice that you pledge
You'll draw another god still closer.   35
With every flagon you will raise
An altar to a friendly god.
Such the delights and pleasures of age.

: 2 :

Ad Elisium Gallutium

Blandis versibus, Elisi, iocamur,
blandis concinimus modis amores
et blandis animum sonis levamus.
Mirum? Blandus Amor, Cupido blandus,
et blandus Iocus est Venusque blanda,
sunt blandae Charitesque Gratiaeque,
blandis templa deum sonis adimus
et blandis precibus Iovem precamur.
Lux blandissima temporum magistra.
    Vale, saeve rigor severitasque,
vale, durities Catoniana:
nil, blandum nisi, quaeritat voluptas.
Tete si mihi, cara Fanniella,
in molli sociam dabis cubili,
in nostro venies sinu fovenda,
sic istaec tibi suxerim labella,
sic istas tibi suxerim papillas,
sic omnem tibi sanguinem resuggam,
ut matri redeas dolor querenti,
ut quae te peperit nec ipsa norit,
sucto gutture, pressulis labellis,
sucto pectore, sicculis ocellis.
Ac ne pallia sint molesta nobis,
nudis corporibus cienda pugna,
nudo pectore, nudulis papillis,

5

10

15

20

25

: 2 :

To Elisius Gallutius

Elisius, sweet poems amuse us,
With sweet songs we sing of love
And with sweet sounds we lift our hearts.
You wonder? Sweet Amor, sweet Cupid,
Jocus sweet and Venus sweet,   5
Charites and Graces sweet,
We near gods' temples with sweet sounds
And pray to Jove with prayers sweet.
Sweetest Light, mistress of time.
 Farewell severity, rigor cruel,   10
Farewell Catonian harshness.
Pleasure seeks nothing unless it's sweet.
If you, my darling Fanniella,
Would share a yielding bed with me,
Warm yourself in my embrace,   15
Thusly would I suck these lips,
Thusly would I suck these breasts,
Thusly drain out all your blood
As, sorrow to a distraught mother,
She'd fail to know the child she bore,   20
Throat deflated, lips squashed flat,
Breasts deflated, eyes dried out.
And lest clothing bother us,
Let war be waged with naked bodies,
Naked chests and naked breasts,   25

nudo pectine, nudulisque coxis
et nudis pedibus genuque nudo,
ac si fert patulis furor fenestris,
nulla ut vulnera in irritum petantur,
30   ut nulli in vacuum ferantur ictus.

Naked bush and slender hips,
Naked feet and naked knee,
And clamor through the open windows:
No sought-for wound is unperformed,
No empty blow endured.   30

: 3 :

De Andrea Contrario

Dilexit iuvenem Thalia, quem nunc
senem candida diligit Sophia;
monstravit iuveni Thalia cantum,
nunc seni sapientiam Sophia;
5   cantavit iuvenis modos Thaliae,
nunc senex sapientiam reponit:
o felix iuvenis senexque felix,
Contrari; o iuvenem, o senem beatum,
quem doctus puerum erudivit Aon,
10   nunc senem erudiunt graves Athenae
casto pectore moribusque castis!

: 3 :

Andreas Contrarius

Thalia loved a youth whom now,
Aged, is loved by bright Sophia.
Thalia taught the boy to sing,
Old now, Sophia gives him wisdom.
The youth sang Thalia's tunes;   5
The old man stores up Sophia's wisdom.
O happy youth and happy old man,
Contrarius, o youth and blessed old man,
Whom learned Helicon taught as a boy,
Now in age grave Athens tutors   10
With a chaste heart and chaste habits!

: 4 :

De Focillae puella ocellis

In tuis Amor insidens ocellis
mira coepit ab arte vulnerare,
nec suetas pharetra iacit sagittas,
nec tendit veterem recurvus arcum,
5   sed, cum lumina poetulosque ocellos
huc illuc agis et subinde rides,
istis utitur ille tunc sagittis,
istis corda quatit feritque amantum:
isti spicula sunt facesque ocelli,
10   quoscunque aspicis ipsa, vulnerantur.
Omnes vulnerat, aspicis quot ipsa,
omnes ustilat, ipsa quot tueris:
isti sunt oculi faces Amoris.
At tu, ne pereas tuis ocellis,
15   in te neu propriis Amor sagittis
utatur, speculum, Focilla, vita,
ne, te cum in speculo vides probasque,
ex ipso speculo nigrisque ocellis
excussas Amor ingerat sagittas
20   atque urare tuis misella flammis,
sit tibi et speculum, fuit quod olim
Narcisso vitrei figura fontis.

: 4 :

Young Focilla's Eyes

Love residing in your darling eyes
Begins to wound with wondrous art,
Fires no wonted arrows from his quiver
Nor bending tightly pulls his ancient bow.
No, when you turn your glowing, glancing eyes,   5
Glancing here and there, and when you smile,
He takes them then and uses them for arrows.
With these he strikes and pierces lovers' breasts,
Your eyes, his torches and his javelins,
And whomsoever you observe is wounded.   10
He wounds them all, as many as you see,
He scorches them, each one whom you regard.
The firebrands of Love they are, your eyes.
But see that you perish not by your own eyes:
Let Amor not make use of your own arrows   15
Against you, Focilla, of life the mirror.
Lest, yourself admiring in the mirror,
Love pour upon you arrows shaken
From that same mirror, those dark, darling eyes,
And scorch you, wretched one, with your own flames   20
So that the mirror do to you what once
A shape in a glassy pool did to Narcissus.

: 5 :

Ad Focillam
de capillis ad frontem sparsis

Quid sparsam digito comam reponis
effusumque vage legis capillum?
Anne ut excrucies, Focilla, amantem?
Ut perdas miserum senem, puella?
5   Ne tu ne, mea, collige: evagari
ad frontem sine, diffluat capillus
circum tempora ventiletque crinis,
auram qui pariat, faces ut ipsas,
blandis quas iacularis ex ocellis,
10   succendas agitans et huc et illuc,
extinctum ut revoces senis calorem.
   Iam tu iam, mea, collige et repone,
crinem contege, subliga et capillum,
auram ne citet exciatque flammas,
15   quae nostrum prope pectus ustilarunt.
Vos, o vos tenerae, precor, puellae,
quae myrtos et amaracum rigatis,
hoc vos, hoc miserum rigate pectus,
imis quod procul ardet ab medullis:
20   en flammas simul, en simul sagittas
ipsae cernitis; hoc rigate pectus
et flammas simul et simul sagittas
ipsae extinguite et usque subrigate.

: 5 :

To Focilla
on Her Bangs

Why do you comb those tresses with your fingers
And gather up those stray and wandering locks?
Focilla, would you crucify your lover?
Would you, my dear, destroy a poor old man?
No, dear, don't be tidy, let your hair   5
Tumble down your forehead, let it flow
About your temples. Let him who makes the breeze
Flutter in your tresses so that they
May kindle the flames you hurl from your sweet eyes,
Agitating them, now here, now there,   10
Till you call back old age's sleeping heat.
   Now, now, my dear, comb and knot them up.
Cover your locks and bind away those tresses
Lest they stir the wind, excite those flames
Which make a fire close to my own heart.   15
And oh, you tender girls, I pray to you
Who irrigate the marjoram and myrtle,
Water now this pitiable heart
Which from afar burns deep within its marrow.
Behold the flames, and at the self-same time   20
The arrows; come, irrigate this heart
And at the self-same time put out the flames
And arrows, and make them leap to life again.

: 6 :

Ad Ioannem Pardum

Inter Socraticos licet libellos
atque inter studium decet sophiae
miscere et teneros, amice, lusus,
o Parde, Aonidum comes dearum.
5   Quare nec medicos lacus nec hortos
Baianos fuge myrteumve litus:
myrtos nam Maro, balneas et inter
Eneam cecinit, petit profundi
Ditis dum hostia, dum parentis umbras,
10 et prolis seriem accipit futurae;
myrtos et Cicero tuus frequentans
fontisque et celebris agros Sibyllae
ornavit Latium potente lingua,
detraxit spolia Atticae et Camenae;
15 has Marcus coluit, pater senatus,
terrarum et dominus parensque Romae
atque omnis sapientiae magister.
Has et tu cole, Parde, nam severam
quandoque et iocus addecet sophiam.
20 Et ludit sapiens: dies et ipse
et soles variant itemque lunae,
est et tristitiae lepor levamen,
Baianis lepor et levamen undis.

: 6 :

To Joannes Pardus

It's all right amid the Socratic books
And amid the pursuit of wisdom, friend,
To intermingle gentle play,
O Pardus, friend of the Aonic Muses.
So don't avoid the healthy lakes,   5
The Baian groves or the myrtled shore.
For Maro, even in myrtled baths,
Sang of Aeneas as he seeks
The way to Dis's depths,
His father's shade and the race to come.   10
Even your Cicero, haunting these myrtles,
The fountains and fields of famous Sibyl,
Bestowed eloquence on Latium
And drew plunder from the Attic Muse.
These Marcus loved, the Senate's father,   15
Lord of the earth, parent to Rome
And master of every wisdom. May you
Also love them, Pardus, for at times
Sport befits even austere wisdom,
And the wise man plays, and even the day,   20
The suns and moons will change their moods;
Humor also relieves sadness,
Relief and humor are in the Baian waves.

: 7 :

Ad Focillam
de cohibendis ocellis

Lascivos cohibe, Focilla, ocellos,
ne perdas miseros videndo amantes;
summissos nec habe, Focilla, ocellos,
ne perdas miseros pudendo amantes;
5   iratos quoque comprimas ocellos,
ne perdas miseros minando amantes;
nec sponde faciles benigna ocellos,
de spe ne perimas benigna amantes,
nec tingas lacrimis misella ocellos,
10   luctu ne perimas misella amantes.
Noli (crede, Focilla, crede) noli
istos exerere, o Focilla, ocellos:
isti quicquid agunt, Focilla, ocelli,
sunt incendia, sunt, Focilla, amantum,
15   funus (crede, Focilla) sunt amantum.

: 7 :

To Focilla
to Restrain her Eyes

Watch out, Focilla, for those sexy eyes.
You'll ruin your poor lovers with a glance.
Nor, Focilla, should you lower those eyes
Lest modesty wreak havoc on your lovers.
And do not let those eyes show any anger   5
Lest with threats you kill your sorry lovers,
Or, feeling gracious, glance as if you're willing;
A single ray of hope would wipe them out.
And even if you're sad you mustn't weep.
Your tearfulness would quite destroy your lovers.   10
Forbear, Focilla, trust me, just forbear
In any manner to reveal your eyes.
It doesn't matter what they do, Focilla.
Your eyes, Focilla, are like fires for lovers.
Trust me, Focilla, they are death to lovers.   15

: 8 :

Ad Focillam

Si rides, veneres, Focilla, rides,
si cantas, veneres, Focilla, cantas,
si saltas, veneres, Focilla, saltas:
demum, sunt veneres, Focilla, quicquid
5 ludisque et loqueris facisque agisque.
At cum nudula lectulo recumbis
inter delicias libidinesque,
tunc non es veneres, Venus sed ipsa,
Venus, ne dubita, Focilla, tunc es.

: 8 :

To Focilla

If you laugh, Focilla, it's love you laugh,
If you sing, Focilla, it's love you sing,
If, Focilla, you dance, it's love you dance.
In short, Focilla, it's always love,
Whatever you laugh or say or touch or do.   5
But naked, slender, lying in a bed
In the midst of pleasure and of lust,
You are not sexy; you are Sex itself;
Venus, Focilla, don't doubt it, is you.

: 9 :

Ad Franciscum Puccium

Quid fontes calidos nemusque Avernum,
Pucci, quid medicos petis recessus?
Baianos habitant sinus Amores,
Baianum Veneres colunt recessum,
5   Baianis Charites aquis foventur.
Adversis cupis an deis valere,
iratas tibi et excitare Baias?
Quin, Pucci mihi care, care Musis,
cum primis Veneri Cupidinique,
10   hoc, sis, hoc age pro tua salute:
unam Sulpitiam precare, et uni
rem sacram facias, roges et unam,
stillet de roseis tibi labellis
tris ut ambrosiae benigna guttas,
15   spiret de teneris tibi papillis
afflatus totidem fragrantis aurae,
his risum adiciat benigniorem.
Sic a Sulpitia salus petenda est,
uno quam liceat tamen parare
20   furtim basiolo repente rapto,
demorsis labiis et ore hiulco
spirantisque animae reflante flore.
Sic fient tibi balneae salubres:
una in Sulpitia salutis est spes.

: 9 :

To Franciscus Puccius

Groves of Avernus, thermal pools, my Puccius,
Salubrious retreats, why do you seek them out?
Amores dwell along Baiae's bay,
Venuses frequent the Baian haunts,
Graces warm themselves in Baiae's waters.   5
Or do you wish to thrive with adverse gods
And stir up Baian wrath against yourself?
No, Puccius, dear to me, dear to the Muses,
But most of all to Venus and to Cupid,
It's here that you must work out your salvation.   10
Pray only to Sulpitia, for her
Alone perform the sacred rite and beg
That, kindly, from her rosy lips she might
Drip upon you three ambrosian drops,
Waft upon you from her tender breasts   15
As many odors from the fragrant air,
Adding the while a very kindly laugh.
Thus you will find salvation in Sulpitia,
Whom one is still permitted to entice
With a secret kiss stolen suddenly,   20
With bitten lips and half-opened mouth,
A flower inhaled out of her breathing soul.
So will these baths inspire good health in you:
Your only hope of health lies in Sulpitia.

: 10 :

Ad Constantiam

Insedere tuis apes labellis:
in labris residens tuis Melissa
Hybleum liquat Atticumque rorem,
quem stillent Paphiaeque Gratiaeque.
5 O qui Castalios lacus, poetae,
quique et Thespiadum sititis amnes,
hinc et Castalii lacus liquores,
hinc et Thespiadum petatis undas:
has Constantia mollibus labellis
10 instillat, quibus Atticae Camenae
rorarunt veneres suas charimque,
quae Musis comes et comes poetis.

: 10 :

To Constantia

Bees reside between your lips,
In these lips the Bee Nymph dwelling,
Attic and Hyblean dew
Distilled by Grace and Paphian.
Oh poets who thirst for Castalian lakes,   5
Who thirst after Thespian streams,
Here you may find the Castalian pool,
Here the Thespian wave:
It flows from Constantia's soft lips
Where the Attic Camenae   10
Distill all grace and love,
Companion both to poet and Muse.

Ioannes Pardus ad Pontanum

Pontane optime, semper haud vocati
cui dii comiter assident deaeque,
cui sales nitidi facetiaeque
semper dulcibus insident labellis,
5   cui perlucida multiplexque vena
aut vinctae pede vocis, aut solutae,
dii magni, ut lepide, ut fluit decenter,
sic sentis male de tuo sodali?
Sic durum potes aut putare ineptum,
10   ut me ad balneolas tuas vocare
te sit suppuditum, invenuste, inepte,
hac in re modo non venuste, inepte,
hac in re male salse vise, ubique
cum sis salsior Atticis salinis?
15   Mene non decet his locis inesse,
ubi tu pater es severitatis,
ubi tu Cato seculi ipse nostri?

: IO BIS :

Joannes Pardus to Pontano

Best Pontanus, at whose slightest nod
The gods and goddesses hasten to encamp,
On whose sweetest lips all brilliant salt
And wit take up their residence,
Out from whom a lucid, complex vein   5
Of metred verse or of spontaneous prose,
Great gods! so charmingly, so nicely flows,
This is how you feel towards your old friend?
You can judge me foolish and inept,
That simply to invite me to your baths   10
You find a cause for shame, inept and charmless,
In this, inept, and quite devoid of charm,
Devoid, in this, of salt who otherwise
Outsalts the salt cellars of Attica?
It doesn't suit *me* to visit these baths   15
Where you're the father of severity,
You, the very Cato of our age?

: II :

Ad Focillam

In somnis tenerum mihi labellum
offers dum male suaviorque utrumque,
decursim lacrimae tibi exciderunt
et largo faciem madore tingis;
atque has dum lacrimas madenti ab ore
detergo simul et simul relingo,
surreptim mihi mordicusque linguam
exceptam rapis opterisque dente,
mox risus lacrimis iocosque miscens:
'Haec nos ludicra imaginesque noctis
has, inquis, simul in die vicissim
et veras faciamus et probemus.'
His te in iudicium voco fidemque:
en linguam tibi, porge mihi labella.

5

10

: II :

To Focilla

Sleeping you offer me your tender lips,
And as I kiss them both just barely
Tears slip down, running softly
Moistening abundantly your face.
And as I make to wipe those tears away   5
From your wet mouth, and as I lick them,
Stealthily snapping, you gain possession of
My caught tongue, and you clench your teeth,
And then, mixing smiles and jokes with tears,
You say, "These games and imaginings of the night,   10
In day time, for a change, let's make them real,
And then let's offer them our full approval."
Now I'll act as judge and keep you to your word:
Take the tongue for yourself; give me those lips.

: 12 :

Ad Focillam

Ni reddis mihi vitreos ocellos,
caecae praesidium meae senectae,
an est, cur ego non tuis papillis
manus iniciam trahamque prensas
5   usque ad basiolum, supina quod des,
quod des ipsa supina, quod supina
cervice excipias, quod ore hiulco,
quodque ipse eripiam tibi supinus?
Atque illud moneo, supina vites
10   ne lapsis pedibus ruas repente,
aut in scriniolo renisa restes.
Nam nec sat fuerit vocare matrem,
furtum aut reddere supplicemve flere,
sed nudo, mihi crede, crure, coxa,
15   nudo pectine et usque ad umbilicum
senem perpetiere verpulentum,
et clames volo: 'Reddo, reddo, reddo!',
pro quo sic ego: 'Subdo, subdo, subdo!'

: 12 :

To Focilla

That you won't give me your clear eyes,
As bulwarks in my sightless age,
Is that the reason that I cannot thrust
This hand upon your breasts and draw them up
And take the kiss that, lying, you bestow,   5
That you bestow, recumbent there, recumbent,
You take upon your throat, your parted lips,
That I myself, recumbant, take from you?
Take my advice. Be careful, lying,
Lest suddenly you rush with slipping feet   10
Or hold your ground unyielding on the desk.
It simply will not do to call your mother,
Return what you've taken or beg for mercy.
No, naked of leg, believe me, and of hip,
Naked of sex, right to the very belly   15
Suffer and receive an old man's tool.
I'll have you cry, "I'll give, I'll give, I'll give!"
And I'll reply, "Take that, take that, take that!"

: 13 :

Ad Focillam

Promissum mihi suavium dedisti,
quod mox, dum repetis revendicatum,
clauso in scriniolo obserans locasti.
Nunc furto quereris, subinde plorans
5   subreptum tibi. Ne, puella, ne fle:
vel triplex tibi basium rependam,
unam si mihi lacrimam resolves.

: 13 :

To Focilla

You gave me the kiss that you promised.
Since you wanted to claim it again,
You put it locked in a desk.
Now you cry "thief!" and you weep
At the loss. Don't cry, my girl.   5
I'll pay you back three kisses
In return for just one tear.

: 14 :

Ad Focillam

Lascivos male temperas ocellos,
nec nostrae miseret tamen senectae.
Quantum vis iuvenes ama foveque,
dum ne me fugias senem, puella;
5   atque hos atque alios ames licebit,
dum ne me abicias, puella, amantem.
Nolo delitias libidinesque:
amisi venerem libidinemque,
lascivos oculos volo precorque.
10   Lascivos quotiens reflectis in me,
et rides simul et doles, ocellos,
inspiras iuvenis mihi vigorem;
quin omnem simul exuo senectam,
si ter blanda, Focilla, suaviaris,
15   si linguam tenero sub ore suggis,
si collo quoque complicata pendes.

: 14 :

To Focilla

Don't take away those sexy eyes,
Show pity on my age.
Love all the young men, go flirt with them,
Only, my girl, don't spurn my years.
Give yourself to this one and that one,   5
Just don't deny me who loves you.
I don't want sex and thrills;
I've given up sexual pleasure.
But I beg you for those sexy eyes.
Whenever you turn towards me,   10
Laughing and weeping, those sexy eyes,
You give me back my youth.
I'd remove the garments of age
If thrice sweet you would kiss, Focilla,
Draw my tongue into your tender mouth,   15
Hang twined about my neck.

: 15 :

Ad Franciscum Pudericum

Quid Baias, Puderice, quidve fontis
suspiras tepidos, amoris expers?
Baias nam Veneres Cypro relicta,
relictis Charites procul Cytheris,
5   desertis Paphiae Uriis vetustis
migrarunt, Amor et migravit una
et blandus Iocus et tener Cupido
altrixque et iuvenum et senum Voluptas.
Quod si tu, Puderice, vina, coenas
10   suspiras, cupis et sales procaces,
nimirum Capimontii recessus
praestent haec tibi, praestet et rosarum
cultrix Antiniana: namque Baias
qui dulcis celebrant, ament necesse est.

: 15 :

To Franciscus Pudericus

Pudericus, why long for warm Baian springs,
Innocent as you are of love?
The Venuses, having forsaken Cyprus,
The Graces, departing from Cythera
And Paphians from ancient Urii,   5
All head for Baiae and Love goes along,
Winning Jest, tender Cupid
And Pleasure, the nurse of young and old.
But if it's wine and food you want,
Pudericus, or witty, wanton talk,   10
In these the Capimontian groves
Excell and so does Antiniana
Where the roses bloom. But those who praise
Sweet Baiae must be willing to love.

: 16 :

Ad Focillam

Accedis quotiens sacras ad aedes
invisisque deos adisque templa,
tecum ne comitem, Focilla, Amorem
adducas moneo domique clausum
5   servari in thalamo iube caveque
ne divos hominesque Amore captos
ad rixam cieas vocesque ad arma
et sis causa tuae volens rapinae.
Quid demens moneo? Nec ipsa Amorem
10   istis vulnerat usque qui ex ocellis,
invitum fugies, Amor nec ipse
tete deseret aut comes relinquet,
regnum qui tenet in tuis ocellis.
Hos tu sub tenui, Focilla, velo
15   compressos tege molliterque vesti
nubemque obice tenuiore vitta,
flammas ne iaculentur et sagittas:
sic et calfacies, Focilla, amantes,
non ures tamen impotente flamma.
20   Quid tum, quid misero seni, calor quem
iam iam destituit, Focilla, fiet?
Fiet quid misero seni, Focilla,
quem frigus prope congelavit omnem,
cui longe est opus ustilante flamma?
25   Iam furtim misero reclude velum,
obliquis refice et, Focilla, ocellis,
furtivo et refove senem calore,
quo primam referet vigor iuventam.

: 16 :

To Focilla

Whenever you visit sacred places,
Visit the gods, approach their temples,
Best not to bring Love along, Focilla.
Order him shut up at home.
Keep watch, I say, within the bedroom,   5
Beware lest you call out gods and men,
Enthralled by Love, to wars and arms,
And be the cause of your own ravishing.
What am I raving about? You yourself,
Won't flee reluctant Love. Love won't,   10
Wounding forever with your eyes,
Forsake or withdraw his friendship,
Who has his kingdom in your eyes.
Cover them, Focilla, with a sheer
Veil, tone down your clothing,   15
Becloud yourself with a slender fillet
Lest flames and arrows fly from them.
Your lovers turn to fire, Focilla,
Flames not devoid of power.
What then becomes of a poor old man   20
Whose warmth has all but failed?
Focilla, what about this poor old man,
Almost frozen through with cold
Who has great need of scorching fire?
Slyly, for the poor man, lower the veil,   25
Focilla, with your slanting eyes,
With hidden fire restore this man,
And give him back the strength of youth.

129

: 17 :

Ad Focillam

E risu in lacrimas, Focilla, vertis,
avertis quotiens gravata ocellos;
in risum e lacrimis, Focilla, mutas,
convertis quotiens benigna ocellos,
5   quis pacem geris et geris duellum,
quis et tristitiamque gaudiumque.
Cur, o cur tenebrae repente obortae?
Cur lux destituit, dies nigrescit?
Obiecitne oculis Focilla velum
10   et lucem obvoluit tegente vitta?
O iam detege, iam, Focilla, velum
et vittam remove et reclude ocellos,
quis lucem simul et diem ministras,
et lucem pariter diemque redde.

: 17 :

To Focilla

Focilla, you turn laughter to tears
When, sad, you take away those eyes.
You change tears to laughter, Focilla
When, kind, you give them back again,
Those eyes that wage both peace and war,   5
Bringing grief and happiness.
O, why these suddenly falling shadows?
Why vanishing light and darkening day?
Did Focilla veil her eyes,
Wrapping up light in concealing cloth?   10
O, put off your veil, Focilla.
Let fall the cloth and disclose your eyes
That minister both light and day,
Bring back the light, bring back the day!

: 18 :

Ad Petrum Summontium

Ducit dum choreas Neera, linquunt
et prata et virides agros Napeae;
pulsat dum citharam Neera, currunt
ad plectrum Dryadesque Oreadesque;
5   cantat dum ad numeros Neera, cultae ad
cantum Naiades ruunt frequentes;
miscent hinc thyasos, Neera ducit,
et ducit simul et canit: canenti
assurgit nemus assonantque ripae
10   et litus resono fragore plaudit,
plaudit ceruleis Avernus undis,
Gaurus de specula superbus alta
diffundit violas, rosam, cyperon
et myrti teneros thymique flores,
15   una et balnea consonant Neeram.
Dic, o dic, age, Petre, quae voluptas,
quae mens tum tibi. Non beatus esse,
non diis persimilis tibi videris?
Quid, cum de Charitum manu capillum
20   ornata ambrosiae et comam liquore,
in te dulciculis tuens ocellis,
in te lacteolo sinu refusa,
instillat placidum tibi venenum
et vultu et labiis et ore hiulco?
25   An non invideant dii tibi ipsi?
Non quod dii dederint, dedit Neera,
indicas etiam ut diis duellum?

: 18 :

To Petrus Summontius

When Neera leads the dance,
Nymphs leave their green meadows and fields;
When she plays the harp, the Oreads
And Dryads run to her strumming.
When she sings, the cultivated   5
Naiads throng to listen.
Bacchantes join, Neera leads,
She leads, she sings, the groves are stirred,
The riverbanks resound, and the shore
Crashes loudly, applauding the singer.   10
Avernus claps with his blue-green waves,
Proud Gaurus from his lookout
Scatters the violet, sedge and rose,
The blossoms of myrtle and thyme,
And together the baths resound: Neera!   15
Come, Petrus, tell what thoughts you have,
What pleasure. Aren't you blessed,
Very like the gods themselves?
Is she not adorned by the Graces' hands,
Her tresses wet with ambrosia,   20
Gazing at you with the sweetest little eyes,
Pouring a calming potion
On you from her milky breast,
On your face and parted lips?
And do the gods themselves not envy you?   25
Neera gave what the gods could not.
Are you challenging the gods to war?

: 19 :

Summontium ad Neeram amator

Stillant de roseis tibi labellis
Hyblei simul Atticique rores;
spirant de niveis tibi papillis
una Coritii Syrique odores;
5   vernos et zephyros, recentem et auram
afflas ambrosio, Neera, ab ore;
tecum ergo Syriam, Neera, Hymetumque
ac defers zephyri recentis auram;
quin ipsas Charites, Neera, et ipsam,
10   dum rides, Veneris refers figuram.
Istam sed remove, Neera, dextram,
ne me, ne digitis, Neera, mulce:
istis articulis, sinistra et ista
quicquid contigeris, repente prurit,
15   et quicquid digito (ah, miser, liquesco)
et quodcunque manu, Neera, tractas,
imis intima pruriunt medullis.
Pruritum digitis, Neera, praefers,
pruritum manibus, Neera, misces,
20   prurigo tua dextera est, Neera.

: 19 :

Summontius Loving Neera

Hyblean dew and Attic
Trickle from your rosy lips;
From your snowy breasts there sighs
Scents of Corycus and Syria.
Neera, fresh and vernal winds   5
Breathe from your ambrosian mouth,
Hymettus, Syria, attend you, Neera,
Air of the freshest zephyr.
When you laugh, you bring to mind
The Graces, and Venus' very form.   10
But take away your hand, Neera,
The pressure of your fingers, Neera:
Whatever these fingers, whatever this hand
Touches once contracts desire.
Whatever this finger or this hand   15
(Alas, I'm gone) strokes, Neera,
Yearns in its deepest marrow.
Your fingers bring desire, Neera,
Your hands stir up desire, Neera.
That hand, Neera, is desire.   20

: 20 :

Ad Antonium Galateum medicum

Gauranae, Galatee, te puellae
expectant, calidis laves ut undis,
expectat medicum salubre litus.
Laetentur medico iocante Baiae,
5   exultent medico lavante thermae!
Qui risus tamen inde, qui cachinni,
senex herniolose, dum lavabis?
Qui lusus tamen inde, qui lepores,
senex ventriculose, cum natabis?
10   His nec te medicum dolere par est,
risus qui soleas ineptiores
ulcisci calido fluore ventri
iniecto et liquidae madore malvae,
tum betae, atque oleo et sale atque melle.

: 20 :

To Antonius Galateus, the Physician

Gauranean girls, Galateus, attend you
Bathing in the thermal pools,
And the healthy shores attend you.
Baiae is pleased when the doctor is pleased.
The baths rejoice when he bathes!   5
What chuckling then, what laughter,
Ruptured old boy, while you bathe!
What jokes and charming games,
Fat-bellied old man, while you swim!
They can't bother you. You're a doctor.   10
When silly people laugh at you
You give them a hot abdominal flush
With an application of mallow juice
And beets and oil and salt and honey.

: 21 :

Ad Petrum Gravinam

Mecum, si sapies, Gravina, mecum
Baias et placidos coles recessus,
quos ipsae et Veneres colunt et illa,
quae mentes hominum regit, Voluptas.
5   Hic vina et choreae iocique regnant,
regnant et Charites facetiaeque,
has sedes Amor, has colit Cupido,
his passim iuvenes puellulaeque
ludunt et tepidis aquis lavantur,
10   coenantque et dapibus leporibusque
miscent delitias venustiores,
miscent gaudia et osculationes
atque una sociis toris foventur.
Has te ad delitias vocant Camenae,
15   invitat mare myrteumque litus,
invitant volucres canorae et ipse
Gaurus pampineas parat corollas,
quis cum, dulciculae accubans Philenae,
ad mensam calices madentiores
20   exicces bibulus citesque somnum.
Haec te, dum tenero sinu quiescis,
dum lento caperis sopore, molli
amplexu foveat vocetque somnos
et cantu et numeris, strepente et aura,
25   componatque genis genas et ori
os blande admoveat, quiete et una

: 21 :

To Petrus Gravina

Gravina, if you're wise, let's you and I
Visit Baiae and her quiet haunts
Which Venuses themselves frequent and Pleasure,
Wielding power over the hearts of men.
Here reigns wine and jest and dance,   5
And wit reigns as do the Charites.
Amor frequents these seats and Cupid too,
And all about youths and tender girls
At play are bathing in the thermal waters,
And dining too, and with their charming feasts   10
They mingle pleasures that are even nicer,
They mingle pleasures and with pleasures kisses
And warm themselves together on shared pillows.
Camenae summon you to these delights,
The sea and all the myrtled shores invite you,   15
And birds invite you with their melodies.
Gaurus himself provides the viny wreaths
Adorned with which, reclining with sweet Philena,
Full of wine you drain still fuller cups
At table, after which you summon sleep.   20
She, while you're resting on her lap,
Taking a little nap, should keep you warm
In her soft embrace, will call forth sleep
With songs and rhythms in the rustling breeze,
Place cheek to cheek and touching mouth   25
With her gentle mouth in the stillness,

coniungat placidos et ipsa somnos.
Haec Baiae dederint tibi, Gravina,
haec capta illecebris tuis Philena;
30   his in delitiis ages beatus,
mecum dum placidos colis recessus.

Add to yours her own quiet sleep.
This, Gravina, Baiae will bestow
And this Philena, taken by your charm;
And blessed, you will dwell in these delights   30
When we seek out these quiet haunts together.

: 22 :

Invitantur pueri et puellae
ad audiendas Charites

Ad myrtum, iuvenes, venite, myrti
laetae dum Charites canunt sub umbra;
ad myrtum, tenerae, simul, puellae,
ludunt dum Charites, venite, cultae;
5   cantant dum Paphiae chorosque ducunt,
et sponsae et iuvenes, favete linguis.
   'Indicit choreas Venus: puellae
immistae pueris agant choreas;
indicit choreas Amor: iuventus
10   misti virginibus choros frequentent.
Libertas sua balneis tributa est.
Custodes abeant, senes valento;
assint blanditiae, valete curae,
et rugae valeant severiores:
15   toto et litore perstrepant cachinni,
ipsa et balnea molliter susurrent
et lusus teneri, et leves lepores.
Libertas iubet hoc Venusque Amorque.
   'Dum lux est, pueri puellulaeque,
20   exercete oculos simul procaces,
exercete iocos benigniores,
et suspiria grata blandiantur.
At dum nox silet et tegunt tenebrae,
in molli thalamo movete rixas,
25   amplexu in cupido ciete pugnas,
nullus sit lateri modus pudorve,
certent oscula morsiunculaeque.

: 22 :

Boys and Girls Are Invited to Hear the Charites

Come to the myrtle, boys, come happy myrtle;
Charites are singing in the shade.
Tender girls, you too, come to the myrtle;
Cultivated Charites are playing.
Paphians are singing, and they're dancing;   5
Youths and betrothed, we bid you keep your silence.
   "Venus proclaims the dance: girls,
Together with boys, begin the dance;
Amor proclaims the dance, youths
Together with virgins crowd the dance.   10
Freedom rules within the baths.
Let guardians go; old men depart!
Come sweetness; farewell cares!
Farewell, wrinkled frowns!
Laughter peals across the shore   15
And even the baths whisper softly,
Tender play, delicate wit:
Freedom and Venus and Amor command it.
   "While it's light, boys and girls
Give each other sexy glances,   20
Make the most agreeable jokes,
Sooth each other with sweet sighs.
When night grows still and shadows fall,
Lead strife into the soft bed-chamber,
Do battle within willing arms,   25
Put modesty and shame aside,
Wield kisses and the smallest nibbles:

143

Libertas iubet hoc Venusque Amorque.
   'Nunc vos, nunc, tenerae, simul, puellae,
30   nobiscum, iuvenes, simul, venusti,
dulcis ad numeros pedes movete,
nobiscum lepidos choros inite.
Libertas iubet hoc Venusque Amorque.
   'Mane roscidulis nitescit hortis
35   frondenti rosa ramulo, recentem
afflans e foliis benigna odorem,
atque hanc horridulo colonus ungui
decerptam variae implicat coronae
vertitque in proprios odoris usus.
40   Manat roridulis fluens puellae
labris ambrosius liquor fragratque
stillans Idalium per ora nectar,
ardor quo iuvenum sitisque amantum
lenitur, socio simul cubili
45   iungunt dum cupidos sinus et una
miscent humidulas per ora linguas
stillatque e roseis fluor labellis.
Hunc, hunc, o iuvenes licentiores,
hunc florem legite, hoc liquate nectar:
50   vobis ambrosii fluant liquores,
vobis Assyrii fragrent odores
et suctis liquor effluat labellis.
Libertas iubet hoc Venusque Amorque.
   'Vos, o vos alios item liquores
55   haurite atque alios, puellae, odores,
novas ambrosias novumque nectar
afflatusque animae fragrantiores:
hos flores legite, has rosas liquate.
Vobis lectulus has rosas parabit,
60   spirans Assyriam simul Cyprumque,

Freedom and Venus and Amor command it.
   "Now you too, tender girls,
Lovely boys along with us,   30
Move your pretty feet in rhythm.
Enter the charming dance with us:
Freedom and Venus and Amor command it.
   "Tomorrow shines in the dewy garden
A rose in the leafy branch, kindly   35
Breathing fresh scents from its petals.
And the farmer with rough finger-nail
Clips and binds it into wreaths
And turns the scent to proper use.
Ambrosian liquid flowing from   40
A maiden's dewy lips, Idalian
Nectar moistens and perfumes.
Then youthful ardor, lover's thirst
Is tempered, as in bed as one
They clasp each other and their wet little   45
Tongues join in each other's mouths
And sweetness flows from rosy lips.
This, oh this, wanton youths,
Pluck this flower, press this nectar,
Ambrosian liquids flow for you,   50
Assyrian odors breathe for you,
Liquor flows from suckled lips.
Freedom and Venus and Amor command it.
   "Now girls, it's time for you
To drink new liquors, breath new odors,   55
New ambrosia and new nectar,
The heart's aromatic breath.
Pick the flowers, press the roses,
Sighing, your bed prepares these roses,
From Cyprus and Assyria,   60

hos flores simul et simul liquores
afflabit thalamus torusque cultus:
hos ergo thalamos torosque, nuptae
et sponsae, colite frequentiores
65   compressu, illecebris, sale et titillis,
lusu et mollitie procaciore;
hic rixas simul et iocos seratis.
Libertas iubet hoc Venusque Amorque.
    'Dens rixas moveat, manus titillans
70   et litis ciat levis querelas,
ast os et lepidos sales, et ipsae
linguae suaviloquos strepant susurros.
Admotae tepido sinu papillae
pacem concilient iocosque paci
75   et lusus similes iocisque verba,
amplexus similes et his et illis.
Libertas iubet hoc Venusque Amorque.
    'Sed iam sol rapidos movens calores
nos oci admonuit meridiani,
80   quocirca, iuvenes nurusque comptae,
post dulcis numeros choris peractis
ite hinc in thalamos meridiatum,
ite in gaudia mutuosque lusus;
nullus delitiis modus sit: ignem
85   succensum Idalia fovete lympha,
quo fessas sopor irriget medullas.
Hoc ipsa ocia nam meridiana
et mulcens simul imperat Voluptas,
hoc nati Veneris Venusque mater:
90   ite atque unanimes fovete somnos.'

The chamber and the neat beds breathe
At once these flowers and liquids:
Therefore tend these rooms and beds,
Brides and husbands, crowding them
With squeezes, charms, jokes and tickles,   65
Play and importunate tenderness.
Intersperse the fray with laughter:
Freedom and Venus and Amor command it.
   "Let teeth do battle, tickling fingers
Stir up strife and frivolous quarrels.   70
Let mouths make pretty jokes, and tongues
Themselves lisp out endearing whispers.
Let nipples pressed on a warmed chest
Make peace dear, and the jokes of peace,
Play and words that go with jokes,   75
Embraces too that go with both:
Freedom and Venus and Amor command it.
   "But now the sun with its racing rays
Warns us of the coming noontime.
So youths and elegant married girls,   80
When the delightful dance is over,
Go then to the noontime chamber,
Go in joy to mutual pleasure.
Let joys have no end. Stir up
Fires by Idalian liquids lit,   85
Where sleep refreshes inwardly.
For now the swift meridian
Holds sway with soothing Pleasure
And Venus, mother of Love's son.
Now go together, go to sleep."   90

: 23 :

De Ioanne Pardo

Dulces balneolae tepensque litus
ac Baiae eliciunt repente Pardum.
Pardumne eliciunt repente Baiae?
Pardum num Venus aut trahit Cupido?
5   Infirmam o sapientiam, cui ipsi
praescribit Venus, imperat Cupido,
et natus puer et puella mater!
Ergo Maeoniae caput palestrae
ducetur Veneris superba pompa,
10   ducetur pueri novus triumphus?
Spectatam o sapientiam omnis aevi:
Baias iam properat meus sodalis,
Baias Mesopiae Cato sophiae
et thermas petit! Euge, dulce litus,
15   dulces balneolae lacusque havete,
orbis delitiae, theatrum amantum!

: 23 :

Joannes Pardus

The mild beach, the sweet little pools,
Baiae has suddenly coaxed out Pardus.
Has Baiae suddenly coaxed out Pardus?
Or does Venus or Cupid draw him out?
Oh tottering wisdom which Venus gives   5
Instruction to, which Cupid commands,
Both the son and the girl, his mother!
So the best of Maeonian wrestlers
Will be led in Venus's proud parade,
Led as the boy's new triumph?   10
Oh famed for wisdom in all time:
Now my friend is running to Baiae,
The Cato of Mopsopian thought
Is making for the baths! Well done, sweet shore,
Sweet little baths and pools, all hail,   15
World of delights, theater of lovers!

: 24 :

Ad Manlium Rallum

Manli, delitiae Attici leporis
atque idem Latiae lepos Camenae,
cantas dum teneros Lycinnae amores
et Coi numeris refers Philitae,
5   dum molles Veneris reponis ignes,
quos dulcis tibi suggerit Tibullus,
nos, Manli, senio gravante pressi,
Miseni aut placidis vagamur oris,
Baiarum aut calidis aquis lavamur
10   et cultis Genio fovemur undis,
hortorum aut resides tenemur umbra,
quos nostra Antiniana, quos Patulcis,
ruris delitiae Maroniani,
oblectant teneri lepore cantus,
15   quos septem assiduis simul choreis
illustrant Cypriae deae ministrae:
septem nam Venerem colunt puellae,
molles, dulciculae, leves, tenellae,
formosae comites, decora pompa.

Euphrosyne

20   Haec curas abigens molestiasque,
iucundi memor et memor leporum,
miscet delitias facetiasque,
ludorum admonet, admonet iocorum
atque ore ac teneris procax labellis

: 24 :

To Manlius Rallus

Manlius, the delight of Attic grace
And grace of Latium's Muse,
While you sing Lycinna's gentle loves
In metres found by Philitas of Cos,
While you restore Venus's soft fires   5
As you were prompted to by sweet Tibullus,
We, Manlius, pressed by harsh old age,
Wander by Misenum's quiet shores,
Bathe ourselves in Baiae's thermal pools,
Warmed by waters fostered by Genius,   10
Or idle in the shadows of the gardens
Which our Antiniana, which Patulcis,
The beauties of the countryside of Maro
And singing and a certain charm beguile,
While the handmaids of the Cyprian goddess   15
Adorn them seven-fold with careless dance.
For seven serving girls attend on Venus,
Soft, a little sweet and light and tender,
Comely companions, decorous parade.

Euphrosyne

  She, casting off all cares and sorrows,   20
Giving thought to charm and thought to fun,
Mingles jokes and pleasure all together,
Urging us to play and to make quips,
Impudent her face and tender lips,

25 afflat blanditias, movet titillos
et circum omnia lusibus serenat.

Aglaia

Illa et munditiem levesque cultus
et curat nitidos beata comptus,
unius studium nitelae et unus
30 ornatus amor elegantiaeque:
ah, labes valeat, valete sordes!

Pasitea

Huic sola et species decorque solus
est curae ratioque et una formae:
spectari cupit undique et probari
35 quis cultus deceat colorque qualis,
qui comptus niveos honestet arctus
omnisque in tenero decore cura est.

Hae, gratae Idaliae deae ministrae,
assistunt thalamo coluntque divam,
40 hae, gratae comites, vagantur una
atque una varias agunt choreas:
hinc nomen Charitesque Gratiaeque.

Opsiglycea et Chariotaris

At poetis oculis, decente nutu
gaudens Opsiglycea, quaeque blandis
45 laetatur Chariotaris susurris,
sollers illecebris, faceta dictis,
quae gratis animos iocis titillat,

Breathes sweet charms, stimulates desire,   25
And makes all things seem brighter by her play.

Aglaia

She cultivates refinement, gentle grooming,
And blessed, has the care of shining locks,
Her only zeal for bright adornment and her
Only love ornament and grace.   30
Ah, farewell, everything unkempt or shabby!

Pasitea

Singular in comeliness and charm,
She is the rule of grace and cultivation,
Wishes to be seen, admired by all
Whom such complexion and such care befit.   35
Coiffed, her snowy arms ennoble her,
Her every care a tender seemliness.

These pleasant maids of the Idalian goddess
Assist in the bedchamber, serve their lady.
These pleasant escorts go around together,   40
Together join in varied choral dance:
Thus they are called the Graces, Charites.

Opsyglycea and Chariotaris

But Opsiglycea with her glancing eyes
Joyous, with eyes cast down, delights
In Chariotaris's alluring whispers,   45
Who, crafty in enticement, quick with words,
Titillates the heart with funny stories.

diversas Veneri faces ministrant,
atque ignes variis fovent venenis
50   et vel melle linunt linuntve felle,
aut acri modo temperant dolore,
aut spe, laetitia, modo ex utrisque
inspersos relinunt simulque miscent
immite et placidum nihilque linquunt,
55   quod sensus moveat vicesque amantum.

Gelopea et Pasirhythmie

Hinc cantu tenero, fide et iocosa
insignis Gelopea nobilisque,
et risu et lepidis decens cachinnis,
atque exculta sinum, comam repexa,
60   passu composito, decora gestu,
omnisque ad numeros modosque prompta
formosis Pasirhythmie lacertis
hamatas acuunt manu sagittas,
immiti puero novantque tela,
65   quae mox Idaliis premunt lacunis,
tingunt et medico recocta succo.
Crudeles calami, truces sagittae,
cuspis quis adamantina; ast inertes,
quis est plumbea vena. Ter beati,
70   felices quater hic et ille, quemque
fixit cuspidis aureae pharetra;
infelix nimium malique fati,
haesit cui lateri aereum verutum!
Hic tot perpetietur ipse totque
75   artes, quot rapidae et levis puellae,

They are in charge of Venus' various torches
And stimulate her flames with magic potions,
Sometimes smearing honey, sometimes gall,   50
And mix together now a piercing sorrow
Or hope or joy, or now, unsealing all
They've interspersed, they mix them up together,
Mercilessly leaving nothing quiet
That moves the feelings or the fates of lovers.   55

Gelopea and Pasirhythmie

  Here, with a tender song and playful lyre,
Noble and distinguished Gelopea,
Graceful in her smile and charming laughter
And exquisite of breast, her locks combed back,
Calm of tread and decorous of mien,   60
And keen for every rhythm, every step,
Lovely of shoulders, Pasirhythmie,
Sharpen both by hand their barbèd arrows,
Refitting the weapons of the Heartless Boy,
Which they then plunge in the Idalian pools,   65
Tincturing them with medicinal juices:
Cruel shafts, most aggressive arrows.
For some the adamantine tips, but others,
Dull, receive the leaden shaft. Three times
Happy, four times blessed are the ones   70
The golden-arrowed quiver finds.
Wretched indeed and full of evil fate
Is he whose side the brazen dart transfixes.
He bears so much suffering, and so many
Tricks as there are quick and shallow girls,   75

quotquot longo in amore sunt labores,
ut possit miser omnibus videri.

At, Manli, Paphiae tibi ministrae
strinxere aureolam liquore pennam
intinctam Cyprio: hinc tibi Lycinna
et risu facilis, benigna et ore,
atque uni tibi se beata comit.
O felix amor, o poeta felix!

80

So many labors in a tedious love
That wretched he might seem to everyone.

    But, Manlius, the serving girls of Paphos
Have grazed you with a golden feather dipped
In Cyprus' waters. Here your Lycinna,   80
Quick to smile and kindly of visage,
Joins her blessed self to you alone.
O happy Love, o happy poet!

: 25 :

De Fabio Lopitio

Quaeris qui Fabium Lopitiumve,
illum quaerere desine in theatris,
aut urbis plateis, foro aut palestris:
Musarum hic tacitos colit recessus
5   et Pucci aediculas eis sacratas;
illic Aonios legit libellos,
ediscens elegos Propertianos,
admirans numeros tuos, Tibulle,
et quos ad citharam refert Corinna,
10   aut magni ad lituos canit Maronis,
divini aut Ciceronis haurit artes,
curans Socraticae instituta vitae.
Hic quaeras Fabium Lopitiumve:
nam Pucci hospitium colunt Camenae,
15   Musarum Fabius colit recessus.

: 25 :

Fabius Lopitius

If it's Fabius or Lopitius you seek,
Stop looking in the theatres for him,
The city's squares, the gym or in the forum.
He cultivates the Muses' silent haunts,
Puccius' little temples, where they dwell.   5
It's here he reads the Muses' little books,
Learning Propertius' elegies by heart,
Admiring your fine rhythms, Tibullus,
And those Corinna rendered on the lyre,
Or sings the clarion songs of noble Maro   10
Or drinks the art of god-like Cicero,
Learning the precepts of Socratic life.
Here you might locate Fabius or Lopitius.
For the Muses are at home with Puccius,
And Fabius haunts the havens of the Muses.   15

: 26 :

Ad Petrum Paulum Sarranum

Effingis veteres, Petre, et recentis
formas grammaticos, nec est iuventus
cui plus debeat ipsa, sive morum
mira simplicitate, seu bonarum
5   summa cognitione litterarum;
idem, Paule, novos colis poetas,
observas veteres facisque et ipse
versus ac numero venustiore,
nescis nec veteris larem Sophiae.
10   Hunc ergo tibi, Petre Paule, nostrum
commendo Iovianulum quatrimum
et matre ingenua, indole et pudenti:
hunc dignum institue et patre et Camenis.

: 26 :

To Petrus Paulus Serranus

Petrus, you imitate the old grammarians
And educate the modern, nor is there one
The young owe more to, for your wonderful
Simplicity of nature, for your brilliance
And deep knowledge of all literature.   5
And also, Paulus, you foster the newer poets,
Respect the old, and you yourself make verses
In a still more captivating rhythm,
Never neglecting old Sophia's lares.
So, Petrus Paulus, I commend to you   10
My little four-year old Gioviano,
His mother's son and decorous by nature:
Make him worthy of his father and the Muses.

: 27 :

De L. Corvino episcopo Triventino

Nymphae Gaurides accolaeque Averni,
quae fontes colitis salubriores,
nymphae, ceruleae decus lacunae,
quas Bacchus fovet et fovet Dione,
5   vos, nymphae, veteri et bono sodali
Corvino et tenera comam cypero
et molli viola et virente myrto,
casta et tempora subligate lauru,
qua Phoebo sacer et sacer Camenis
10   intret balnea cognitus sacerdos;
Corvino et nemus assonent et aurae,
tota et litora sentiant poetam.

: 27 :

Leonardus Corvinus, Bishop of Trivento

Gauran nymphs, Avernus' neighbors,
Dwelling in the healthy waters,
Nymphs who grace the caerulean pools
Which Bacchus and Dione love,
You nymphs, my good and trusty friend   5
Corvinus, bind his hair and brow
With rush and tender violets,
Fresh myrtle and chaste laurel
As, sacred to Phoebus and the Muses,
A known priest, he may enter the baths;   10
Now groves and winds resound: Corvinus!
And all the shore knows its poet.

: 28 :

Ad Marinum Tomacellum et Petrum Compatrem

Annos sex novies, Marine, amici
una viximus integello amore;
annos tot pariter quiete et una
terni, Compater, egimus nec ullas
5   sensit noster amor per haec querelas,
exemplum fidei atque amoris unum.
Hanc mentem, hos animos sibi requirunt
Lucrinae quoque balneationes,
hanc legem et cyathi frequentiores.
10   Quare hoc nunc agite, o mei sodales:
aequatis numeris, tenore eodem
scyphos tergeminemus ac trientes.
Sit triplex acies triplexque Mavors,
ac Marte in medio calente rixa
15   ternas, i, puer, evoca et puellas,
nostram ut calfaciant simul senectam,
quaeque inter pateras, furore in ipso,
pacis commoneant serantque lusus,
interque oscula mollibus labellis
20   includant animae senilis auras
contingantque animae virentis aura.
Haec est illa, Marine, lenis aura,
flat quae de tenerae sinu puellae,
qua mulcet iuvenum Venus calores,
25   senum et frigida corda confocillat.

: 28 :

Marinus Tomacellus and Petrus Compater

Marinus, six years multiplied by nine
We dwelt in friendship with an unspoilt love,
And just as many years the three of us,
Compater, spent in harmony without
A trace of trouble to disturb our love,   5
Of love a prime example and of faith.
Lucrine bathing and a crowd of cups
Have need of such good dispositions and
Of hearts like ours and also stipulations.
Wherefore, oh my comrades, let's begin   10
In matching metres and in unison
To multiply by three the cups and goblets,
Wage tripled battles under triple Mars,
And in hot struggles, in the midst of strife.
Go, boy, now and call for tripled girls   15
To fire up three old fellows all together
And mid the cups and right in mid-excitement
Engender thoughts of peace and merriment,
And mid the kisses with soft tender lips
Hold the breath exhaled from aged hearts   20
And join it with the breath of youthful hearts.
Marinus, this soft air, the very air
That breathes from the breasts of tender girls,
Venus softens with it youthful fire
Warming up the frozen hearts of age.   25

: 29 :

Ad Uxorem

Oblita es thalami torique nostri,
o fallax senii mei levamen,
connubi immemor immemorque amorum,
o fallax amor, o nihil fidele!
5   Ergo sub tremula, miser, senecta
a te destituor, mihi nec ipsa,
in somnis veniens, levas senectae
ipsius gravidas dolore curas,
natum nec memorem senis parentis,
10   ah dura, esse sinis. Valete uterque:
has vobis sine perferam procellas,
languens, frigidus atque destitutus.
Vana o nomina spesque liberorum,
heu res coniugii parum fideles!

: 29 :

To His Wife

Unmindful of our bedroom and our bed,
Of my old age deceitful consolation,
Forgetful of our promises and loves,
Oh you false and utterly faithless love!
Therefore sadly into frail old age   5
I go, by you abandoned, nor do you
Coming to me in dreams, yourself relieve
My age's heavy burden of its grief.
Nor, cruel one, do you suffer a son
To recollect his father. Farewell both: 10
I shall endure these storms without you both,
Faint and freezing and by all abandoned.
Vain names, alas, vain hope of children,
Marriage itself, unreliable!

: 30 :

De Annibale Famatio in balneis

'Dic, o dic, puer, Annibalne lavit?'
'Lavit, sed latitat puellae in ulnis:
hic Famatiolus latet litatque,
persolvens Veneri sacrum, quod olim
5   vovit pro tenerae salute Hyellae.
Tu ne pollue sacra neve turba.'
'Verum! Ipsas Charites videre fas est,
una dum violas legunt rosasque
et gratas Veneri parant corollas.
10   Mollis en digitos, manus tenellas!
Ecquis de niveis nitor papillis,
quaen ore e roseo refragat aura!
Iam Famatiolum litasse verum est.'

: 30 :

Hannibal Famatius in the Baths

"Tell me, my boy, is Hannibal bathing?"
"He's bathing and hiding within a girl's thighs:
Here little Famatius hides, propitiates,
Observing the rites of Venus which he
Vowed on young Hyella's behalf.   5
Take care not to defile them."
"Indeed! We can see the Graces themselves
Gathering roses and violets together
And weaving Venus's delicate wreaths.
Such soft fingers, such tender hands!   10
And the brightness of her snowy breasts,
The fragrance from her rosy mouth!
Now did Famatius truly propitiate."

: 31 :

De Federico rege ad balneas accedente

Quid, quod plus solito serenus aer
et gramen viret et nitescit arbos?
Quid, quod plus solito canunt volucres,
cantant gutture leniore cygni,
5   Progne et lugubrioribus querelis?
En spirant zephyri salubriores
et rident pelago silente arenae,
nullo et murmure litus opstrepescit;
en ducunt choreas per arva nymphae
10   et Musae numeris suis sequuntur,
ipsa et balnea perstrepunt cachinnis.
An non adveniente Federico
ipsa et balnea molliter cachinnent,
ipsa et litora suaviter susurrent?
15   Agnoscunt dominum suum lacunae,
regem balneolae suum salutant,
assurgunt et hero suo liquores.
Adventat decus elegantiarum
et flos advenit omnium leporum;
20   illum delitiae sequuntur omnes,
illum munditiaeque gratiaeque
et sceptro species potente digna.
Ne, ne, balneolae, timete, ne, ne
Mavortem socium trucesque vultus,
25   Mavortem socium nihil timete:
iussa nam timet ipse Federici
paretque imperio et veretur illum.

: 31 :

King Federigo Approaching the Baths

Is not the air now unusually serene,
Green the grass and the orchards shining?
Aren't the birds uncustomarily songful,
The swans singing with a gentler voice
And Procne even gloomier than usual?   5
Look, Zephyr's breath's uncommonly benign,
And the beaches laugh beside a silent sea,
The shore untroubled by the slightest murmur;
Look, nymphs come dancing all through the fields,
And Muses follow with their own rhythms,   10
And the very baths burst into laughter;
Do not the baths laugh softly,
At Federigo's approach
The very beaches whisper sweetly?
The pools recognize their lord,   15
The baths greet their royal master,
The waters rise to greet their hero.
The model of elegance arrives,
The flower of every charm approaches;
All that's delightful follows him,   20
All partaking of grace and refinement,
A vision befitting a powerful scepter.
Have no fear, baths, have no fear
Of Mars, his companion of threatening visage.
Have no fear of his warlike companion.   25
Even he obeys Federigo's commands,
Obeys his authority and quakes before it.

Felices domino lavante thermae,
felices et hero iocante Baiae,
30   o felix spatiante rege litus!
Myrti, dicite: 'Io, euge Federice!',
'Euge, io' canite 'euge, Federice!'

Happy the waters when their lord bathes,
Happy Baiae when their hero laughs,
Happy beach where the King strolls!   30
Say it, myrtle, "Bravo, Federigo!"
Sing "Bravo," sing "Bravo, Federigo!"

: 32 :

De Marte in balneis lavante

Marsne in balneolis? Valete, castra!
Marsne et ipse lavat? Valete, bella!
Cumque illo et Cytherea? Pax, adesto!
Hoc sors imperat ipsa Federici.
5   Tu vero, Venerilla, dulce coeli
et terrae decus, unicum et levamen,
mollis illecebras decoro amanti,
blandos Martiolo tuo susurros
fac et delitias libidinesque,
10   misce et suavia, iunge dulce murmur;
his lusus adhibe beatiores,
mox tinge ambrosio liquore fessum,
somnus quo placidus per ossa serpat
et belli rapidus furor quiescat:
15   hoc, hoc te rogat ipse Federicus.

: 32 :

Mars Washing in the Baths

Isn't that Mars in the baths? Farewell to arms!
And isn't that Mars bathing? All wars, goodbye!
And with him, Cytherea? Peace is at hand!
Federigo's destiny is commanding it.
Darling little Venus, heaven and earth's   5
Sweet ornament and solitary solace,
Give soft enticements to your handsome swain,
Honey'd whispers to your little Mars.
Make everything delightful and lubricious;
Offer kisses mingled with sweet murmurs,   10
And to these add even more blissful games.
Moisten with ambrosia the tired one
And make a quiet sleep creep through his limbs
And still the sudden thunderstorm of war.
It's this that Federigo asks of you.   15

: 33 :

De Batilla

Lavit delitium meum, Batilla,
laverunt Charites simul, Venusque
intrans balneolum lavatque et haeret,
quae sit de numero choroque quarta,
5 quaenam sit Charis, extera aut puella,
unus cum decor esset, una forma.
Dum haeret dubitans et hanc et illam
per risumque iocumque suaviatur,
spiravit roseo Batillae ab ore
10 fragrans ambrosii liquoris aura,
quae iam de Charitum coma suesset
spirare artifici manu reposta,
stillatim et medico liquore tincta.
Tum ridens Cypris: 'Extera o puella,
15 vicisti Charites meas, ab arte
quis spirat coma, cum tibi e labellis
stillent ambrosiae perennis aurae.'

: 33 :

Batilla

My darling Batilla bathes herself.
The Graces bathe as well, and Venus
Entering the baths, bathes and wonders
Who is this fourth girl in the choir?
Is it a Grace or some other girl,   5
Identical in charm and beauty?
And wondering, gives each one a kiss
Amid the jokes and laughter,
And breathes from Batilla's rosy mouth,
A fragrance of ambrosian liquor   10
Such as perfumes the Graces' hair
When applied by artful hand,
Dropwise applied, a medicament.
Then Cypris laughs, "Oh, unknown girl,
You've bested my Graces, who, by art,   15
Perfume their hair, while from your lips
Ambrosian breath forever wafts."

: 34 :

De Hieronymo Carbone patricio Neapolitano

Cur ille in fluidis calescit undis
Carbo? Cur fluidus liquor coruscat?
Carbo cur tepet, incalescit unda?
An non et Venus, e liquore nata,
5   ignescit face? Vis amoris haec est.
Ergo balneolis meus sub ipsis
Carbo aut aestuat impotente flamma,
aut rursum nimio e gelu tepescit,
ut frigus modo, nunc calor recurset.
10   Tabet nobilitas amore victa.
Tu vero, Theonilla, dum lavaris,
ferventem simul et simul tepentem
Carbonem cole, sic tibi e capillis
stillent semper amoma, sic ab ore
15   spirent ambrosiae liquentis aurae.

: 34 :

Girolamo Carbone, a Neapolitan Noble

Why does Carbo grow warm in the flowing
Water? Why does the water glow?
Why is he warm, the water warm?
Well, did not Venus, born of the wave,
Ignite a torch? It's the power of love.   5
So my own Carbo in the baths
Either burns with ungoverned fire
Or cools again from excess of frost.
Just now cold, now he's hot,
Nobility gives way to love.   10
Now Theonilla, while you're bathing
Take care of Carbo when he's boiling
And when he cools, amoma dripping
From your hair, and from your mouth
Exhaling the scent of clear ambrosia.   15

: 35 :

Ad Marinum Tomacellum

Et vino venus et viro puella
et ludo iuvenis, senex quiete
et gratis animus iocis fovetur;
quocirca cole balneas, Marine:
5   hic vina, hic requies senem iocusque
effoetum foveant, manus titillis
ludant in venerem, Venus sed ipsa
adsit rancidulo seni. Puella,
postquam obdormieris, parem requirat,
10   quicum lusitet excitetque pugnam
et rixas agitet ferociores;
nam tactu et teneris venus titillis
exercenda seni: senex papillas
contrectet digitis, iocetur ore,
15   voce et pruriat et gemat senile.
Hoc tantum liceat. Iuventa nervis
et tento valet et valet duello:
haec ergo iuvenis movebit arma.
Ast lingua et digitis valet senectus,
20   et lingua et digitis senex tuendus,
et lingua et digitis venus fovenda:
has te delicias movere oportet
et vina et venerem et suam quietem
instillent tibi balneae salubres,
25   infundant tibi thermulae beatae.
His ludis animus senis levandus.

: 35 :

To Marinus Tomacellus

Sex by wine, a girl by a man,
A youth by sport, an old man by quiet,
And the heart is warmed by pleasant wit.
So go to the baths, Marinus.
Here wine and peace and wit warm up   5
A tired old man, playful hands
Play at sex, but Venus herself
Is there for the broken-down fellow. Girl,
After you've rested, find a mate
To play with, to start the struggle,   10
Get the savage contest going.
Now sex for the elderly comes from touch,
From tender titillations. Breasts
Are stroked by hand, his mouth makes jokes,
He arouses moans with his elderly voice.   15
This much is allowed. Youth prevails
With his bow and arrow, prevails in the fight.
Therefore these are the arms he deploys.
But old age succeeds with tongue and hands,
Tongue and hands protect old men,   20
For Venus is warmed with tongue and hands:
These are the pleasures you should deploy.
May wine and healthy baths instill
Sex and its peacefulness in you,
May blessed little baths pour over you: 25
These games lighten an old man's heart.

: 36 :

Ad Terinam

Tecum si liceat, velim, Terina,
me tussis licet et premat gravedo,
tecum has frigidulas fovere noctes.
O noctes mihi ter quater beatas,
5   o somnos sine fine prurientes,
me cum sub tepido, Terina, lecto,
me cum sub teneris fovebis ulnis,
me cum roscidulis procax labellis
et sugges simul osculaberisque!
10 O noctes mihi ter quater beatas!
Ne tu, ne digitis, Terina, saevi,
ne saevi aridulo, Terina, dente.
Ah, quid pallia lectulo excidere?
Ah, quid lectulus ipse subtremiscit?
15 Ne saevi, rogo, ne, Terina, saevi.
Sic, sic, o mea, saevias licebit,
hac mecum ratione litigato:
nunc vinci patiare, nunc repugna,
et nunc oscula porge, nunc negato,
20 nunc risum lacrimis iocisque fletum
misce et dulcia verba tinge amaris.
Haec cum feceris, o Terina, mox te
ad lusus placidos resolve mecum,
complexa et teneris senem lacertis
25 ludas delitias venustiores,

: 36 :

To Terina

Terina, if I might, I'd like,
Although I have a frightful cold,
To warm these chilly nights with you.
Oh three and four-times blessed nights,
Sleeps with endless sexual teasing,   5
In a snug little bed with you, Terina,
While you warm me with your tender legs
And wicked, with those rosy lips
Suck and kiss me all at once!
Oh three and four-times blessed nights!   10
Don't scratch me with your nails, Terina,
Nor bite, Terina, with grating teeth.
Ah, why do the covers fall to the floor?
Ah, why is the very bed trembling?
Don't fight, Terina, please don't fight.   15
This, my girl, is the way to fight.
Litigate with me this way:
Suffer yourself to lose, then fight back,
Be free with your kisses, then deny them,
Mix laughter with tears, weeping with jokes,   20
And stain sweet words with bitter ones.
This done, Terina, presently
Relax with me in quiet sport.
Hold an old man in your delicate arms,
Bring on still more ravishing pleasures.   25

dicas blanditias procaciores,
fingas nequitiam proterviorem,
et ludos, age, fac licentiores
et noctem quoque duc amantiorem,
30   dum lassis sopor instet ex ocellis.

Utter still more exciting endearments,
Concoct for me still sexier crimes.
Come, play still more wanton games
And bring on nights more amorous still,
Till sleep fills our eyes with exhaustion.   30

∶ 37 ∶

Ad Suardinum Suardum

Et noster quoque balneas frequentat,
Cumanum colit et sinum Suardus.
Adeste, hendecasyllabi, lavanti,
Romano et sale et Attico lepore
5   mulcete et placidos sinus legentem
et cantu et numeris Catullianis.
Ne tu, ne mea Syrmioni desis
intactos calamis modos referre;
o blandis comes atque amica cygnis,
10   dic, o dic aliquid meo Suardo,
quod dulce et lepidum, quod et venustum:
sic nostra Antiniana, sic Patulcis
nunquam non roseas tibi corollas,
nunquam non tibi myrteos liquores
15   gratae sufficiant, et usque laetas
Sebethus salicum ministret umbras.
       'Regnabat Veneris puer iugoque
heroas, superos, Iovemque et ipsum
victor subdiderat coegeratque
20   victos servitium pati superbum:
supplex Acrisii ad fores iaceret
regnator superum, futurus himber;
ductaret niveos greges Apollo,
Amphriso teneras levante curas;
25   Neptunnus liquidos subiret amnes,
Eleae ut foveat sinum puellae;
esset Persephone rapina Ditis,
ludus Mars Veneris; senex equinos

: 37 :

To Suardinus Suardus

And our Suardus also haunts the baths
And cultivates the Cumaean shore.
Hendecasyllables, greet the bather
Walking on the quiet shore,
With Roman salt and Attic charm,   5
With song and with Catullan verses.
And you, my Sirmio, never cease
Playing those unheard melodies.
Sweet friend, companion to the swans,
Speak something to my Suardus,   10
Charming, sweet and ravishing.
Thus our Patulcis, our Antiniana,
Welcome you ever with rosy wreaths,
Offer you ever their myrtle liquors
While the willows of Sebethos   15
Serve you with their pleasant shade.
  "The son of Venus was reigning over
Heroes and gods, and Jove himself
He put to the yoke and forced him, vanquished,
To suffer haughty servitude: 20
The king of the gods, a suppliant, lay
At the gates of Acrisius. A shower was coming.
Apollo led the snowy flocks
By Amphrysos, lifter of cares;
Neptune hid in the watery floods   25
To kindle the Elean maiden's breast;
Persephone would be ravished by Dis,
Mars a game for Venus. Ah,

ah divum pater induisset armos;
30   ire ad Lamidas osculationes
ornato properaret ore Luna.
Ergo hinc vulnifico superbus arcu,
prostratorque hominum deumque victor
et coeli domitor puer solique,
35   ausus Pallada Palladisque pectus
intorto penitus ferire telo,
innisusque humeris manu genuque
lunato iaculum tetendit arcu
irato minitante vulnus ictu.
40   Avertit dea tortiles sagittas
ac vanas iaculi refregit iras
praetenta aegide Gorgonisque crine.
    'Quo viso pueri repente ocelli,
afflati tacito veneno, ibidem
45   obducunt tenebras. Vocatque matrem
infelix puer optegitque vultum
et flens lumina capta pergravatur,
infelix Amor, abdit et pharetram.
Ah moerens Amor, ah puer miselle,
50   et caecus simul atque inermis erras;
ah terrae domitor simulque coeli,
rideris pariter diis virisque,
imbellis pariter puerque Amorque,
infelix iterum puer deusque!
55   Delapsae interea polo sagittae,
iussu Palladis aegidisque tractu
quae fixae steterant, rotante penna
saxosi procul Ansuris recessu
subsidunt parili simul ruina.
60   Hic illas dea vertit in virentis
silvam suberis ac referre iussit

The old father of gods put on equine limbs;
On the way to Latmian kisses   30
Luna hastened with painted face.
At last, proud with his wounding bow,
Subduer of gods as well as men,
A boy, tamer of heaven and earth,
Dared to strike with springing arrow   35
Pallas and the Palladian breast;
To his shoulder, resting on hand and knee,
He stretched the dart on its crescent bow,
Threatening an angry strike.
The goddess turned the flying shafts,   40
Breaking the missiles' useless wrath.
The gorgon's tress protected her.
   "At the sight the boy's eyes suddenly
Swelled with instant silent poison,
Shadowed over. The wretched boy   45
Called to his mother, hid his face,
Weeping, cursed his sightless eyes,
And wretched Love undid his quiver.
Ah, grieving Amor, sorry boy,
You wander unarmed now and blind.   50
Ah, tamer of earth, tamer of heaven,
Mocked alike by gods and man,
Harmless Amor, harmless boy,
Wretched boy and wretched god!
Now arrows fallen from the sky   55
By Pallas' will and her aegis's power,
Standing stuck with fluttering feathers
Far by Anxur's rocky reach,
Collapsed together in a heap.
There the goddess gave them life   60
Commanding them to turn to cork

atro cortice fungidisque venis:
conatus fragiles minasque inanis
et vanos sine viribus tumultus.
65   In fungos igitur repente versae,
egerunt faciles solo meatus,
egerunt teneras repente fibras,
mox sese tenues agunt in auras
surguntque in solidum subinde robur,
70   scabro cortice fungidisque libris,
quo post in soleas pedumque in usus
vertant, opprobrium perenne secli.
Quid saevis, dea? Quid fremens minaris?
Aut cur aegida concutisque parmam?
75   'Nam mater pueri, dolore victa,
Phoebum consuluit. Recludit ille
fatorum seriem, docens salutem
Baianis fore fontibus petendam,
quod mox contigit annuente fato.
80   Cumanos puer ut sinus pererrans
intravit placidos lacus et ipsis
lavit fontibus ac calente lympha
(ter ludens oculos puer lavabat,
ter natans puer ora surrigabat),
85   illi candida lux repente fulsit,
fulserunt nitidae ad latus pharetrae,
effulsit nitor aureus metalli,
fulserunt nitidi lacus sinusque,
fulsit plus solito serenus aer
90   et toto micuere litore undae.
Tum felix Amor et puer deusque
tinxit spicula fervidis in undis,
mox laeto pariter salutat ore:
    "'Salvete, o liquidi lacus et undae,

190

With black bark and spongy fiber:
Frail their blows and harmless their threats,
Vain their violence, devoid of force.
Then, rendered spongy, suddenly   65
They slipped their way into the earth,
Quickly put out slender shoots,
Forced themselves into thin air
And rose forthwith as solid wood,
Rough of bark and soft of pith,   70
Later used for shoes and sandals,
A deep disgrace for all the ages.
Why rage so, goddess? Why roar threats?
Why do you strike the gorgon's shield?
   "Then the boy's mother, crushed by grief,   75
Consulted Phoebus. He uncovered
All the future, teaching the way
To health was in the Baian fount,
Which soon transpired at Fate's command.
When at last the wandering boy arrived   80
At the Bay of Cumae and its quiet waters,
Bathed in those fonts and warming waters
(Playing, he washed his eyes three times,
Swimming, he bathed his face three times),
A brilliant light shone suddenly.   85
At his side the brilliant arrows gleamed,
The golden gleam of metal shone,
And the bay and the gleaming lake shone forth,
The air shone with unaccustomed light,
And waves glittered all along the shore.   90
Then happy love, both boy and god,
Dipped his darts in the boiling water
And called out with a joyful voice:
   "'Hail, my watery pools and waves,

95   salvete, o latices mihi salubres,
       o salve mihi, Tulliana lympha,
       de cuius merito resumo tela,
       cuius munere et hic resurgit arcus.
       Quo sitis memores meae salutis
100   hocque ut secula posterique norint,
       quae vis est mihi, quae meis sagittis,
       haec ipsa et tibi sit, salubris unda;
       quae vis est mihi, quae meae pharetrae,
       sit vobis, latices bonaeque thermae.
105   Mecum vos pariter fovete amantes
       et curas iuvenum et puellularum,
       mecum hos et capite et tenete captos
       gratis illecebris leporibusque;
       nunquam blanditiae iocique desint
110   et nunquam choreae levesque cantus,
       semper desidiae libidinesque
       et coenae et lepidi sales et ipsae
       assint nequitiae procaxque lusus,
       o dulces mihi balneae et salubres,
115   dulces balneolae venustulaeque;
       ipsa et litora et ipsi ament recessus
       et tellus amet atque ament lacunae."
        'Dixit. Mox residem tetendit arcum
       et strinxit volucres manu sagittas,
120   quis et flumina fixit et paludes
       et colles simul atque opaca lustra.
       Confestim volucres simul feraeque
       et pisces simul in furorem adacti
       senserunt pueri trucem pharetram,
125   senserunt siluaeque flosculique,
       Baianis Amor ipse ut insit undis.'
        Haec ludens mihi Syrmionis. At tu

Hail health-giving waters,   95
Tullian pools, all hail,
Whose merit gave me my arrows back,
Whose gift, my bow restored to me.
That you be mindful of my rescue,
That this and succeeding ages know,   100
What power is in me and my arrows
Shall be in you, salubrious wave.
What power I and my quiver have
Is yours, good and warming waters.
Along with me you'll warm up lovers,   105
Warm the thoughts of boys and girls.
With me you'll take and hold them captive
By means of sweet and pleasant snares.
There'll be no end to charm and jokes,
No end to dances and soft singing.   110
Leisure and libido, always,
And feasts and lovely wit will come,
Wickedness and sexy games.
Oh, my sweet and healthy baths,
Sweet, ravishing little baths,   115
May the shores and the very grottos love
And the earth love and the pools love.'
   "He spoke. He stretched his idle bow
And delivered winging arrows
Which struck the rivers and the marsh   120
And struck the hills and lairs of beasts.
All at once the birds and beasts
And fishes, driven into madness
Felt the boy's fierce quiver,
And the forests and the flowerets felt   125
Amor himself in the Baian waves."
   Thus Sirmio sang to me.

sic nostras cole balneas, Suarde,
sic nostri lege litoris recessum,
130   ut leges teneas Amoris, ut te
et litus sciat et sciant lacunae
et colles quoque sentiant te amare:
qui Baias colis, et colas amores.

But you, Suardus, visit our baths,
Stroll the grottos of our shore
That you may hold to Amor's rule,   130
That the beach know you and the pools know you
And the hills acknowledge that you love:
Who visits Baiae, visits Love.

: 38 :

Ad Hendecasyllabos

Havete, hendecasyllabi, meorum,
havete, illecebrae ducesque amorum,
havete, o comites meae senectae,
ruris delitiae atque balnearum.
5   Sit lusum satis et satis iocatum:
et finem lepidi sales requirunt,
est certus quoque terminus cachinnis.
Ergo qui, iuvenes, meas legetis
nugas, qui tenerae iocos Thaliae,
10   optetis cineri meo quietem:
    'Sit tellus levis et perenni in urna
non unquam violae rosaeque desint,
tecumque Elisiis beata campis
uxor perpetuas agat choreas
15   et sparsim ambrosii irrigent liquores.'
    Sic vobis in amore nil amarum,
nil insit nisi dulce; sic amando
et noctes pariter diesque agatis,
assistat lateri et comes Voluptas.

: 38 :

To His Hendecasyllables

Hail, hendecasyllables, and hail,
You who entice me into love affairs.
Hail, of my old age best companions,
Pleasures of the country, of the baths.
We've had enough of playing and of jokes.   5
Our pleasant cleverness desires an end
And certain terminus to all this laughter.
And you boys, whenever you should read
My trifles, tender Thalia's wit,
Pray for some quiet for my ashes: 10
    "May the earth be light, may violets and roses
Ever bloom by your eternal urn,
And in Elysium may your dearest wife
Accompany you in an endless dance,
Moistly sprinkling ambrosian liquors."   15
    Let bitterness be absent from your loving.
Let everything be sweetness. Thus in loving
You'll while away the night-times and the day-times
With Pleasure at your side as your companion.

Note on the Text

茶冬茶

This I Tatti edition of the *Baiae* reproduces the Latin text of Liliana Monti Sabia (Naples: Associazione di studi tardoantichi, 1978), but without the critical apparatus. The translator is grateful to Prof. Monti Sabia and to the publishers for their permission to reprint. Readers who wish to learn more about the textual basis of the work are advised to consult this excellent edition.

Notes to the Translation

❧❧❧

I.1

1. Muse: Pieris. The Pierides were daughters of Pieros, king of Emathia.

4. Nymphs: Napeae are nymphs of the dell.

5. Sirmio's sweet waters: Catullus's villa at Sirmio, a promontory in Lake Garda (Catullus 31). Also mentioned at the beginning and end of Book II.

10. Verses: hendecasyllabi. The Phalaecium or eleven-syllable meter favored by Catullus and used throughout the *Baiae*. This line echoes Catullus 42: "Adeste, hendecasyllabi quot estis" ("Come, all you hendecasyllables"). The collection closes "Havete, hendecasyllabi" ("Hail, hendecasyllables"), making a ring form.

31. Marinus Tomacellus: Marino Tomacelli, 1429–1515, member of the Accademia Pontaniana, Pontano's life-long friend, receives the dedication of the entire work. See especially II.28.

38. Petrus Compater: Pietro Golino, 1431–1501. Perhaps Pontano's closest friend. See also II.28.

I.2

27. Cyprian dove: Cyprus is sacred to Venus. See I.7.16 and I.22.

I.3

Title. Batilla also appears in I.14, I.15 and II.33. For her name, see Horace, *Epodes* XIV, 9–10: "non aliter Samio dicunt arsisse Bathyllo / Anacreonta Teium" ("not otherwise did Teian Anacreon burn for Samian Bathyllus"). For changing gender of names, see I.26.8.

I.4

Title. Hermione was the daughter of Helen and Menelaus. See Propertius I.4.5–6: "tu / Spartanae referas laudibus Hermionae" ("You recall the praises of Spartan Hermione").

20. Tithonus, the mortal husband of Aurora, grew old but could not die.

I.5

Title. Marino Tomacelli: see I.1.31.

17. Romulan hearth: Romulus and Remus, twin founders of Rome, were born of a Vestal Virgin who had been violated by Mars.

I.6

Title. Marino Tomacelli: see I.1.31.

25. Bacchus/Lyaeus, a cult title of Dionysus as wine personified. See Tibullus, III.2.19: "et primum annoso spargent collecta Lyaeo" ("and, gathered, first they sprinkled the vintage wine").

I.7

16–17. "salaciorque / verno passere, martiis columbis" ("randier than a sparrow in the Spring / or than combative doves"). The sparrow and the dove, linked here as in Martial and Catullus: "Issa est passere nequior Catulli / Issa et prior osculo columbae" ("Issa is sexier than Catullus's sparrow and purer than a dove's kiss"): Martial I.109.1–2; "nec tantum niveo gavisa est ulla columbo / compar, quae multo dicitur improbius / oscula mordenti semper decerpere rostro" ("nor does any dove find in her snowy companion / such joy, though one says that they hook at constant / kisses with their beaks"): Catullus 68.125–7. See I.22 and I.29.11.

24. "setosum Hectora" ("bristling Hector"): Possibly in reference to Hector's "squalentem barbam et concretos sanguine crinis" ("his beard filthy, his hair stiff with blood"): Virgil, *Aeneid* II.277.

I.8

Title. Deianira: a reference to Heracles's wife, who killed him with a poisoned robe, seems doubtful. On Hermione see I.4.

3. *poetulosque: sc. paetulosque.*

I.9

Title. Compater: see I.1.38.

5–6. Apollo . . . Thalia: The pleasures of poetry are not enough to console him.

6. Thalia: one of the three graces or Charites, according to Hesiod, daughters of Zeus: Aglaea (Radiance), Euphrosyne (Joy) and Thalia (Flowering). Here however she is the muse of light verse as in Martial X.20 and elsewhere. See Swann, *Martial's Catullus*, p. 105n.

I.10

Title. Franciscus Aelius: Franceschello Marchese, d. 1517, a political exile in Rome, 1463–1476, where, around 1475, he edited a very early edition of Horace. See Rosanna Rocca-Red in *Enciclopedia Oraziana* (Rome, 1996), I, p. 357. The party celebrates his return, and the poem refers to Horace, *Ode* II.7, that celebrates the return of Horace's friend, Pompeius Varus (lines 27–28): "recepto / dulce mihi furere est amico" ("It is nice to go wild when your friend comes back").

11. Elizio Calenzio, ca. 1430–1502, a poet and tutor to Federigo, the future king of Naples. He had returned from France in 1476. Giovanni Albino, d. 1496, an early member of the Academy. Compater is Golino: see I.1.38. Gabriele Altilio, ca. 1440–1501, later Bishop of Policastro. Michael Marullus, 1453–1530, Latin poet and soldier; there is an interesting biography of him by Carol Kidwell, *Marullus: Soldier Poet of the Renaissance* (London, 1989).

15. Nine is the canonical number of the Muses.

16. Hercules' labors, twelve in number.

17. Perhaps fourteen here is twice seven. Pausanias (II.17.4) describes a statue of Hera wearing a crown adorned with the Graces (three) and the Horae (four). Marullus was to drink twice as many as these. See II.24 for seven maidens of Venus.

18–20. The goddess is Thetis, worrying about Achilles, her son. The snowy servants are her sisters, the Nereids. They were fifty in number. Of the Nereids who mourned for Patroklos (see *Iliad* XVIII), thirty-three were singled out by name.

23. At Dido's feast for exiled Aeneas it took two hundred servants to set the table: "centum aliae totidemque pares aetate ministri / qui dapibus mensas onerant et pocula ponant" ("A hundred and as many of equal age set the table and put out the cups"): Virgil, *Aeneid* I.705–706.

28–29. Oceanus, Thetis's maternal grandfather, seems in Catullus 64.30ff. to be the host at the wedding of Peleus and Thetis.

I.II

Title. Actius Sincerus: an academic name, bestowed by Pontano on the Virgilian poet Jacopo Sannazaro, 1458–1530.

1–3. The reference is to Virgil, *Eclogues*, I.2: "silvestrem tenui musam meditari averna" ("You practise the muse with slender oaten step"). And IV.1–2: "Sicilides musae, paulo maiora canamus / non omnis arbusto iuvant humilesque myricae" ("Sicilian muses, we sing something greater. Orchards and humble shrubs don't please everyone"). The substitution of *Partheniae* for *humiles*: Parthenas, according to Servius, was Virgil's nickname, i.e., "the Maiden." Sannazaro was a famous Virgilian. He wrote eclogues about the sea, and in Pontano's dialogue *Actius* he discourses on Virgil's metrics. Meliseus was Pontano's name for himself as a singing shepherd in his early eclogue *Acon* as well as later in the pastoral *Meliseus*, and elsewhere.

4–5. In *Acon* Meliseus sings "dulce in pratis dum gramina tondant / cernere capreolos variato tergere, pictis / distinctos maculis" ("sweet to watch while they clip the grass, the little goats with different coats, distinct with their colored spots").

4 and 6. "Golden apples" refers to Pontano's poem about citrus trees, *De hortis hesperidum*.

9. Maenalus is a mountain in Arcadia. See "Incipe Maenalios mecum, mea tibia, versus" ("My flute, begin with a Maenalean song"): Virgil, *Eclogues* VIII.21 and repeated.

10. Compare "tu, Tityre, lentus in umbra / formosam resonare doces Amaryllida silvas" ("Tityrus, soft in the shade, you teach the woods to sing of beautiful Amaryllis"): ibid. I.4–5.

11–12. According to Petrus Summontius' annotations at the end of his 1505 edition of the *Baiae*, "Tebenna and Tanager: the former is a mountain, the latter a river in Picene territory."

1.12

Title. Pontano married Ariane Sassone in 1461. She died in 1490. His three daughters were Aurelia Domitilla, Eugenia and Lucia Marzia, born 1462, 1463 and 1464 respectively. Lucio Francesco was born in 1469, the subject of Pontano's celebrated lullabies. Lucilio, Pontano's son by his mistress Stella, is not included here. Pontano gave his own birthday as March 7th, but this date is not certain. His birth year, traditionally 1426, is also not certain (Kidwell, *Pontano*, p. 22). Ludwig, "Catullus Renatus," p. 173, n. 45, cites Monti Sabia as authority for the date of 1429.

24–26. Myrtle and Cyprian scent refer to Venus. Cyprus was sacred to Venus.

28–29. Genius: the spirit of the birthday party. See Tibullus II.2.5 on Cornutus's birthday party: "Ipse suos Genius adsit visurus honores" ("Genius himself is there to observe the celebration"); wine and nard are also present and young children playing at Cornutus's feet. See also Messalla's birthday party in Tibullus I.7.49–50: "hunc ades et Genium ludis Geniumque choreis / concelebra et multo tempora fronde mero" ("Come then with a hundred games and dances, celebrate Genius. Drench his head with our finest wine").

1.13

Title. On Ariane, see I.12. Much in this poem recalls Catullus 61.

11. "Ut flos in saeptis secretus nascitur hortis" ("As a secret flower grows in a closed garden"): Catullus 62.39. And "iam licet venies, marito / uxor in thalamo tibi est / ore floridulo nitens, / alba parthenice velut / luteumve papaver" ("husband, now it's time for you: your wife is in the bridal chamber, shining her sweet flowering face, like the white camomile, like the yellow poppy"): Catullus 61.191–195.

25. Charites: see I.9.6.

26. The "Gnidia dea" is Venus of Cnidos.

39. *Refragat: sc. refragrat.*

40. "Tithoni croceum linquens Aurora cubile" ("Aurora leaving Tithonus's saffron chamber"): found in Virgil, three times: *Georgics* I.447, *Aeneid* IV.585, and IX.460.

1.14

Title. For Batilla, see I.3.

12. "frigens aestuat aestuansque friget / infelix simul et simul beatus" ("And freezing burns and burning freezes, and wretched is and blessed at once"). See also I.22. On this, see Ludwig, "Catullus Renatus," p. 191. The lover is at once *misellus* and *beatus*. Heat and cold have various meanings. See II.34.

18. Hybla, one of the southeastern slopes of Mt. Etna, famous for bees and honey. Mopsopius: Mopsopia is the name given to Attica by Callimachus. Pontano wrote *Mesopii* and his editors have disagreed. Soldati (1902), p. 259, retained Pontano's word; Oeschger (1948), p. 293, printed *Mopsopii*, calling *Mesopii* "incomprehensible" and suggesting it was the corruption of the text of a classical author; Monti Sabia (1978) restored *Mesopii* and called it a *hapax*. *Mesopii* is a corruption attested in the Tibullan textual tradition. In Tibullus I.7, 54, where the word is unquestionably *Mopsopio*, some MSS have *Mesopio*, as does MS Guelferbytanus 82.6, f. 11, a manuscript entirely in Pontano's hand (see the facsimile edition of the MS, *Tibulli carmina*, cited in the Bibliography). So we have re-

tained Monti Sabia's text, which reflects Pontano's wishes, but corrected the word in the translation.

20. Hymettus: Mountain southeast of Athens: "the Attic mountain."

22. Panormus: A city of Sicily on the site of modern Palermo. A juxtaposition of Sicilian and Attic mountains.

1.15

1–7. The unity of pleasure and grief: "non est dea nescia nostri, / quae dulcem curis miscet amaritium" ("nor was the goddess unmindful who mixes the sweet with the bitter"). Catullus 68.17–18.

1.16

Title. King Alfonso II of Aragon, before his accession in 1495, was Duke of Calabria.

1. Drusula: Trusia Gazella was a mistress of Alfonso and the mother of his son, Alfonso.

1–9. The kiss: "Suaviolum dulci dulcius ambrosia" ("a kiss sweeter than sweet ambrosia"): Catullus 99.2. In Catullus there is ambrosia in that stolen kiss, but only there. Tongues are not mentioned in kissing in Catullus. "Et dare anhelanti pugnantibus umida linguis / oscula et in collo figere dente notas" ("And you'll give the breathless fellow wet kisses, a tongue-lashing, and bury your teeth in his neck"): Tibullus I.8.37–38. Ludwig, "Catullus Renatus," p. 183 ff., has traced the source of the notion of the transmission of souls in Pontano and his imitators (to whom we might add Robert Herrick and John Donne) to Gellius, *Noctes Atticae* XIX.11, a distich attributed to Plato in his youth.

8. Idalian goddess: Venus, to whom Idalium, a city of Cyprus, was sacred.

10ff. Ludwig, "Catullus Renatus," p. 183ff., remarks that the three-part form and basic movement of the poem derive from Catullus 45, the love of Acme and Septimius, while the refrain echos Catullus 51.1–2: "Ille mi par esse deo videtur / ille, si fas est, superare divos" ("that one seems to me like a god, that one, if I may, seems higher than the gods").

35ff. Drusula is like Venus with the Graces. "circumcursans hinc illinc saepe Cupido / fulgebat crocina candidus in tunica" ("Cupid racing here and there shining in his yellow dress"). I.e., if Cupid accompanies Lesbia in the act of love, Lesbia is Venus.

39. *poetulos: sc. paetulos.*

1.17

Title. Martinalia: The feast of St. Martin of Tours, 11th of November. The word Martinalia, which occurs only in the title, may be a coinage on the model of the Saturnalia, a December feast in honor of Saturn. The latter, too, was a time for drinking: "at ipsi / Saturnalibus huc fugisti sobrius" ("You fled here somewhat sober even during the Saturnalia"): Horace, *Satires* II.3.5–6. Pontanus, in the dialogue *Charon*, has Mercury state "the French, the Spanish, the Germans, the Italians celebrate Martin so that it is shameful on his festive day not to be soaking drunk. And there is nothing on earth winier and more wanton than that day."

8. Petrucianus's cellars: Giovanni Antonio Petrucci, d. 1486 on December 11. He was involved in the Second Barons' War against Ferrante, king of Naples, and was beheaded. While awaiting execution, he wrote sonnets. Poggio Bracciolini thought (probably incorrectly) that Petrucci was satirized as the donkey in Pontano's satire *Asinus*.

12. The wines: Falernian, Massic and Caecuban in antiquity were (and remained in the Renaissance) the three great wines of the central Tyrrhenian coast (Pliny, *Natural History* XVI, passim). Wines of Lesbos and Chios were also known in antiquity and regarded as of high quality. Most of the other wines mentioned were traded at Naples, "the most important Mediterranean wine trading post of the fourteenth century" (Jancis Robinson, *Oxford Companion to Wine*, 1999, s.v.). Vernaccia of Liguria was exported; Barolum (Barolo), made from the Nebbiola grape, came from Piedmont; Monti Sabia finds Moroan wine mysterious, "a hapax." Cretensis was thought inferior to Falernian: see A. Tchernia, *Le vin de l'italie romaine*, 1986; the latter lists Tarentum as among the "grands crus marginaux." Melfi is near Venusia (Horace's birthplace) in ancient Lucania; Cairano (Clariana?) is on the Aufidus.

25. Bartolomeo Scala, 1430–1497, poet and politician, had acted as Ferrante's ambassador to Innocent VIII in 1484.

28. Zebethan liquors: unidentified.

1.18

Title. Joannes Brancatus or Giovanni Brancaccio, son of Pontano's friend Marino Brancaccio whom Pontano described as a great eater and conversationalist (*De prudentia*).

7. Castalian throng: The muses at the Castalian Fountain on Mt. Parnassus. Associated with Apollo "qui rore puro Castaliae lavit / crinis solutos" ("Who washes his long hair in pure Castalian dew"): Horace, *Odes* III.4.61–62.

8. Dulichium's lady: i.e. Penelope. Dulichium was an island in the Ionian Sea belonging to Ulysses.

13 ff. Advice about the wedding night considerably more precise than that found in Catullus 61, 62, or 64.

21–22. Teeth marks: compare "tunc sucos herbasque dedi quis livor abiret / quem facit impresso mutua dente venus" ("I gave her herbs and juices to eradicate the marks left here and there by both our teeth"): Tibullus I.6.13–14.

29. In reference to another wedding night, Catullus 66.13–14, Berenice's husband goes to war the morning after, "dulcia nocturnae portans vestigia rixae / quam de vigineis generat exuvies" ("carrying sweet traces of last night's struggle when he had exulted in a virgin's prize"). *Rixae*, which Catullus uses quite literally, becomes in Pontano a frequent term for sexual embrace, or perhaps foreplay: I.3.5, I.20.8, etc.

30. One should perhaps read the rare Plautine word *vinnula* in place of the hapax *vinula*, in which case one would translate "a tender little girl."

1.19

Title. Fannia was a favorite of Pontano in the poems of Book I of his earlier work *Parthenopeus*. Parthenopeus I.5, an imitation of Catullus 2, apparently to Fanny, speaks of her rosy lips and honey tongue, but

Neera, II.19 and Constantia, II.10, also have Hyblean dew on their lips. At the end of his life Pontano gave Fannia a place of honor at the conclusion of *Urania:* "resonat virides formosa per umbras Fannia" ("beautiful Fannia sounds through the green shades"). See Virgil, *Eclogues* I.4–5, lines also cited here under I.11.

I.20

Title. The defense of dark complexion: See "alba ligustra cadunt, vaccinia nigra leguntur" ("white privet blossoms fall, the dark hyacinths are gathered"): Virgil, *Eclogues* II.18.

3. Quid tum? Compare "quid tum, si fuscus Amyntas? / et nigrae violae sunt et vaccinia nigra" ("what then if Amyntas is dark? Violets are black and hyacinths are black"): Virgil, *Eclogues* X, 38–39. Clausen, *Eclogues,* p. 303, sees these lines as a conflation of lines by Asclepiades and Theocritus.

I.21

1. Who sucks these lips? "Cui labella mordebis?" ("whose lips will you bite?"): Catullus, 8.18.

13. Virgil, *Eclogue* VIII.60: "extremum hoc munus morientis habeto" ("have in death the final reward"). Here Damon kills himself for love. Catullus, above, resolves to endure his jealousy. Pontano's poem sounds a new, almost operatic note.

I.22

Title. For the purity of doves, see Catullus 68.125–7, and above I.7.16–17.

11 ff. Heat and cold: see I.14.12.

23. Doves, an example of love: he repeats line 8, a Catullan device. The line is also repeated in II.28.6. It derives from Propertius, II.15.27: "exemplo iunctae tibi sint in amore columbae" ("Let doves joined in love be an example to you").

1.23

Title. Dazzling: "Urit me Glycerae nitor / splendentis Pario marmore purius" ("The brilliance of shining Glycera burns me, clearer than Parian marble"): Horace, *Odes*, I.19.5–6.

1.24

Title. Pietro Summonte, 1453–1526. Pontano's old friend, successor as head of the Academy and literary executor. In a letter to Angelo Colucci written after Pontano's death, Summonte praises Pontano's "continence and sanctity" (cited by Oeschger, in his *Pontani carmina*, 1948, p. 472).

1. Neera, a name probably taken from Lygdamus's mistress, Tibullus III and passim, given to Summonte's beloved three times in this work: here, II.18 and 19 and in *Eridanus* II.15. In *De Tumulis* II.33, Summonte mourns at Neera's grave. For another Tibullan name, see II.9.11.

1.25

Title. For Gabriele Altilio, see I.10.12.

1.26

Title. For Michael Murullus, see I.10.16.

9. Septimilla: the name and the poem are based on Catullus 45. Acme calls Septimius "Septimille." The practise of taking an old name and changing it from male to female is also seen in I.3 and I.14.

12. Happy union, mutual fires: "Mutuis animis amant amantur" ("they love, are loved with mutual souls": Catullus 45.19. I.16 is also based on Catullus 45. Marullus was about fifteen years younger that Pontano, so the comparison with the young lovers in Catullus is not inapt.

1.27

Title. Francesco Caracciolo was a Neapolitan poet. In 1536 Petrus Gravina wrote at his grave: "Haec vivent dum Parthenope sirenes habebit / Sebetusque humili fonte refondet aquas" ("They [your poems] will live as long as Naples has her sirens, and the Sebetus fills its waters from a humble spring").

11. Harmosine, a Neapolitan girl, has a poem in *De tumulis*, II.56; Erycina herself (Sicilian Venus) has extinguished her torches: "extinxitque suas ipsa Erycina faces."

18. Whom you may visit for a little nap: compare "amabo, mea dulcis Ipsitilla . . . iube ad te veniam meridiatum" ("I'll love, my sweet Ipsitilla. Let me come to you for a noontime nap"): Catullus 32.1–3.

1.28

Title. Stella: Pontano met the girl he called Stella in Ferrara in 1483. She inspired his *Eridanus* (the Po), later moved to Naples and gave birth to Pontano's son Lucilio. She left him after his wife died. This poem is based in part on Catullus 51, which may be the first poem Catullus wrote to Lesbia and which itself is a translation from Sappho.

5–7. Now drop by drop my innards melt: Compare "lingua sed torpet tenuis sub artus / flamma demanat, sonitu suopte / tintinant aures, gemina teguntur / lumina nocte" ("but my words got jumbled and little flames went through my arms and legs, my ears began ringing, and then twin nighttimes clothed my eyes"): Catullus 51.9–12.

10ff. Pontano always associated Stella with brilliant light. In *Urania* (V, 293ff.), at the end of his life, he recalls seeing her by the banks of the Po. She turns her glance to the river and sets it on fire. Cicero (*Pro Caelio* 20, 49), who did not intend to flatter, in speaking about Clodia Pulcher (Catullus's Lesbia), alludes to her *flagrantia oculorum* (blazing eyes). See also II.4.

1.29

Title. Michael Marullus: see I.10 and I.26.

3. Menaliae puellae: see I.11.9.

5. Aonian sisters: the Muses, who live in the Aonian Mountains in Boetia.

9. Septimilla: see I.26.9.

11. A hundred kisses, Catullan ones: the ultimate source is "da mi basia mille, deinde centum" ("give me a thousand kisses, then a hundred"): Catullus 5.7. But the latter is mediated by "da mi basia, sed Catulliana / quae si tot fuerint quot ille dixit / donabo tibi passerem Catulli" ("give me kisses, but Catullan ones which, if as many as he said, I'll give you Catullus's sparrow"): Martial XI.6.14–16. Lines that gave rise to a (probably incorrect) reading of Catullus 2 that deeply affected Catullus's image in the renaissance and thereafter. See Gaisser, *Catullus*, 226ff., and the Introduction, p. xv ff.

1.30

Title. Benedetto Chariteo, ca. 1450–ca. 1520; Italian name of the Catalan poet Benet Gareth. The Academy named him to underline his encounters with the Graces (Charites).

1–7. Pontano contrasts his age with that of the younger Chariteo.

11. *poetulisque: sc. paetulisque.*

15. Endymion and the Latmian rock: compare "ut Triviam furtim sub Latmia saxa relegans / dulcis amor gyro devocet aerio" ("how sweet love summoning her from her high gyre quietly calls Luna to the Latmian rocks"): Catullus 66.5–6. The Endymion story prepares the way for Luna, 31 and passim, the name given to one of Chariteo's girls, at whose grave he mourns in *De tumulis* II.35.

39. Ambrosian essence (see I.16 and Catullus 99) liquefies.

45. Assyrian bed: Assyrian fortifies the Syrian and Cyprian scent of line 43. See "ac Syrio fragrans olivo" ("fragrant with Syrian olive"): Catullus 6.8, and "fragrantem Assyrio venit odore domum" ("to a house fragrant with Assyrian scent"): Catullus 68.144.

1.31

Title. Masius Aquosa: Tommaso Aquosa, born in Messina, was named Magnificus Masius Aquosa by the Academy in 1495. He was secretary to Alfonso I and later to Federigo II. Pontano mentions him in *De Sermone* II.15.

8. The following lines refer to Athens in various ways: 13. Hippolyta, an Amazon queen who mated with Theseus, legendary king of Athens, washes in Baian waters. 15. "Cecropio sinu:" Cecrops was a mythical king of Athens (see Catullus 64.172, where "Cecropiae . . . puppes" are Athenian ships). See also Martial V, 2: "coram Cecropia . . . puella" ("in the presence of the Cecropian girl"), i.e., Minerva, as here.

18–19. Placed upon his throne. Perhaps Theseus returning to Athens from Crete under the direction of Pallas Athena.

25. Pierides: see I.1. The Muses, invoked at the beginning.

26. Cicero wrote part of his dialogue *De finibus bonorum et malorum* at his villa in Cumae. See II.6 and 25. *Anchisiaden*, Aeneas, son of Anchises.

I.32

Title. Giovanni Albino, d. 1496, member of the Academy and once tutor of Alfonso, Duke of Calabria; see I.16. The address to Alfonso as Duke of Calabria dates the poem to before Alfonso's accession to the throne in 1495. The attitude toward Drusula has changed.

II.1

Title. Marino Tomacelli: see I.1.31. The first poems of both books are addressed to Tomacelli. Both mention Sirmio as does the penultimate poem of Book I.

1. Camenae: the native Italian muses. Book I invokes the Pierides, who came from Thessaly.

13. Peace for Italy: it is uncertain which time of hope is alluded to. See II.32.

17–18. Jewel of islands, Sirmio, Come, and come Catullan ashes [Catullus's spirit?]. Compare: "Paene insularum, Sirmio, insularumque, ocelle" ("Of almost islands, Sirmio, and of islands the jewel"): Catullus 30, 1–2. Catullus had greeted his home in Sirmio on his return from visiting his brother's ashes (Catullus 101). This may explain the word *cineres* in line 18.

26. The wines of Melfi are mentioned in I.17.21.

29–30. Dried up, frigid, minuscule, hung with just a little pickle: Compare "languidior tenera cui pendens sicula beta" ("hung with a penis limper than a tender beet"): Catullus 67.21.

32–33. Please, my boy! Set out the little chalices: compare "Minister vetuli puer Falerni / inger mi calices amariores" ("Boy with the old Falernian, pour me a fiercer chalice"): Catullus 28.1–2, and see Gaisser, *Catullus*, p. 227.

II.2

Title. Elisius Gallutius or Luigi Gallucci: Latin poet, given the name Elisio Calenzio in the Academy. See I.10.11.

4. Sweet Amor, sweet Cupid, Jocus sweet and Venus sweet: compare "Erycina ridens / quam Iocus circumvolat et Cupido" ("Venus laughing around whom Iocus and Cupid fly"): Horace, *Odes* I.2.33–34.

11. Catonian harshness: Cato, orator known for his moral severity and hostility to all things Greek.

13. Fanniella: see I.19.

II.3

Title. Andrea Contrario, humanist and student of philosophy, born in Venice, settled in Naples after 1471. He is mentioned in the dialogue *Antonius* where, together with Elisius (see previous poem) he discusses Cicero and Virgil: "Who is more learned in Virgil than Andrea? And a sharper critic of the excellence of his poem and work?" Note the placement of poems II.2 and II.3 together.

3. Thalia as the Muse of light verse: see I.9.6.

9. Aon: see I.29.5. Contrario may have learned Greek from Nicolaus Secundinus, a bilingual Greek who served both the Venetian state and the papal court; his education was overseen by the Venetian Francesco Barbaro.

II.4

Title. Focilla: ten poems to Focilla, many of them on her flashing eyes, form an important part of Book II. She is not mentioned in Pontano's other poems. Her name suggests "a little brightness" or "a little fireplace."

5. *poetulosque: sc. paetulosque.*

6. He takes them then and uses them for arrows. See *Eridanus* I.21: "Neve, puer, neu fle, mater; dant spicula mille Stellae oculi" ("Son and mother, do not weep. Stella's eyes provide a thousand arrows"). There are parallels between Stella, who may have already abandoned Pontano, and Focilla: see I.28.

22. Narcissus, male in Ovid, *Metamorphoses* III.339–401, and other ancient sources, has turned into a girl. See I.26, etc.

II.6

Title. Giovanni Pardo, d. after 1512. One of the speakers, with Sannazaro and Summontius, in Pontano's dialogue *Actius*. As here among the Focilla poems, a poem is dedicated to him in *Eridanus* I.31 among the Stella poems, again concerning the arrows from Stella's eyes. Pardo in the baths is in company with Virgil composing Books V and VI of the *Aeneid* and with Cicero. The cave of the Cumaean Sibyl near Naples was visited by Cicero and, before him, by Aeneas. See I.31.26.

15. Marcus Aurelius, emperor and philosopher.

II.9

Title. Francesco Pucci, former student of Angelo Poliziano, speaks in Pontano's dialogue *Aegidius* about the death of Gabriele Altilio and the decline of grammar in the Middle Ages.

1. Avernus: a volcanic lake east of Baiae thought to have been an entrance to the Underworld.

3. Amores: not love songs but Cupids.

5. Graces: see I.9.6.

11. Sulpicia: the name, suspiciously noble for one of the girls at Baiae, is probably taken from the Roman poet Sulpicia, associated with Tibullus in the circle around Messalla. See I.24.1.

II.10

Title. Constantia: Constanza d'Avalos, ca. 1460–ca. 1541, evidently a poetess. Chariteo called her "Heliconian Goddess." After 1483 she was a widow in a politically influential family.

2. Melissa: a bee-nymph.

3. Hyblean dew: see I.14.19.

4. Paphian: the Paphians are attendants to Venus to whom Paphos is sacred.

5. Castalian lakes: sacred to Apollo. See I.18.7.

6. Thespian streams: frequented by the Muses. Mt. Helicon was near Thespia in Boetia.

10. Attic Camenae: the Camenae, native Italian Muses, here are of Attic origin. See II.1.1.

II.10 (BIS)

Title. Joannes Pardus: see II.6, Title. And see Monti Sabia's edition (1978), p. 15, for her complex reasoning behind the placement of this poem.

3–4. All shining salt and witticisms: compare "qui tum denique habent salem ac leporem" ("as long as they [the poems] have salt and charm"): Catullus 16.7.

6. "aut vinctae pede vocis, aut solutae," "of metred verse or of spontaneous prose." Compare "undique quique canent vincto pede quique soluto" ("Whoever sing either in verse or in prose"): Tibullus, III.7.36. Literally, singing with a chained or free foot.

14. [You . . . who . . .] Outsalts the cellars of Attica? B. W. Swann notes that Martial distinguishes between Roman salt and Attic charm (*Mar-*

tial's Catullus, p. 61). Pontano follows Catullus (16.7) in equating the two; but see II.37.4, below.

15. Cato: see II.2.11.

II.15

Title. Franciscus Pudericus or Francesco Poderico, d. 1528, an early and long-time member of the Academy, a speaker in *Actius* and elsewhere. Pontano dedicated several works to him.

3. Cythera: an island southwest of the promontory Malea sacred to Venus.

5. Paphos: see II.10, 4.

5. Urii: uncertain place sacred to Venus, possibly the cult center founded by Idomeneus in the Salentino. Probably not the same as Urium on the coast of Apulia. In antiquity found in this form only in Catullus 36.12: "Uriosque apertos" ("exposed to the winds").

11. Capimontian groves: according to Summontius' notes to his 1505 edition, this is "a place not far from Naples, a city in the hills seen from the north, very cultivated with fields and villas, which he celebrates in thanks to Franciscus Pudericus, who had a villa there." I.e., modern Capodimonte. See I.11.11–12.

13. Antiniana: Pontano's villa on the Vomero hill overlooking the bay of Naples. See II.37.12.

II.16

This poem and the next continue the theme of the brightness of Focilla's eyes, an attribute that had hitherto characterized Stella. The eyes are arrows, etc. See I.4.

20 ff. Hot and cold, which had described the lover as *beatus* and *misellus* (see I.14 and I.22), now stand for youth and age.

II.17

11–13. "et vittam remove et reclude ocellos / quis lucem simul et diem ministras / et lucem pariter diemque redde" ("Let fall the cloth and disclose your eyes, / That minister both light and day, / Bring back the light, bring back the day!"). Compare "In medio, mea Stella, die sub sole nitescis, / clarior et per te solque diesque venit." ("My Stella, you shine in the midday sun. Through you the sun and the day shine brighter"): *Eridanus* I.10.

II.18

Title. Petrus Summontius: see I.24.

1. Neera: see I.24.

2 ff. Napeae, Dryades, Oreades, Naiades: nymphs of the dell, the woods, the mountains and the sea, respectively.

7. Thyasos: worshipers, particularly of Dionysus.

11. Avernus: see II.9.1.

12. Gaurus: a mountain in Campania famous for its wine. Now Monte Barbaro.

18 and 25. Aren't you blessed, Very like the gods themselves? . . . And do the gods not envy you? Expressions modelled on Catullus 51.1–2. See I.16.10ff.

II.19

Title. Summontius and Neera: see I.24. Ludwig, "Catullus Renatus," p. 183, cites this poem in particular for its sexual explicitness: "it certainly goes far beyond Catullus."

2. Hyblean roses: see I.14.19.

4. Scents of Corycus: from Corycus in Cilicia, known for its saffron; not, probably, the Corycian cave in Mt. Parnassus.

5. Hymettus: see I.14.19.

II.20

Title. Antonius Galateus or Antonio de Farrariis, known as "il Galateo," ca. 1448–1517. Member of the Academy, physician to Alfonso II, left Naples in 1495 and did not return until a year or two before Pontano's death. Portrayed in *De sermone* as a model of *humanitas*.

1. Gauran girls: mountain nymphs. See II.18.12.

6–7. "Qui risus tamen inde, qui cachinni, / senex herniolose, dum lavabis?" ("What chuckling then, what laughter, / ruptured old boy, while you bathe!"). Compare "Derisor Fabianus hirnearum . . . in thermis subito Neronianis / vidit se miser et tacere coepit" ("Fabianus who made fun of hernias . . . suddenly saw himself in the Neronian baths, Felt sad and stopped talking"): Martial XII.83.1 and 5–6.

II.21

Title. Petrus Gravina or Pietro Gravina, ca. 1453–1528, poet and humanist. Lived in Naples after 1494; known for his *iocunditas*. Galateus (see II.20, title) in a letter to Pontano praised his lack of pedantry.

4. Pleasure, wielding power over the hearts of men. Compare "trahit sua quemque voluptas" ("each man is drawn by his own pleasure"): Virgil, *Eclogues*, II.65. Ludwig, "Catullus Renatus," p. 186: "The ruling concept of *Hendecasyllabi . . . libri II* is *voluptas*."

6. Charites: see I.9.6 etc.

14. Camenae: see II.1.1.

17. Gaurus: see II.18.12.

18. Philena: Philaenis, a poetess, ca. 400 B.C.

II.22

Based on Catullus 62. Eight sections, each, excepting the first, ends with a refrain. Catullus 62, as we have it, is in nine sections with refrain. The invocation is to boys and girls to make love in Pontano, to get married in Catullus. Compare Catullus's first line, "Vesper adest: iuvenes, consurgite! Vesper Olympo" ("Vesper is here: get up, boys. Vesper from

Olympus"), and Pontano's, "Ad myrtum, iuvenes, venite, myrti" ("To the myrtle, boys, come to the myrtle"), which are strikingly similar. But Catullus's poem is about harsh reality; Pontano's is about pleasure. Compare "idem cum tenui carptus defloruit ungui / nulli illum pueri, nullae optavere puellae" ("when it [the blossom] is deflowered, clipped by a sharp fingernail, no boys want it, nor do any girls") in Catullus 62.43–44, with "atque hanc horridulo colonus ungui decerptam variae implicit coronae" ("and the farmer with his rough fingernail clips and binds it into wreathes") in lines 37–38 of Pontano's poem.

2. Charites: see I.9.6.

5. Paphiae: see II.10, 4.

41. Ambrosian liquor: see I.16.1.

42. Idalium: see I.16.8.

II.23

Title. Joannes Pardus: see II.6.

8. Maeonian wrestlers (gymnasiums): unlikely to refer to homosexual wrestling. Virgil (*Aeneid* IV, 216) uses Maeonian, i.e., Lydian, as a word for effeminacy. Otherwise, Homeric wrestling or Etruscan wrestling.

13. The Cato of Mopsopian thought: for *Mopsopius* see I.14.8. For Cato see II.2.

II.24

Title. Manlius Rallus or Manilio Cabacio Rallo, ca. 1447–1523, poet and humanist; wrote *Juveniles ingenii lusus* (Naples, 1520); born in Sparta, came to Italy in 1466.

1–2. Poliziano called Cabacio "a Greek man, but with the highest refinement in Latin letters." Gravina wrote: "Huc mirere magis quod vir Lacedemone natus / Romano potuit cultius ore loqui." ("It is wonderful that a man from Sparta could speak such refined Latin"); see his liminal epigram printed in Cabacio's *Juveniles*.

3. Lycinna is Cabacio's mistress in his collected poems, also the girl who introduced Propertius to love (Propertius III.15.6).

4. Philitas of Cos, an Alexandrian poet (b. ca. 340 BC) and tutor to Ptolemy II Philadelphus. Known to Pontano probably from Propertius III.I.I: "Callimachi manes et Coi sacra Philitae" ("Shades of Callimachus and rites of Coan Philitas"). He is also alluded to in Ovid's *Tristia* I.6.2.

6. sweet Tibullus: most of the poems in Cabacio's collection are in elegiac distichs. The epithet, the manuscript of Tibullus in Wolfenbüttel (see I.14.18) and the number of Tibullan allusions here suggest that, although Cabacio clearly favoured Propertius, Pontano inclined toward Tibullus.

8. Misenum: a promontory just south of Baiae, in antiquity a Roman naval base.

12. Antiniana: see II.15.13 and II.38.12; Patulcis is Pontano's villa by the sea near Virgil's tomb at Posillipo, associated in Pontano's poems with Virgil, as in the following line. Patulcus is an epithet of Janus (Servius, *In Aeneidem* VI.710) and is a word also attested in inscriptions near Puteoli.

15. The seven handmaidens of Venus consist of three Charites (see I.9.6, but here Pasithea substitutes for Thalia) and four others, apparently Horae (daughters of Zeus and Themis associated with the seasons), but given new Greek names, doubtless in honor of Cabacio the Lacedaemonian: Opsiglycea, "eyes-sweet;" Chariotaris, "joking;" Gelopea, "provoking laughter;" and Pasirhythmie, "all-rhythmic."

16. Cyprian: see I.12.26.

43. *poetis: sc. paetis.*

63. Compare "eque sagittifera prompsit duo tela pharetra / diversorum operum: fugat hoc, facit illud amorem; / quod facit, auratum est et cuspide fulget acuta / quod fugat, obtusum est et habet sub harundine plumbum." ("he plucked from his quiver two arrows of differing use: one causes flight, the other love, the first is gold and its sharp tip shines, the other is dull and has a leaden tip"): Ovid, *Metamorphoses* I.468–471.

65. Idalian pools: see I.16.8. In II.37, Amor himself plunges his arrows into the waters there called Tullian.

II.25

Title. Fabius Lopitius: unidentified. The meaning of Fabius or Lopitius (lines 1 and 13) is unclear.

5. Francesco Pucci: see II.9. The opening is reminiscent of the search for Camerarius in Catullus 55. Camerarius is with the girls while Lopitius is studying.

6. Aon: see I.29.5.

9. Corinna: Ovid's mistress.

II.26

Title. Petrus Paulus Sarranus: A grammarian, poet and tutor.

11. Iovanulus is Lucio Pontano, Pontano's only son by his wife Ariane. Lucilio, a son by the woman called Stella, only lived for fifty days. Since Lucio was born in 1469, this poem can be dated to 1473, the earliest dateable poem in the collection.

II.27

Title. Leonardus Corvinus, bishop of Trivento, a churchman and poet who dedicated a poem to Petrus Gravina in the latter's *Oratio de Christo*. He was made bishop of Potenza in 1491 and translated to Trivento in 1499.

1. Gaurides: see II.18.12; for Avernus, see II.9.1.

II.28

Title. Marino Tomacelli: see I.1. Petrus Compater (Pietro Golino): see I.1.38. Tomacelli came to Naples around 1447. Ludwig, "Catullus Renatus," p. 183 n. 89, dates the poem to 1501, counting 54 years from 1447; Compater died in that year.

6. Of love a prime example and of faith. Repeats I.22.23 exactly; repeating a line in this way is a practice also found in Catullus and Virgil.

7. The Lucrine Lake on the east coast of Campania near Baiae.

II.29

Title. Ariane Pontano: see I.12, died in 1490. Lucio Francesco, Pontano's only son by Ariane, died in 1498 at the age of 29. *Eridanus* II begins with a poem on Ariane's death: until he sees her in Elisium (see II.38) Stella will be his light. This poem may be addressed to Stella, who abandoned him after his wife died.

3. "connubi immemor, immemorque amorum" ("Forgetful of our promises and loves"). Compare "nec te noster amor nec te data dextero quondam . . . tenet?" ("Does not our love hold you, our hands once pledged?"): Virgil, *Aeneid* IV, 307–8. Also "immemor . . . ? Et non haec quondam blanda promissa dedisti?" ("Unmindful . . . But did you not give sweet vows once?"): Catullus 64.135, 139. Especially in an intensely personal situation, there are classical models.

II.30

Title. Annibal Famatius: unidentified.

2. He's hiding within a girl's thighs. Compare: "en hic in roseis latet papillis" ("Look, he's hiding in my rosy breasts!"): Catullus 55.12.

5. Hyella: perhaps "transparent." Compare: "vellera nymphae / carpebant hyali saturo fucata colore" ("[water] nymphs spun cloth dyed with a glassy color"): Virgil, *Georgics*, IV, 334–5.

12. *Refragat: sc. refragrat.*

II.31

Title. Federigo of Aragon, king of Naples, 1451–1504. Federigo's reign lasted from 1496 to 1501 when he was taken into exile.

5. Progne/Procne, mythological wife of Tereus, killed her son Itys in a rage and was turned into a sparrow or a nightingale. She mourned her son. Compare "qualia sub densis ramorum concinit umbris / Daulias absumpti fata gemens Itali" ("as Procne sings deep in the woods" thick shade about Itys, about her own son's death"): Catullus 65.13–14. These words are found in Pontano's hand in the margin of his manuscript copy

of Ovid, *Heroides* XV, where mention is made of Procne: see Introduction, pp. xviii–xix.

24. Mars must stand for a real person: see II.32.

II.32

1–2. The peace hoped for on the accession of Federigo was certainly over by 1499 when the French entered Milan.

3. Cytherea: Venus of Cythera. See II.15.3.

II.33

Title. Batilla's only appearance in Book II. For her name, see I.3. This poem, like II.26, may be an earlier work placed late in the collection for variety. In arranging his "polymetric poems," 1–60, Catullus too seems to have intentionally disrupted chronology.

10. ambrosia: see I.16.1–9.

14. Cypris, i.e. Venus: see I.12.28.

II.34

Title. Hieronymus Carbo: Girolamo Carbone, ca. 1465-after 1527, poet, was head of the Academy between Summonte and Sannazaro. He appears frequently in Pontano's writings. The wit of the verses comes from the meaning of *carbo* in Latin: a piece of coal.

10. Just now cold, now he's hot. Heat and cold: I.14, I.22, II.16, happiness and sadness, youth and age. Here it is simple changeability.

11. Theonilla: In Pontano's *De tumulis* II.32, Carbone performs rites before the tomb of a girl named Variana.

13–14. Compare "sic tibi e capellis / stillent semper amoma" ("amoma dripping from your hair") to "pinguescat nimio madidus mihi crinis amomo" ("let my wet hair grow sleek with excess of amoma"): Martial, V.64.3.

II.35

Title. Marino Tomacelli: see I.1 and throughout. This may be the frankest evocation of elderly sexuality in the lyric canon.

II.36

Title. Terina appears in Pontano's *De amore coniugali* I.II.2, mentioned along with Margara, Greciana and Iunepra; in *Eridanus* II.9, she is in a group with Thelesina and Venerilla, i.e., she is one of the girls.

14. "Ah, quid lectulus ipse subtremiscit?" ("Ah, why is the very bed trembling?"). Compare "tremulique quassa lecti / argutatio inambulatione" ("the creaking and the marching of the trembling bed"): Catullus, 6.10–11.

II.37

Title. Suardo Suardino, d. 1536, a speaker in Pontano's dialogue *Aegidius*. Pontano sent Suardino his works, *Urania*, *Meteora* and the *Horti Hesperidum* in 1502 for publication by Aldus. Suardino wrote *In metamorphosim Ovidii praelectio* (Brescia, 1499).

2. Cumaean shore: Cumae, just North of Baiae (see II.6), home of the Cumaean sibyl.

3, 6, 7. Adeste, hendecasyllabi . . . numeris Catullianis . . . Syrmioni. This is properly the last poem in the work (II.38 is a postlude), and it begins, as did I.1, with references to Catullus, to his metre and to Sirmio.

4. "Romano et sale et Attico lepore" ("with Roman salt and Attic charm"): see II.10bis, 14. The distinction is from Martial and not from Catullus.

9. Catullus is asked for a song. But what issues is in the style of Ovid.

12. Summontius in his 1505 edition comments on the place names: "A mountain rising to the west of Naples, notable for its fresh air and numerous villas, on which is a place called Antinianum where Pontanus had a villa . . . And on this mountain is Patulcium . . . famous for the tomb

of Maro, which Pontanus often mentions by naming the Nymphs of Patulcis, celebrating Virgil himself." See I.11.11–12.

16. Sebethus. Summontius comments: "A river, often sung by Pontano, that flows near the walls of Naples. Referred to by Virgil, Statius and Columella".

17–126. A story in the form and style of an Ovidian metamorphosis.

17–31. The seven allusions are: (1) Acrisius, the father of Danaë to whom Jupiter came as a shower of gold. (2) Amphrysos, a river in Thessaly where Apollo tended the sheep of his lover Admetus to whom he was in bondage. (3) Neptune loved Iphimedea, the daughter of Aloeus. (4) Persephone was raped by Dis. (5) Mars and Venus, discovered by Vulcan. (6) Saturn, in the form of a horse, sired Chiron, the centaur, on Philyra. (7) Luna visited Endymion on Mt. Latmos. Nos. 1, 2, 3, 5 and 6 are the *caelestia crimina*, sins of the gods, depicted by Arachne in *Metamorphoses* VI.103ff. Arachne was punished by Athena. For (4) see *Metamorphoses.* V, 366ff. (7) The Endymion story has only a passing mention in Ovid, *Ars Amatoria* III.83. Pontano's source may be Catullus 66.5–6. See I.30, 15ff.

37–38. To his shoulder, resting on hand and knee. As Apollo had spotted Amor and mocked him. Compare *Metamorphoses* I.454.

42. Athena's Aegis, a shield or bib carrying the face with snakey hair of the Gorgon Medusa. The stories of Perseus with Medusa's head (that turned viewers into stone) are in *Metamorphoses* IV, 604-V, 249.

58. Anxur/Terracina, colony on the coast of Latium, northwest of Naples, an ancient stronghold of the Volsci, with prominent remains of the temple of Jupiter Anxur.

75. The boy's mother is Venus.

92. Thrust his darts: see II.24.65.

96. Tullian pools: the Bay of Cumae, with its Idalian Pools (see above). They are called Tullian pools here because Cicero was known to have frequented them. See I.31.26.

127. Sirmio—i.e. Catullus—sang, but in this poem it was certainly Ovid.

11.38

Hail, hendecasyllables. This concludes what started as "Here, here, you thronging verses" at I.1.10. The word "hail" (havete) recalls Catullus's farewell to his brother (Catullus 101.10) and anticipates the seriousness of the poem's conclusion.

5. Of playing and of jokes: "lepidi sales," i.e. "charming wit." The distinction is now lifted; see II.10 bis, 14 and II.37.4.

9. Nonsense: *nugae*. Compare "namque tu solebas / meas esse aliquid putare nugas" ("For you used to think my nonsense was worth something"): Catullus 1.3–4.

9. Thalia: see I.9.6.

13. Elysium: the extremely conciliatory tone provides a remarkable conclusion, especially following Pontano's poem to his wife at the beginning of *Eridanus* II, where he expects to see her in Elysium but has, in the meantime, illumination from Stella, and II.29 in this work, which expresses anger at her "desertion" of him in death.

19. Voluptas: the last word, and the theme of the whole. See II.21.4.

Bibliography

ℬ✦ℬ

WORKS OF PONTANO CONSULTED

Ioannis Ioviani Pontani Opera. De fortitudine libri duo [etc.]. Venice: Bernardinus Vercellensis, 1501. Contains the moral treatises and the dialogue *Antonius*.

Ioannis Ioviani Pontani Opera. Urania, sive de stellis libri quinque [etc.]. Venice: Aldus, 1505. Contains *Urania, Meteora, De hortis Hesperidum, Lepidina, Meliseus, Acon, Baiae, De tumulis, Neniae,* and *Epigrammata.*

[*Ioannis Ioviani Pontani*] *Hoc in volumine opera continentur. Parthenopei libri duo* [etc.]. Naples: S. Mayr, 1505. Contains *Parthenopeus, De amore coniugali, De tumulis, De divinis laudibus, Baiae, Sapphici,* and *Eridanus,* edited by Pietro Summonte.

Ioannis Ioviani Pontani Carmina, ed. Benedetto Soldati. 2 vols. Florence: G. Barbèra, 1902.

Giovanni Gioviano Pontano. *I Dialoghi,* ed. Carmelo Previtera. Florence: Sansoni, 1943.

Giovanni Gioviano Pontano. *De sermone libri sex,* ed. Sergio Lupi and Antonino Risicato. Lugano: Thesaurus Mundi, 1954.

Ioannis Ioviana Pontani Carmina: ecloghe, elegie, liriche, ed. Johannes Oeschger. Bari: Laterza, 1948.

Hendecasyllaborum libri Ioannis Ioviani Pontani, ed. Liliana Monti Sabia. Naples: Associazione di studi tardoantichi, 1978.

Poeti latini del Quattrocento, ed. Francesco Arnaldi, Lucia Gualdo Rosa and Liliana Monti Sabia. Milan: Ricciardi, 1964. Contains Latin texts and Italian translations of a number of the hendecasyllabic poems.

SELECTED MODERN STUDIES

Clausen, Wendell. *A Commentary on Virgil, Eclogues.* Oxford: Clarendon Press, 1994.

Gaisser, Julia Haig. *Catullus and his Renaissance Readers*. Oxford: Clarendon Press, 1993. Comprehensive monograph on the Renaissance reception of Catullus.

Kidwell, Carol. *Pontano: Poet and Prime Minister*. London: Duckworth, 1991. Comprehensive biography with extensive excerpts from Pontano's poetry in English translation.

Ludwig, Walther. "Catullus Renatus." In *Litterae neolatinae, Schriften sur neulateinischen Literatur*, 162–194. Munich: W. Fink, 1989. Pioneering essay on Catullus' Renaissance reception.

———. "The Catullan Style in Neo-Latin Poetry." In Peter Godman and Oswyn Murray, eds., *Latin Poetry and the Classical Tradition, Essays in Medieval and Renaissance Literature*, 183–197. Oxford: Clarendon Press, 1990. A brief version of the previous essay.

———. *Miscella Neolatina: Ausgewählte Aufsätze, 1989–2003*. Edited by Astrid Steiner-Weber. 3 vols. Hildesheim: Georg Olms, 2004–2005. Contains two essays on Pontano's influence on later Neo-Latin poetry.

Minieri Riccio, Camillo. *Biografie degli accademici alfonsini*. Naples: Furchheim, 1881. Photo-reprint, Bologna: Forni, 1969.

Swann, Bruce W. *Martial's Catullus: The Reception of an Epigrammatic Rival*. Hildesheim: Georg Olms, 1994.

Thompson, D. F. S. *Catullus, edited with a textual and interpretative commentary*. Toronto: University of Toronto Press, 1997.

Tibulli Carmina; Sapphus Epistula Ovidiana; Codex Guelferbytanus 82.6. Aug. Preface by Friedrich Leo. Leiden: Sijthoff, 1910. Facsimile edition of a MS, now in Wolfenbüttel, written in Pontano's hand.

Index

References are by book, poem, and (where appropriate) line number. Roman numerals refer to page numbers in the Introduction.

grasses drink drafts of divine milk, why does rust impede the
sown crops and blight the vines; what can drive away the clouds
and repel storms; what is the nature of the wind; what is it that
turns clouds into a clear sky; what does the absence of the moon   460
portend, or the moon in the interlunar period, or when it is full or
when it begins to wane again. The provident farmer also observes
the numbers and the laws of the days.[50] He knows what the sev-
enth day brings, on which day Diana welcomed her newly-born
brother; he knows what tasks the stars enjoin on the eleventh and   465
twelfth days; wherefore he either shears the fleece-wool or cuts the
ripe ears of wheat and collects them in heavy sheaves or sets up his
wife's loom (for on the second of these days the hanging spider
also spins her web).   470

The next day is good for planting shrubs, but unfavorable for
sowing crops; therefore he avoids what is harmful and presses on
with what is advantageous. He knows what day is inimical to mat-
ings and births and which day favors them; on which day he
should castrate the fat kid, enclose the flock in a pen; what day is
good for uniting lovers and what day gives license to share clandes-   475
tine whisperings; on what day the dog will cease its snarling, and
evil-counselling cares will torment the heart too much; on what
night the grim Fury will be abroad. He cuts wood on a day of his
choosing, tastes the wine in the barrel, puts the young bull under
the yoke. Concerning winds also, and rain and clear skies, he con-   480
sults the setting or the rising of the moon. He sets to work on a
task if it is shining brightly; but if it disappears into the dark or if
on the fifth day it is vertical or blunted in the middle of the disk,
or does not have a thin crescent, or if it is adorned with a triple
halo, he returns to the shelter of his home, fearing a storm; if it   485
has a red glow, then he is certain that there will be winds and he
knows also with which horn Cynthia calls forth Boreas and with
which one Auster.[51] He consults as well the fires of Phoebus,
whether he foretells hail when he is pale, or promises rain with his

490 palleat; an radiis monstret discordibus imbrem;
an prae se exoriens nubis agat; an niger orbem
circulus extremum claudens, qua rumpitur, acres
carceris Aeolii moneat consurgere flatus.
Adnotat et caeli faciem: num stella sereno
495 aethere lapsa cadat, rapidi praenuntia Cauri;
conscia num subita semet caligine obumbrent
astra trahantque hiemem; gemino Thaumantias arcu
quid ferat aut curto cum vix secat aera gyro,
et paene unicolor taurina fronte minatur.
500 Nunc Praesepe oculis, nunc Bacchi spectat asellos,
quique Noton cernit quique est obversus ad Arcton;
fulgores, tonitrus, inspersaque vellera caelo
brumalemque diem et totum semel aspicit annum.
Necnon et nautis ruiturum in carbasa nimbum
505 augurat, undisonum si fors mare surrigit Aegon
canaque conspergit sale saxa et litora frangit.
Tunc et tristifico reboant montana fragore
et repetunt siccum mergi atque ex aequore clamant;
ipsa volans sublime auras aethramque lacessit
510 ardea; colludunt fulicae plauduntque gregatae;
at lasciva lacus alis praestringit hirundo
et summas prope radit aquas ranaeque coaxant ;
fusca gradu cornix lento metitur harenas,
aut fluvium capite et madida cervice receptat
515 crocituque gravi pluviam increpat usque morantem;
clangunt Naupliadae volucres et pervia pinnis
nubila conscribunt; incertus in aequore delphin
difflat aquas; latrant corvi vocemque resorbent.
Progerit ova cavis patiens formica laborum;
520 blanda canis terram pedibus scabit; ore lapillos
tardigradus prendit cancer seseque saburrat
atque haeret ripae; densum occinit improbulus mus

divergent rays, or at his rising drives the clouds before him, or   490
when a black ring encircles his orbit, he warns that, at the point
where this ring is broken, raging winds will burst forth from
Aeolus' prison.[52] He observes, too, the face of the sky: whether a
falling star shoots down from a serene sky, heralding Caurus, the
rapid northwest wind; whether the stars, with prescient knowl-   495
edge, suddenly veil themselves in a mist, announcing a storm. He
knows what the daughter of Thaumas[53] brings with her double
rainbow, or when she barely cleaves the air with an imperfect semi-
circle and, almost having but a single color, has the menacing ap-
pearance of a bull's brow. Now he turns his eyes toward Praesepe
[the Crib], now he observes the Asses of Bacchus,[54] of which one   500
is oriented toward the South Wind and the other is opposite the
Bear. He observes flashes of lightning, thunder, and fleecy clouds
in the heavens, the winter solstice — in a word, the whole year.

He also predicts to sailors the storm that will swoop down
upon their sails if perchance the Aegean raises the roaring sea and   505
spatters the white rocks with salt and breaks upon the shore. Then
the mountains resound with an ominous crashing sound and the
gulls seek dry land and waft their cries from over sea; the heron,
soaring aloft, defies the winds and the aether; the coots, flocking
together, sport playfully and flap their wings; but the playful swal-   510
low skims over the ponds and almost grazes the waters, and the
frogs croak. The black raven walks up and down the sands with
measured step or dips its head and dripping neck in the river, and
with raucous croaking chides the rain that is slow in coming; the   515
cranes, birds of Palamedes,[55] scream and trace letters in the pass-
ing clouds with their wings; the dolphin, unsure of himself, dis-
perses the waters with his blowing; the crows squawk and suck in
their sounds; the hard-working ant carries the eggs out of their
holes; the fawning dog scratches the earth with its feet; the slow-   520
moving crab takes little stones into its mouth, filling itself with
ballast, and clings to the shore; the rather impudent mouse inter-

straminaque exculcat; quin centipedes scolopendrae
parietibus repant; aures pigra motat asella;
525   dependent bullae lychno, sitiensque cruoris
musca redit summosque proboscide mordicat artus;
nec longe a tectis apis ingeniosa recedit,
prunaque concretusque ima cinis haeret in olla
carboque pellucet. Neque non praenuntiat Euros
530   pluma natans foliumve errans pappique volantes,
flammaque cum flectit, cum sese elidit et ipsis
vix sedet in stuppis scintillamque excutit udam.
Vos quoque, pastores, ventos horretis et imbres,
cum temere excursans pecus ampla in pascua fertur
535   cumque alacres ludunt agni calcisque protervos
subsultim incutiunt inter se et cornibus haerent,
aut cum se e pastu vi vix aegreque revellunt;
cumque boves liquidi suspectant lumina caeli
olfactantque auras et sucos naribus udos
540   crebra trahunt dextrumque latus consternere gaudent,
aut lingunt adversa pilos, aut vespere sero
mugitu ingenti redeunt caulasque fatigant;
cum sibi non factos sus dissipat ore maniplos,
cumque antro lupus exululat cumque improbus idem
545   nec metuens hominum propius consistit et offert
se mendicanti similem ac loca culta pererrat.
Ergo in consilium maria advocat aethera terras
naturamque omnem vivitque auctoribus astris,
cura deum, agricola atque animo praescita recenset
550   et rerum eventus sensu praesagit acuto.
    Hanc, o caelicolae magni, concedite vitam!
Sic mihi delicias, sic blandimenta laborum,
sic faciles date semper opes; hac improba sunto
vota tenus. Numquam certe, numquam illa precabor,

poses its unceasing squeak and stamps down the straw; the hundred-footed scolopendras creep along the wall; the lazy she-ass shakes its ears; bubbles hang from the lamp; the fly, thirsty for blood, returns and bites the extremities with its proboscis; the ingenious bee does not move far from its hive; the hot coals and the condensed ashes stick to the bottom of the pot, and the coal is incandescent. The last winds are announced by the floating feathers or the drifting leaf and the flying pappus and the flickering flame that extinguishes itself and barely adheres to the tow and emits a humid spark. You too, shepherds, dread the winds and the rains, when the flock recklessly dashes off to broad pastures and when the lively lambs play and jump into the air, kicking each other impetuously and locking horns, or when they can be torn away from pasture only by force and with difficulty; and when the oxen look up at the radiance of the sky and sniff the air and draw in the moisture repeatedly with their nostrils and like to lie down on their right side or lick their skin against the fur or return in the late evening and fill the stalls with their lowing; or when the pig tosses with his snout the bundles of straw not destined for him; and when the wolf howls inside his cave and audaciously, without fear of humans, comes closer and presents himself like a beggar and wanders over the cultivated fields. Thus the farmer, beloved of the gods, takes counsel with the seas, the air, the lands and all of nature, and lives by the guidance of the stars and goes over in his mind what is known of the future with acute understanding.

O great dwellers of the heavens, grant me this way of life! Give me always these delights, these pleasures from toil, these simple riches; let this be the limit of my greedy ambitions. Never, certainly, never shall I pray that my brow, attracting envy to itself,

555   splendeat ut rutilo frons invidiosa galero
    tergeminaque gravis surgat mihi mitra corona.
       Talia Faesuleo lentus meditabar in antro
    rure suburbano Medicum, qua mons sacer urbem
    Maeoniam longique volumina despicit Arni,
560   qua bonus hospitium felix placidamque quietem
    indulget Laurens, Laurens haud ultima Phoebi
    gloria, iactatis Laurens fida ancora Musis.
    Qui si certa magis permiserit otia nobis,
    afflabor maiore deo nec iam ardua tantum
565   silva meas voces montanaque saxa loquentur,
    sed tu (si qua fides), tu nostrum forsitan olim,
    o mea blanda altrix, non aspernabere carmen,
    quamvis magnorum genetrix, Florentia, vatum,
    doctaque me triplici recinet facundia lingua.

shall be resplendent with the red hat or that the heavy miter with   555
threefold crown should rest upon my head.

Such verses I composed in the peace of my Fiesolan cave,[56] at
the suburban farm of the Medici, where the sacred hill looks down
on the Maeonian city[57] and the curves of the long Arno, where the
good Lorenzo bestows a happy sojourn and placid tranquility —
Lorenzo, not the least glory of Phoebus; Lorenzo, faithful anchor   560
of the Muses tossed by tempests. If he shall accord me more se-
cure tranquillity, a greater god will inspire me; then no longer the
tall forests and the mountain rocks will re-echo my verses, but you   565
(if I may so hope), you one day, perhaps, my sweet nurse, Flor-
ence, will not despise my song, though you be the mother of illus-
trious poets; and learned eloquence will sing my works in three
languages.[58]

AMBRA

Angelus Politianus Laurentio Tornabono suo S. D.

Debetur haec silva tibi, vel argumento vel titulo, nam et Homeri studiosus es quasique noster consectaneus, et propinquus Laurentii Medicis, summi praecellentisque viri, qui scilicet Ambram ipsam Caianam, praedium (ut ita dixerim) omniferum, quasi pro laxamento sibi delegit civilium laborum. Tibi ergo poemation hoc, qualecumque est, nuncupamus, ut sit amoris nostri monimentum, sit incitamentum tibi ad studia litterarum praesertimque graecarum, in quibus tamen ita tantum processisti, ut videare ad summum brevi, si modo perrexeris, evasurus. Vale. Florentiae, pridie nonas Novembres MCCCCLXXXV.

AMBRA

Angelo Poliziano to His Friend Lorenzo Tornabuoni,[1] Greeting.

This *silva* is owed to you, both in its theme and in its title, for you are also a student of Homer and, one might say, a member of the same sect as I. And you are a relative of Lorenzo de' Medici, an illustrious and pre-eminent man, who, as we know, selected Ambra[2] at Poggio a Caiano, an estate, so to speak, that produces everything, as a place of relaxation from civic responsibilities. Therefore, I dedicate this little poem to you, whatever its worth, as a token of my affection, and as an incentive for the study of letters, especially Greek literature, in which you have made such progress that you seem destined in a short time to reach the summit of perfection, if you persevere. Farewell. At Florence, 4 November 1485.

Angeli Politiani silva cui titulus Ambra
in poetae Homeri narratione pronuntiata

Spicea si Cereris templo suspensa corona
donum erat agricolae quondam; si vinitor uvam
seposuit Bromio, quoties praedivite cornu
copia se fudit; placidam si lacte recenti
pastores sparsere Palem, spumantia postquam
complerant olidam supra caput ubera mulctram;
primitias et quisque sui fert muneris auctor ;
cur ego non vocem hanc, aut si quid spiritus olim
concipit egregium, si quid mens ardua conscit
rarum insigne sibi, si quo se murmure iactat
lingua potens, cur non totum in praeconia solvam
Maeonidae magni, cuius de gurgite vivo
combibit arcanos vatum omnis turba furores?
Utque laboriferi ferrum lapis Herculis alte
erigit et longos Chalybum procul implicat orbes
vimque suam aspirat cunctis, ita prorsus ab uno
impetus ille sacer vatum dependet Homero.
Ille, Iovis mensae accumbens, dat pocula nobis
Iliaca porrecta manu, quae triste repellant
annorum senium vitamque in saecla propagent.
Ille deum vultus, ille ardua semina laudum
ostentat populis ac mentis praepete nisu
pervolitat chaos, immensum caelum, aequora, terras
vimque omnem exsinuat rerum vocesque refundit,
quas fera, quas volucris, quas venti atque aetheris ignes,
quas maria atque amnes, quas dique hominesque loquantur.
Quin nudam virtutem ipsam complexus, honores
fastidit vanos et ineptae praemia famae

If at one time the farmer's offering was a wreath made from ears of
wheat; if the vine-dresser set aside a bunch of grapes for Bromius[3]
whenever Abundance lavished gifts from her rich horn of plenty;
if shepherds sprinkled peaceful Pales with fresh milk after the   5
foamy udders had filled the sweet-smelling milk-pails to over-
flowing and each one brings the first fruits of his tribute; why
should I not give free rein to this song, or if my inspiration one
day conceives some marvelous work, if my lofty mind is conscious
of some rare quality in itself, if the power of my eloquence vaunts 10
some muted utterance, why should I not devote all of this to the
praise of the great Maeonian,[4] from whose fresh-flowing torrent
the whole throng of poets imbibed their secret frenzies? As the
stone[5] of the laboring Hercules draws the iron upwards and inter-
twines at a distance the long rings of metal and breathes its power 15
into them all, so the sacred impulse of poets depends entirely on
Homer alone. He, reclining at the table of Jupiter, gives us to
drink from cups offered by the Trojan youth[6] that drive away the
sad decrepitude of the years and prolong life into eternity. He   20
shows the faces of the gods to peoples and the sublime beginnings
of deeds of glory, and in a soaring flight of the mind he flies over
vast chaos, sky, seas and lands and reveals all the power of the ele-
ments and reproduces the language that wild beasts, winged crea-
tures, winds and fires of the aether, that seas and rivers, gods and   25
men speak. Indeed, embracing naked virtue, he disdains empty
honors and, far-removed from the crowd, despises the rewards of

despicit, exemptus vulgo ac iam monte potitus,
30   ridet anhelantem dura ad fastigia turbam.
       Vos, age nunc, tanti, precor, incunabula vatis
     divinosque ortus, Clio, dictate canenti;
     muneris hoc vestri, longis siquidem obsita saeclis
     Fama tacet centumque deae premit ora vetustas.
35   Iverat Aethiopum solitas invisere mensas
     Oceanumque senem et fecundae Tethyos antra
     Iuppiter Aetnaeoque manum exarmaverat igni
     contentus sceptris; frontem tranquilla serenat
     maiestas sanctoque nitet pax aurea vultu,
40   nimbi, hiemes tonitrusque procul; regem omne deorum
     concilium facie cultuque insigne sequuntur.
     Bistoniis Mars instat equis; tu iungis olores,
     Phoebe, Therapnaeos; Getica Mars fulgurat hasta;
     contendis tu, Phoebe, fides arcusque retendis;
45   lyncas agit Bromius, pavos Saturnia pictos,
     tardos Luna boves, annosas Delia cervas,
     grypas Hyperboreos Nemesis, Cytherea columbas.
     Fert pedibus pinnas puer Arcas, crine galerum
     et chelyn incurvam atque incurvam sustinet harpen
50   paciferaque duos virga discriminat angues;
     goryton puer Idalius calamosque facemque,
     Alcides clavam et Nemeaei vellera monstri,
     Tartaream Pallas galeam et Phorcynida gestat.
     Concordes gemino radiantur Castores astro;
55   claviger in semet redeuntem computat annum
     iam dextra deus. At Saturnum lanea compes
     Mulcibero iubet ire parem; nec dextra, Prometheu,
     non tua Caucaseae meminit ferrata catenae.
     Arma deos sua quemque decent.
                           Nec segnius alti
60   numina conveniunt pelagi: rex ipse biformes

hollow fame; having reached the summit, he laughs at the multitude panting to scale the steep heights.   30

But now, you, Clio[7], I pray, dictate to me as I sing of the birth and divine origins of so great a poet (for this is your role) since Fame, enveloped in the darkness of long centuries, is silent, and antiquity suppresses the hundred mouths of the goddess. Jupiter had gone as usual to visit the banquets of the Ethiopians[8] and old   35 Oceanus[9] and the caves of fecund Tethys,[10] and he had disarmed himself of Etna's fire, content with his scepter; a tranquil majesty gladdens his brow and golden peace shines in his holy countenance; clouds, storms and thunder are far away; the entire council   40 of the gods, magnificent in aspect and adornment, follows their king. Mars spurs on his Bistonian steeds;[11] you, Phoebus, yoke your Therapnean swans,[12] Mars blazes with his Getic spear; Phoebus, you stretch the strings of your lyre and unbend your bow. Bromius drives his lynxes, Saturnia her multi-colored pea-   45 cocks, the moon her slow oxen, Delia[13] her long-lived hinds, Nemesis her Hyperborean griffins, Cytherea her doves. The Arcadian youth,[14] wings on his feet and cap on his head, holds a curved lyre and a curved sword, and with his rod, symbol of peace, he separates the two serpents; the Idalian youth[15] bears his quiver, arrows   50 and torch, Alcides[16] carries his club and the skin of the Nemean monster,[17] Pallas her Tartarean helmet[18] and the head of the Medusa.[19] The inseparable Dioscuri[20] radiate with the effulgence of their twin stars; the key-bearing god[21] already counts in his right hand the course of the year that returns upon itself. The   55 woolen fetters on his feet oblige Saturn[22] to walk at the same pace as Vulcan,[23] and your right hand, Prometheus,[24] bound with iron, does not forget the Caucasian chain. Each god is distinguished by his proper implements.

No less quickly the divinities of the deep ocean convene: the king himself, his head held high, urges on his biform sea-horses   60

arduus urget equos saevoque tridente minatur
Euroque Boreaeque et vultu temperat Austros;
solus equo Zephyrus tremulis persultat in undis,
ipse sinu facilem molli fovet Amphitriten.

65 Ludunt Nereidum simplex chorus: illa sororem
provocat et blando certat superare natatu;
haec iunctum delphina regit, premit illa leonem,
trux vehit hanc aries, olido sedet illa iuvenco;
insultant aliae monstris quae plurima vastus

70 subluit Oceanus scopulis, horrentia cete,
balaenam pistrinque et physetera, marinos
— siqua fides vero est — efflantem ad sidera fluctus.
Quasdam et semiferi dorso Tritones amico
excipiunt bifidaeque ligant curvamine caudae,

75 et nunc tortilibus permulcent aequora conchis,
dulcia nunc flexis cervicibus oscula captant.
It Phorcus pater, it Glaucus longamque per undas
canitiem trahit et nymphis luctantibus instat.
Inousque puer glauca cum matre repulsas

80 nunc subter lascivit aquas, nunc improbus exstat
pube tenus conchasque et rubra corallia vellit.
Tu quoque non dubio frontem laxare severam
tandem ausus risu, Proteu.

                                    Verum una peremptum
plorat adhuc natum Thetis et crudelia divum

85 numina, crudeles Parcas miseranda lacessit
ac precibus mixtas obliquans saeva querelas
exitiique reum citat et convicia fundit.
Tum, vix passa toro primos accumbere divum,
procurrit turbata comas et pectore nudo

90 (sic dolor ille monet) laevaque amplexa verendi
genua Iovis dextraque attentans supplice barbam,
talibus affata est: 'O qui stellantia nutu

and menaces the East, and the North wind with his fierce trident and with a look controls the South wind; only Zephyr leaps over the tremulous waves on his horse, and comforts acquiescent Amphitrite[25] in his soft bosom. A simple band of Nereids[26] play together; one challenges her sister and strives to defeat her in graceful swimming, another directs the course of a bridled dolphin, while yet another mounts a sea-lion; a fierce ram draws another in a chariot, while still another bestrides a foul-smelling seal. Others leap about mounted on monsters that the vast Ocean bathes in great numbers on the reefs: the hideous cetaceans, the whale and the sawfish and the sperm whale, which, if it can be believed, sprays the sea's waves to the stars; half-wild Tritons[27] take other Nereids on their friendly backs and hold them fast in the curve of their forked tail, and now they soothe the surface of the waters with their twisted conches, now, turning their heads, steal sweet kisses. Father Phorcus[28] arrives, and Glaucus,[29] who drags his long white beard across the waves and harasses the resisting nymphs. The son of Ino,[30] in the company of his mother who is the color of the sea now sports frolicsomely beneath the resisting waves, now daringly emerges up to his groin and collects shells and red coral. You also, Proteus,[31] finally dared to relax your severe brow in a frank smile.

But Thetis[32] alone still mourns the death of her son and pitifully accuses the cruel will of the gods and the cruel fates; in her rage she alternates complaint with supplication and charges by name the one guilty of his death and covers him with insults. Then, hardly waiting for the first gods to recline on their couches, she bursts forth, her hair dishevelled and her breast bared (so her sorrow ordains), and with her left hand embracing the knees of awe-inspiring Jupiter and touching his beard with her right hand in a gesture of supplication, she addressed him in these words: 'O thou who shakest the starry realms with a nod of thy head, dost

regna quatis, viden ut magna de gente dearum
sola ego perpetuo (quid enim mea vulnera celem?)
95   tabescam luctu vestrasque infesta profanem
has epulas? Quodnam ob meritum, pater optime? Certe
non ego vincla tibi—scis, o scis ipse!—parabam,
magne sator; non Corycio tua tela sub antro
servabat Thetis anguipedi iurata Typhoeo.
100   Nec nunc mortales thalamos humilemque maritum
conquerimur; fuerint Parcarum vellera iustis
invida connubiis, liceat timuisse Tonanti.
Quamquam o! . . . sed taceo. Cur autem, summe deorum,
cum meus Aeacides Latoia tela cruentat,
105   te minor? Anne etiam subolem damnavimus ipsae
aut faciem, Titani, tuam? Sed vertite, quaeso,
me quoque iam dudum in silicem nec marmora solum
tristibus aeternum lacrimis Sipyleia manent.
Hos certe ingrato cineri mutisque sepulchris
110   (quando aliud quid sit?) genetrix persolvat honores,
si neque perpetuae saltem illum munere laudis
dignaris, pater, et Lethen parva accolet umbra.'
    Talia verba refert genibusque affixa Tonantis
haeret, inexhaustum lacrimans sparsisque capillis.
115   Iamque deos omnes dictis et imagine maesta
flexerat; invidiam sensit vultusque retorsit
ad Venerem Phoebus. Tum divam, pauca moratus,
sublevat omnipotens verbisque ita mulcet amicis:
'Ne crede aeterno incisas adamante revelli
120   posse deum leges. Stant omne immota per aevum
quae triplices nevere colus, nec funera nati
flet Thetis una sui. Communes desine casus
adnumerare tibi ac totam hanc circumspice turbam;
scilicet invenies consortes undique luctus,

76

thou not see that I alone of the great assembly of the gods waste away with unending grief (for why should I conceal my wounds?) and like an enemy profane these festivities? What have I done to 95 merit this, most excellent father? It was not I, certainly — ah! you know it well, you yourself know it! — who prepared chains for you, great creator; it was not Thetis who hid your weapon in a Corycian cave in conspiracy with serpent-footed Typhoeus.[33] Nor do I complain now of mortal nuptials and a lowly husband; the 100 threads of the Fates may have been envious of a just marriage; the Thunderer may have been afraid.[34] And yet, oh . . . but I shall be silent. But why, O greatest among the gods, does my Achilles, descendant of Aeacus, though no rival to you, bloody the arrows of Latona's son[35]? Or did I ever find fault with your offspring or 105 your beauty, Latona? But turn me into a stone immediately, I beg of you, and the marble of Sipylus[36] will not remain alone forever in its sad tears. Let a mother pay these honors at least to the thankless ashes and the silent tomb (what else is there?), if you, 110 father, do not even consider him worthy of the prize of eternal praise, and he will dwell, an insignificant shade by the waters of Lethe.

Such were her words, and embracing the knees of Jupiter, she clung there weeping ceaselessly, her hair streaming out in all directions. By this time she had moved all the gods with her words and mournful demeanor; Phoebus sensed her hatred and turned his 115 face towards Venus. Then, after a brief pause, the almighty helps her arise and consoles her with these kindly words: "Do not think that the laws of the gods inscribed forever in adamantine steel can be erased; that which the three distaffs have spun remains un- 120 changed for all ages. Thetis is not the only one to weep over the death of her son; cease viewing common misfortunes as your own peculiar fate; since Nereids are gods, not mortal, look around you at this company; you will find companions of your grief on every side, me also among them, since the lance of the Opuntian war-

125 me quoque in his, siquidem transegit Opuntia cuspis
ductorem Lyciae et moribundum in pulvere mersit.
Nec tu digna tamen, fateor, ni fata repugnent,
quae tam saeva gemas, quae mortales hymenaeos,
Nerei, pertuleris; nec solus Apollinis arcus
130 pignora divarum Phrygiis tamen obruit arvis;
est etiam cui Memnoniam Pallantias urnam
imputet. Atque adeo tristes ut pectore curas
excutias animumque leves, reddetur Achilli
ingens tantorum pretium, mihi crede, laborum.
135 Nam neque Cerbereos rictus nec Erynnidas atris
anguibus implicitas inamoenaque Tartara passus,
Elysium tenet. Hic magna venerabilis umbra
mutatis pulchram auspiciis sibi Colchida iunget,
Solis et Oceani volventi progener aevo.
140 Utque Rhodos Solem, Venerem Paphos atque Cythera,
Iunonemque Samos, Cereremque Typhoias Aetne,
me mea Creta colit, sic nato candida Leuce,
Leuce quae Scythicis procul insula personat undis,
templa tuo ponet; nautis hic ille sub alto
145 fata canet luco venturae nuntia sortis.
Adde quod et pulchro tradetur pulchra marito
Tyndaris Aeacidae, stellis fulgentibus ardens,
meque dabit socerum. Thalamis, en, sternuit istis
pulcher Hymen gratasque vices sortita Voluptas
150 iam nunc dividuos iuveni despondet amores.
Utque tuos artus nunc dulci Gratia nodo,
nunc Paphie roseis nectit, Vulcane, lacertis,
sic illum formosa Helene, formosa Cytaeis
auferet alternum et lentus festa otia ducet.
155 Famaque, ne dubita, centeno gutture vestros
indefessa canet caeloque aequabit honores.
Audiet hos et quem torrenti flammeus astro

rior[37] transfixed the king of Lycia[38] and plunged him, dying, into 125
the dust. Yet you did not deserve to lament so bitterly, I admit, if
the fates were not contrary, nor to endure a mortal marriage, O
daughter of Nereus; nevertheless not only did Apollo's bow lay
low the children of the gods in the Phrygian fields: there is also 130
the one whom the sister of Pallas can blame for the urn of
Memnon.[39] And so that you may dispel these dismal cares from
your heart and relieve your mind, an immense reward will be ren-
dered to Achilles (believe me) for his great labors. For he has been
spared the gaping jaws of Cerberus[40] and the Erinyes,[41] entangled 135
in their grisly snakes, and unlovely Tartarus. He dwells in Ely-
sium;[42] here, venerated as a great shade, he will join himself to the
beautiful princess of Colchis[43] under different auspices and will
become the husband of the grand-daughter of the Sun and Ocean
for all eternity. As Rhodes honors the Sun, Paphos[44] and Cythera
Venus, Samos Juno, Etna Ceres, daughter of Typhoeus, my land 140
of Crete honors me; so white Leuke, Leuke the distant island that
resounds with the Scythian wave, will raise up a temple to your
son; there in the depths of a grove he will predict future fates to
sailors. In addition, the beautiful daughter of Tyndarus,[45] radiant 145
with brilliant stars, will be given to the beautiful descendant of
Aeacus,[46] making me his father-in-law; behold beautiful Hymen
gives his sneeze of approval to this wedding, and Pleasure, in an
agreeable turn of events, already promises a two-fold love to the
young man. And just as now one of the Graces enfolds your 150
limbs in a sweet embrace, O Vulcan, now the goddess of Paphos
holds you in her rosy arms, so beautiful Helen and the beautiful
Colchian will have him in turn and he will enjoy a festive leisure in
tranquillity. And Fame (doubt it not) with a hundred mouths will
sing the praises of both of you tirelessly and raise them to the 155
skies. They will be heard by those whom flaming Cancer with its

Carcinus aestiferis late dispescit harenis
et quos Herculeae summorunt orbe columnae
160 atque hominum primi Blemyae quosque altior axis
cogit Hyperboreos subter durare triones.
Nulla virum gens, nulla dies, nusquam ulla tacebit
posteritas, nulla teget invida nube vetustas.
Quippe deum sancta nascetur origine vates,
165 qui lucem aeternam factis immanibus addat,
qui regum fera bella tonet grandique tremendas
obruat ore tubas, cuius vocalia Siren
pectora et Aonidum miretur prima sororum.
Ille tuum, Theti, Peliden venientibus annis
170 dedet honoratum serisque nepotibus unum
Thessalus exemplum virtutis habebitur heros.
Quondam etiam nostro iuvenis de sanguine cretus,
dux bello invictus, Gangen domiturus et Indos
atque Semiramias fracturus cuspide turres,
175 felicem tanto praecone vocabit Achillem.
Et dubitabis adhuc obductae nubila frontis
atque importunas Euris mandare querelas?
Quin audes laxare animum vultusque priores
induis et laetis hilarem te coetibus infers?'
180 Dixerat. Illa oculis iam dudum absterserat imbrem
laeta omnem, aetherio grates agit inde Tonanti
instauratque comas cultusque habitusque decoros
accipit. Hic divam glaucarum tota sororum
circumfusa cohors studio excolit. Ipsa sibi obstat
185 sedulitas: pars multifidi discrimine dentis
caesariem comit, molli pars colligit auro
effusam, pars fingit acu crinemque lapillis
spargit Hydaspeis; hae baccas auribus addunt
restituuntque sinus, illa aurea cingula donat,

scorching star sequesters on far-off sultry sands, and by those cut
off from the world by the pillars of Hercules and by the Blemyes,[47]
the first humans, and by those whom the North Pole forces to live   160
under the Hyperborean oxen.[48] No people, no time, no future
generation will ever pass over his name in silence, nor will envious
antiquity obscure it with any cloud. For a poet, drawing his sacred
origin from the gods, will be born, who will add eternal luster to
his tremendous exploits, who will sing in thunderous tones of the   165
cruel wars of kings and with his magniloquent voice will drown
out the terrifying trumpets, whose sonorous tones will elicit the
wonder of the Siren and the most illustrious of the Aonian sisters.
He will deliver to future ages, Thetis, your beloved Pelides laden
with honors, and to later descendants the Thessalian hero will be   170
held as a unique example of courage. One day also a young man
sprung from our blood, a leader unconquered in war, destined to
subdue the Ganges and the people of India and to smash the tow-
ers of Semiramis[49] with his lance, will call Achilles fortunate for
having such a one to proclaim his praise.[50] And will you still hesi-   175
tate to disperse the clouds that darken your brow and banish your
relentless laments to the winds? Why not take courage to relax
your spirit and assume your former appearance and join yourself
cheerfully to this joyful throng?"

So he spoke. She had long since dried the tears from her eyes,   180
overjoyed, and rendering thanks to the heavenly Thunderer, she
rearranges her hair and receives fine apparel and adornments.
Hereupon the whole band of green-eyed sisters, crowding around
the goddess, eagerly attend to her adornment; their very assiduity
stands in the way of itself; some of them arrange her long, flowing
hair, parting it with the help of a many-toothed comb, others   185
gather her loose locks in a soft gold mesh, others shape her tresses
with a pin, and fleck it with precious stones from the Hydaspes;[51]
these nymphs adorn her ears with pearls and dispose the folds of
her garment; that nymph presents her with a golden belt; another

190   donat Erythraeis haec plena monilia conchis;
            laetantur Nereusque pater grandaevaque Doris.
            Continuo redit ille decor suffusaque pulchris
            fax radiat tranquilla genis; procul exulat omnis
            tristitia, insuetam tentant nova gaudia mentem.
195   Haud aliter verno cum pulsa rosaria nimbo
            frondentis rutilum virgae spoliantur honorem,
            defluit exspirans dominae cruor ictaque lapsis
            commoritur foliis halantum gratia florum,
            ast ubi mox clarum iubar aureus exseruit sol,
200   augescunt recidiva novis tum germina truncis
            laetaque nativas ostentat purpura gemmas.

               Iamque implere fidem divini coeperat oris
            Aeacides thalamo et templis et honoribus auctus,
            cum partum ingentem memor extulit Ilithyia.
205   Hermaeo praetenta sinu fuit inclyta quondam
            urbs toti praelata Asiae. Boebeius illam
            coniugis extinctae monimentum nobile Theseus
            esse dedit Smyrnes arcemque in monte locavit
            prospectantem undas semel et sua tecta tuentem,
210   quo flet maesta silex Niobe Niobesque sepulchrum.
            Hic placido fluit amne Meles auditque sub altis
            ipse tacens antris meditantes carmina cycnos.

               Haec vatem eximium tellus (ita sancta vetustas
            credidit), haec illum dias in luminis oras
215   prima tulit. Pater, Aonii deus incola luci,
            ductare assuetus thiasos sacrisque sororum
            responsare choris et par contendere Phoebo,
            furtivo pulchram implerat Critheida fetu.
            Inde capax nato ingenium largusque verendae
220   scilicet haustus aquae. Primo (si credimus) ille
            vagitu horrisoni sternebat murmura ponti,
            pacabat ventos, mollibat corda ferarum,

gives her necklaces filled with shells from Eritrea. Her father   190
Nereus and aged Doris rejoice. Immediately her former beauty re-
turns and a serene glow diffused on her beautiful cheeks radiates
light: all sorrow is banished far away and fresh joys steal upon a
mind unused to them. In the same way when the rose-gardens,   195
lashed by the spring rains, are stripped of the ruddy effulgence of
the leafy branches, the blood of the goddess, issuing forth, flows
away and the loveliness of the aromatic flowers, affected by the
falling leaves, dies with them; but as soon as the golden rays of the
sun reveal the first light of day, then the renascent buds grow
larger on the new branches and joyously the purple shows forth its   200
new-born buds.

And already Achilles had begun to fulfill the promise uttered
by the divine mouth, blessed by a marriage, temples and honors,
when Ilithyia,[52] true to her promise, produced a prodigious birth.
Stretched out along the Hermean Gulf there was once a cele-
brated city[53] exalted above all of Asia; the Thessalian Theseus[54]   205
made it the noble memorial of his deceased wife Smyrne, and built
a citadel on the top of a mountain looking out on the sea and at
the same time protecting his home, where sad Niobe, turned into
a stone, weeps, and the tomb of Niobe stands. Here the river   210
Meles[55] flows peacefully and in silence listens in its deep caves to
the swans practicing their songs.

This land (so venerable antiquity believed) first brought forth
the greatest of poets into the sunlit shores of light. His father, a
god who inhabited the Aonian grove, who used to lead the sacred   215
processions of Bacchus and echo the sacred choruses of the Muses
and rival Phoebus as an equal, had secretly made the beautiful
Criteis[56] pregnant. Thence came capacious genius to her son and a
generous draught of the sacred stream, to be sure; with his first
wails (if it is to be believed) he stilled the dreadful rumbling of the   220
sea, he calmed the winds, he softened the hearts of wild beasts;

83

ipsa etiam lacrimas Sipyleia fundere cautes
destitit audito. Reptabat maximus infans
225   fluminis in ripa; reptantem mollibus ulnis
nais harenivagum rapiebat saepe sub amnem
ostensura patri et rursum exponebat in ulva
flore breves cinctum aut apio rorante capillos.
Vosque, Eteocleae (ni mendax fama) sorores,
230   misistis lectas Horarum a fonte corollas
flavaque virgineam puero immulsisse papillam
dicitur, Actaeo ceu quondam Pallas Erechtheo.

     Ipse ut iam certo vestigia ponere nisu
utque datum varia voces effingere lingua,
235   gaudebat calamos Hyblaeis iungere ceris,
dilectos Bromio calamos, gaudebat et uncam
ore inflare pio ac digitis percurrere loton.
Grande tamen calami reboant, grande unca remugit
tibia. Saepe illum vicina faunus in umbra
240   demirans auris tacitus tendebat acutas
et subito puerum satyri cinxere theatro;
cum satyrisque ferae, sed quae nil triste minentur,
cumque feris silvae, sed quae alta cacumina motent
multifidaeque sacris adnutent legibus aurae.
245   Ipsi quin etiam riguo Pactolus et Hermus
certatim affluxere auro; iussosque tacere
ripa ab utraque suos Maeander misit olores,
Maeander sibimet refluis saepe obvius undis,
Maeander sub humum pudibundo flumine labens,
250   quod puerum ignarus Carpon, dum ludit in unda,
delicias nati, mox natum merserat alveo,
infelix genitor, sed venti id crimen amantis.
Verum ubi primaevae dubio se flore iuventae
induit ac plenis adolevit fortior annis,
255   carmen amat, carmen, proh maxima numina vatum!

the very Siplyean rock ceased to shed tears, merely on hearing of
him. The wondrous child crawled along the riverbank; as he   225
crawled the naiad often took him in her soft arms beneath the
stream that wandered over the sands to show him to her father
and laid him again in the sedge, garlanding his short locks with
flowers or parsley wet with dew. And you, Eteoclean sisters,[57] if
fame does not lie, sent garlands picked from the springs of the
Hours; and it is said that blond Pallas Athena nourished him at   230
her virginal breast, as she once did Athenian Erechtheus.[58]

And as soon as he was able to walk with firm footing and fash-
ion words with different sounds, he enjoyed joining reeds together
with Hyblaean wax,[59] the pipes beloved of Bromius, and enjoyed   235
also blowing with his consecrated lips on the curved lotus flute,
moving his fingers along it. Yet the reeds emit a loud sound and
the curved flute reverberates loudly. Often in the nearby shade a
faun, in wonder, pricked up his pointed ears without making a
sound and suddenly the satyrs surrounded the boy, as in a theater;   240
with the satyrs were wild beasts, but those that pose no grim
threat; and with the wild beasts the woods, those that sway their
high treetops and bow to the sacred laws of the many-stringed
airs. Even the Pactolus[60] and the Hermus,[61] their waters rich with   245
gold, flowed towards him, rivalling each other; the Meander[62]
sends its swans from its two banks, ordering them to be still, the
Meander that often returns upon itself in its refluent waters, the
Meander that sinks down under the earth as if ashamed because
unknowingly it had drowned the boy Carpos[63] in its current while
he was playing in the waves, the darling of his son, and then the   250
unhappy father drowned his own son; but this was the crime of
the wind in love. Then when Homer clothed himself in the uncer-
tain flower of adolescence and grew stronger in his more mature
years, he loved song (O great supernatural powers of the poet!),[64]   255

85

carmen Apollineo tantum modulabile plectro,
carmen Caucaseas silices cautemque Sicanam
quod trahat et rigidi leges infringat Averni
exarmetque Iovis minitantem fulmine dextram.

260   Iamque insana sacrum vis insertusque medullis
exstimulat vatem Aeacides, iam parturit altum
mens opus et magnis animosa accingitur ausis.
Ille tamen quaenam ora sui, qui vultus Achilli
quive oculi, quantus maternis fulguret armis,

265   scire avet (ah nimius voti!), violentaque fundens
murmura, terribilem tumulo ciet improbus umbram.
Continuo Sigeus apex concussus in aequor
procumbit raucumque gemit Rhaeteia contra
litora et effusis tremit ardua fontibus Ide

270   semiustumque cavo Xanthus crinem abdidit antro.
Ecce tuens torvum nec vati impune videndus,
Phthius honoratis heros adstabat in armis,
qualis Peliaca Teucros obtriverat hasta,
Priamiden versa a Danais dum quaereret ira

275   ultor et heu! fluviis miseros campisque fugaret.
Flammeus ignescit thorax auroque minatur
terrifico radiatus apex, in nubila surgit
fraxinus et longa rursum Hectora vulnerat umbra.
Ipse ardens clypeo ostentat terramque fretumque

280   atque indefessum Solem Solisque sororem
iam plenam et tacito volventia sidera mundo.
Ergo his defixus vates, dum singula visu
explorat miser incauto, dum lumina figit,
lumina nox pepulit; tum vero exterritus haesit

285   voxque repressa metu et gelidos tremor impulit artus.
At iuvenem sacer Aonium miseratus Achilles
(quandoquidem, Saturne, tuas inflectere leges
haud licitum cuiquam) clypeo excipit oraque iungens

86

song that can be played only on Apollo's lyre, song that can attract
to itself the Caucasian boulders and the Sicilian cliffs and can in-
fringe the laws of unbending Avernus and disarm the right hand
of Jupiter that wields the lightning-bolt.

And already the frenzied violence of Achilles had penetrated   260
into the inmost fiber of the sacred poet, spurring him on; already
his mind conceives the noble work and boldly girds itself for
mighty exploits. Yet he longs to know (ah! inordinate desire!) the
features, the expression, the eyes of Achilles, and how he glitters
in his mother's armor; and giving vent to primitive mumblings,
presumptuously he summons the fearsome shade from the tomb.   265
Immediately the Sigean promontory, shaken, plunges into the sea
and sends forth a loud mournful sound against the Trojan shore,
and towering Mount Ida trembles, pouring out her springs of wa-
ter, and the river Xanthus hid his scorched locks in his hollow
cave. Behold, with fierce glance, a vision the poet would not look   270
upon with impunity, the Thessalian hero stood there in his glori-
ous armor, just as he had devastated the Trojans with his spear
fashioned from wood from Mt. Pelion, while, seeking vengeance,
he turned his anger from the Greeks and sought the son of Priam,
and ah! chased the poor victims into the rivers and plains. His   275
flaming cuirass glistens, the crest of his helmet, radiant with terri-
fying gold, menaces; his ashen spear rises towards the clouds and
casting a long shadow it wounds Hector again. Raging, Achilles
shows on his shield the land and the sea, and the tireless Sun and
the Sun's sister, already full, and the stars revolving in the silent   280
firmament. So while the poet, his eyes fixed upon this vision,
scans each detail, unhappy man, as he fixes his eyes upon it with
incautious gaze, night took away his sight;[65] then, terrified, he be-
came motionless and his voice was choked with fear, and trem-
bling took hold of his icy limbs. But divine Achilles, taking pity on   285
the Aonian youth,[66] (since, Saturn, it is not permitted to anyone
to alter your laws) scoops him up with his shield and kissing him,

inspuit augurium. Baculum dat deinde potentem
Tiresiae magni, qui quondam Pallada nudam
vidit et hoc raptam pensavit munere lucem,
suetus inoffensos baculo duce tendere gressus.
Nec deest ipse sibi, quin sacro instincta furore
ora movet tantique parat solatia damni.
Aeaciden tamen, Aeaciden caelo aequat et astris,
Aeaciden famae levat arduus alite curru,
unum Dardanidis, unum componit Achivis
Aeaciden, unum ante omnes miratur amatque.
    Ac primum irarum causas trepidique tumultus
expedit utque luem neglecta induxerit aegris
religio populis; ut regem irritet amantem
Thestorides; ut acerba fremens vix temperet ipso
ense puer Thetidis, vix magni sanguine Atridae
abstineat divae admonitu; quae iurgia contra
dux ferat incensus dictis; quo vulnera Nestor
melle riget; quantum amisso dux frendeat alter
munere; quos nato genetrix exoret honores;
quid doleat Iuno; caelo quid portet ab alto
insidiosa quies; quae rex obliquet inertis
tentamenta fugae; faciat Laertius heros
quantum operae pretium, cum dulcibus aspera miscet,
cum vaga clamosae reprimit convicia linguae,
cum suadet durent castris praesagaque monstrat
fata deum; memorat platanum infantesque volucres
cum matre absumptas versumque in saxa draconem;
quo Pylius fremat ore senex, ut pacta fidemque
deploret dextrasque datas, ut fulmina narret
missa polo ac pretium ostentet victoribus urbem;
quae facies Danaum, cum sese in munia Martis
accingunt, quantum dux ore et pectore et armis

88

spat into him the gift of prophecy; then he gives him the powerful
staff of the great Tiresias, who once saw Pallas naked, and with   290
this gift he compensated for the loss of his sight, by becoming
used to directing his unobstructed steps with the staff as his guide.
Nor does the poet fail to do his part, but moves his lips, inspired
by a sacred frenzy, and provides solace for so great a loss. In com-
pensation, he exalts Achilles to the sky and to the stars, and with   295
lofty spirit he elevates Achilles on the winged chariot of fame;
Achilles alone he compares to the Trojans, Achilles alone to the
Greeks, him alone above all others he admires and loves.

   First he narrates the causes of wrath and the alarming tumult,
and how the neglect of religion brought pestilence to the afflicted
people, how the son of Thestor[67] provokes the smitten king; how,   300
snarling with anger, the son of Thetis barely refrains from drawing
his sword, barely keeps from shedding the blood of the mighty son
of Atreus, at the behest of the goddess; what abuse the leader of
the host hurls at him, incensed by his words; with what honeyed
words Nestor soothes their wounds; how the other leader gnashes   305
his teeth in anger at the loss of his prize; what honors the mother
implores for her son; the cause of Juno's grief; the consequences of
a deceitful dream sent from the heights of heaven; how the king
simulates a cowardly attempt to escape; the salutary intervention
of the son of Laertes when he mixes sweet words with harsh ones,   310
represses the abusive language of an uncontrolled tongue,[68] per-
suades them to remain in the camp, and interprets the portentous
signs sent by the fates; he recalls the plane tree and the fledglings
devoured together with their mother and the dragon turned to
stone,[69] the reproaches made by the old man from Pylos, how he   315
laments the pacts and the trust and pledges given, his account of
the thunder-bolts sent from heaven and the city made a prize for
the victors; he narrates the expressions on the faces of the Greeks
when they gird themselves for the work of Mars, and how their
leader stands out in his bearing, courage and armor. Then he in-   320

emineat. Tum Pieridas, sua numina, rursum
consulit Hectoreasque Agamemnoniasque phalangas
enumerans; ipsos icto mox foedere amantes
committit victumque rapit Phryga nubibus atris,
325   victorem Atriden necopino vulnerat arcu.
Tum pugnam instaurans toto dat funera campo,
haud dubitans alta Tydiden strage cruentum
Dardanio Lycioque duci totidemque repente
obiectare deis, Glauci post munere pulchro
330   insignem auratis ostentaturus in armis.
Quid nunc Sidonio tentatam Pallada peplo,
quid memorem lacrimas Thebaeae coniugis et te,
parve puer, cristas et cassidis aera timentem?
Teque, heros, longe gradientem et torva tuentem
335   quassantemque procul metuendam cuspidis umbram
atque ausum corde impavido solum Hectora contra
stare diu? Quid te populorum fata duorum
lancibus aequantem imparibus, rex magne deorum,
aut miseros tonitru Danaos et lampade saeva
340   terrentem? Quid te vallo castrisque minantem,
Priamide armipotens? His rursum adiungitur ardens
heu! precibus nihil et donis inflexus Achilles
exceptusque Dolon et somno proditus heros
Othrysius tacitaque aversi nocte iugales,
345   qui superent candore nives, qui cursibus aequent
flamina. Mox ipsi ferro telisque repulsi
ductores Danaum clypeoque interritus Aiax,
tutari sociam classem Iliacumque paratus
ductorem et ferrum et flammam exceptare Iovemque,
350   quem caesto tamen Idalio coniunxque sororque
implicat et Somni facies mentita volucrem,
dum pater aequoreus fessis aspirat Achivis.
Nec mora: Peliacis cum longe horrendus in armis

vokes again the Muses, his divinities, and enumerates the pha-
lanxes of Hector and Agamemnon; next he sets the two lovers[70]
against each other in accordance with the treaty joined, and carries
off the vanquished Phrygian in a black cloud. Then he tells how
the son of Atreus was wounded by an unexpected arrow; then re-   325
newing the battle he sows destruction over the plain, not hesitat-
ing to oppose Diomedes,[71] bloodied from the rampant slaughter,
to the Dardanian and the Lycian leader[72] and suddenly to as many
gods, and to show him resplendent in the gilded armor he received
as a gift from Glaucus.[73] Why should I make mention of the woo-   330
ing of Pallas Athena with the Sidonian peplum,[74] the tears of the
Theban spouse,[75] and you, tiny child,[76] shrinking back from the
plumes of the bronze helmet? And you, hero,[77] taking long strides
and casting grim looks about you and brandishing the spear,
whose shadow inspires fear even from afar, and daring to stand up   335
to Hector for a long time, alone, with fearless heart? And why
should I mention you, great king of the gods, who weigh the desti-
nies of two peoples in unequal scales, or terrify the luckless Greeks
with thunder and cruel lightning? And you, son of Priam, valiant
in war, threatening the fortifications and the camp of the Greeks?
To them the raging Achilles joins himself again, alas! unmoved   340
by prayers or gifts; and Dolon,[78] captured by ambush, and the
Thracian hero[79] betrayed by sleep, and the twin steeds, whiter
than snow, stolen in the silence of the night, that are equal to the
winds in their speed; then the leaders of the Greek host, repulsed   345
by sword and arrows; and Ajax, whose shield renders him fearless,
prepared to defend the allied fleet and to withstand the Trojan
leader, fire and sword and Jupiter, whom his sister-wife entangles
with the girdle of Venus with the help also of sleep, who takes on   350
the appearance of a bird while the father of the seas lends his aid
to the exhausted Greeks. Without delay Patroclus springs up, for-
midable even from afar, clad in the armor of Achilles and he averts

emicat et nubem belli defensat Achivis
355 Actorides ac sanguineo Sarpedona campo
obruit, heu magni prolem Iovis! Inde secundis
elatus rerum Balium Xanthumque iugales,
quos Zephyro peperit geminos Harpyia Podarge,
et te captivo funalem, Pedase, collo
360 igneus exstimulat Scaeaeque in limine portae
concidit, ah, tanti nimium securus amici.
Nam quid Panthoiden foedantem sanguine crinis
illos (proh dolor!) argentoque auroque micantes,
quid primos querar heroum pro corpore functo
365 certatim obnisos inter se haud cedere certos
atque animam exanimum funus super exhalantes?
Ecce suum tandem cantor Smyrnaeus Achillem
suscitat, ardentem clypeo atque Hyperionis orbem
orbe lacessentem pulchro et caelestibus armis
370 ingentique manu Centaurica tela tenentem
atque immortalis adigentem in proelia bigas.
Hic vero obversis Victoria remigat alis,
dum rapit inferias, dum curribus ille virisque
atque armis et equis minitantem infestior implet
375 Xanthon et arsuras angustat caedibus undas.
Vix ego nunc si mille sonent mea pectora linguis
voxque adamante rigens atque indefessus anhelet
spiritus infusum totos paeana per artus,
bella deum narrem, terram ipsam immane gementem
380 clangentemque polum Martemque in iugera septem
porrectum multoque comas in pulvere mersum;
aegidaque horrificam protectamque aegide pectus
Pallada, nil magni metuentem fulmina patris;
imbellemque deum Venerem et te, Phoebe, tridenti
385 submittentem arcus et te, Latonia virgo,
iam pavidam ac vacua linquentem castra pharetra.

the cloud of war from the Argives[80] and massacres Sarpedon on
the bloody field of battle, alas! offspring of mighty Jupiter; then   355
elated by his successes, with ardor he spurs on the team of Balios
and Xanthus, the twin horses that the harpy Podarge bore to
Zephyr, and you, Pedasus, the trace-horse fastened by the neck,
and at the threshold of the Scaean gate falls to the ground, ah! un-   360
heeding of the advice of his great friend. Why should I lament the
fate of the son of Panthous,[81] befouling with gore his beautiful
locks (what sorrow!) that gleamed with gold and silver, why bewail
the foremost of the heroes who strove with one another for a life-
less corpse, resolved not to yield, and breathed out their lives upon   365
the lifeless cadaver? Behold at last the Smyrnean bard rouses his
hero Achilles, gleaming in the brilliance of his disk-shaped shield
that challenges the disk of Hyperion[82] for beauty and in his divine
armor, wielding the centaur's spear in his huge hand, and driving   370
his immortal two-horsed chariot into the fray. And now Victory
flies with its wings pointed in the opposite direction, as Achilles
carries off his sacrificial victims and with savage fury fills the
Xanthus river, a constant threat, with chariots, warriors, armor
and horses, and chokes its waters with corpses, waters that will   375
soon be set ablaze. Even if my breast now resounded with a thou-
sand tongues and had a voice of steel, and my unflagging spirit
could gasp forth the paean that is infused through all my limbs, I
could scarcely narrate the war between gods, the earth itself heav-
ing a tremendous groan, the heavens ringing, and Mars stretched
out over seven acres, his hair immersed in the dust; and the terri-   380
ble aegis and Pallas Athena, her breast protected by the aegis, with
no fear of the lightning bolts of her great father; and Venus,
unwarlike goddess, and you, Phoebus,[83] submitting your bow to
the trident, and you, Latonian virgin,[84] suddenly terror-stricken   385
and abandoning the field of battle with empty quiver. Not if my

Nec si Castalios ipsis a fontibus amnes
hauriat os avidum nec si Pirenida lympham
Pimpleosque bibat latices, aequare canendo
390 Hectora sanguineum violentumque ausit Achillem;
Hectora pro patria carisque penatibus unum
stantem animis contra, qualis draco pastus amaros
per brumam sucos venientem expectat iniquus
pastorem et tumido furiatus felle cruentum
395 spectat hians immane cavoque advolvitur ingens;
Aeaciden autem caedem et crudele ferentem
exitium, qualis vasti canis Orionis
per noctem exercet radios saevumque minatur.
Iamque illum ante oculos amborum ante ora parentum
400 raptatum Haemonio circum sua moenia curru,
iam funus, Patrocle, tuum Priamumque superbos
porrectum ante pedes atque auro supplice victum
dixerat invictum iuvenem lamentaque saeva
Iliadum maestosque rogos cineremque sepultum,
405 cum subito in somnis Ithaci experientis imago
visa viro sic ampla humeros, sic pectora fundens,
sed letale gerens vulnus. Namque inscia nati
dextera quae situm per caerula vasta parentem
protinus aequoreae viroso trigonos ictu
410 perculerat, sive ira deum seu fata iubebant.
    Atque ait: 'O magnae qui princeps debita laudi
praemia persolvis, qui lenta oblivia saeclis
excutis et seros famam producis in annos,
anne tot exhaustos nobis terraque marique
415 Lethaeo mersos fluvio patiere labores
nec sua reddetur virtuti gloria merces?
Namque licet virtus semet contenta quiescat,
sola tamen iustos virtus adsciscit honores
solaque se merito laudum fulgore coronat.

94

eager mouth were to quaff the springs of Castalia itself, not if it were to drink the waters of Pirene[85] or the streams of Pimpla,[86] would it dare to equal in its singing blood-stained Hector and the raging Achilles: Hector standing alone, courageously, in defense of his country and his dear household gods, like a dragon, fed on bitter juices through the winter, who treacherously awaits the shepherd, and driven mad by the venom that swells its veins, casting bloodthirsty looks at him, its monstrous jaws gaping wide, it glides toward him from its hole in huge coils; while Achilles, bearing slaughter and cruel death, like the dog of giant Orion,[87] pierces the darkness of the night with his menacing glances. And now he had narrated how the Trojan hero was dragged, before the eyes and gaze of both his parents, around the walls of his own city by the Thessalian's chariot; now your funeral rites, Patroclus, and Priam, prostrate at the feet of the proud Achilles, and the unconquered young man conquered by gold and supplication, and the bitter lamentations of the Trojans, and the sad funeral pyres and the buried ashes, when suddenly in his sleep the image of all-suffering Ulysses appeared to the poet, with those same wide shoulders and broad chest, but bearing a mortal wound: for his son[88] unknowingly had pierced his own father, whom he had sought over the vast expanse of the sea, with the foul-smelling sting of the marine sting-ray, whether this was because of the wrath of the gods or willed by fate.

And he said: "O you who first pay fitting tribute to great renown, who shake off the enduring oblivion of the ages and prolong fame into later years, will you allow the toils I endured on sea and land to be drowned in the river of Lethe? And will due glory, virtue's reward, not be paid me? For although virtue rests content with itself, nevertheless virtue alone makes claim to just honors, and she alone crowns herself with well-deserved brilliance of praise; nay more, leading the way, she desires to bear the torch in

390

395

400

405

410

415

420 Quin etiam ignaris praeferre nepotibus optat
prima facem ac monstrare viam quae tendat in altum
culmen et e celso scandenti porgere dextram.
Quem neque posteritas neque tangit fama superstes,
nempe aliis exempla, sibi vitam invidet amens.
425 Ergo sub Iliacis tractantem proelia muris
Graius Achilleis populus donaverit armis;
tu vero emenso quae gessi plurima ponto
quaeque tuli nullo, vates, dignabere cantu,
quem solum vocat iste labor, cui pectore pleno
430 defluit illa meae felix opulentia linguae?
Incipe, namque adero et praesens tua coepta iuvabo.'
     Haec ait, et pariter somnusque Ithacusque recessit.
Ille, novo rursus Musarum percitus oestro,
concinit abiegnae Danaos compagibus alvi
435 occultos et equi molem fraudemque Sinonis
indiciique metu praeclusum pollice fauces
Anticlon Ortygiden, populataque Pergama flammis
disiectasque rates patriumque a Pallade missum
fulmen; Oilidenque ignes et sulfura fixo
440 pectore proflantem teque, importune Caphareu,
nec faciles Ciconas fortunatosque ciborum
Lotophagos vinoque gravem Cyclopa per antrum
exporrectum ingens humanaque frusta vomentem
mixta mero inque bovis constrictos tergore ventos;
445 et Lamium Antiphaten et virgam et pocula Circes
Cimmerionque domos Everidenque locutum
vera senem fusoque allectos sanguine Manes
et maris illecebras vocemque impune canorae
virginis auditam Scyllamque avidamque Charybdin;
450 Lampetienque patri violata armenta querentem
immersosque undis socios ipsumque natantem

front of her ignorant descendants and to show the way that leads   420
up to the lofty summit and to stretch out her right hand from
above to the one scaling the heights. He who has no care for fu-
ture generations or lasting fame foolishly refuses to give example
to others and denies life for himself. Therefore while the Greek
people awarded the arms of Achilles[89] to me for my doing battle   425
under the walls of Troy, will you, poet, not consider the many ex-
ploits I accomplished in my wanderings over the sea and my many
sufferings worthy of song, since this is your task alone, to whom
the fertile opulence of my oratory flowed down with full inspira-   430
tion? Begin, for I shall be present and by my presence will aid
your enterprise."

Thus he spoke; and together the dream and the Ithacan de-
parted. The poet, stirred again by the new frenzy sent by the
Muses, sang of the Greeks hidden in the framework of the fir-
wood belly, and of the huge hulk of the horse, and of the deceit of
Sinon, and of Anticlon of Ortygia,[90] whose mouth they closed   435
with their fists for fear of being discovered; he sang of Pergamum
ravaged by flames and the scattered ships and the father's light-
ning bolt sent by Pallas Athena; and of Ajax, son of Oileus,[91] his
breast transfixed, exhaling fire and sulphur, and you, insidious
Caphareus,[92] the inhospitable Ciconians[93] and the Lotus-eaters[94]   440
blessed with food, and the Cyclops heavy with wine, stretched out
in his huge cave, vomiting gobs of human flesh mixed with wine;
and the winds confined in the ox-hide bag,[95] and Antiphates,[96]
son of Lamos, and the wand and goblets of Circe,[97] and the land   445
of the Cimmerians,[98] and the old man, son of Everus,[99] and his
true prophecies; and the Manes[100] placated by the spilling of
blood, and the seductions of the sea and the voice of the melodi-
ous virgin heard without dire consequences, and Scylla and vora-
cious Charybdis,[101] and Lampetie[102] lamenting to her father for
the slaughter of her herds; and the companions drowned in the   450
waves, and the hero himself swimming to the shore of Ogygia and

litus ad Ogygies et Atlantidos antra Calypsus;
Neptunumque iterum ventosque undasque cientem,
Leucotheamque piam Corcyraeosque recessus
455   hospitio faciles subitumque in gurgite montem;
assertumque larem tandem ultricesque sagittas.
    Ergo tegunt geminae victricia tempora laurus
vatis Apollinei; geminis ergo arduus alis
fugit humo celsumque altis caput intulit astris,
460   par superis ipsique Iovi, quo nulla rebellis
spicula Livor agat, quo nulla aspiret iniquae
tempestas foeda Invidiae. Sic eminet extra
liber et innocuus, toto sic ille sereno
perfruitur gaudens, magni ceu purus Olympi
465   supra imbres vertex et rauca tonitrua surgit
despectatque procul ventorum proelia tutus.
Quo nunc divitias animosi carminis ore
exsequar? Haud illi plena se conferat urna
Hermus et aurata radians Pactolus harena
470   et Tagus et Durius, latebris quodque eruit audax
Dalmata quodque procul Bessus rimatur et Astur,
fusile Callaica quodque in fornace liquescit,
decolor in toto quodque invenit Indus Hydaspe,
quemque Rhodos fulvis hausit de nubibus imbrem,
475   quodque manu dea caeca tenet praedivite cornu.
Utque parens rerum fontes et flumina magnae
suggerit Oceanus terrae, sic omnis ab istis
docta per ora virum decurrit gratia chartis;
hinc fusa innumeris felix opulentia saeclis
480   ditavit mentes tacitoque infloruit aevo.
    Omnia ab his et in his sunt omnia, sive beati
te decor eloquii seu rerum pondera tangunt.
Nam quae tam varium Memphitis stamen harundo
separat aut quae sic Babylonos texta potentis

the caves of Calypso, daughter of Atlas; and Neptune unleashing
once more the winds and the waves, and the pious Leucothea,[103]
and the secluded recesses of Corcyra,[104] accommodating with their
hospitality, and the mountain suddenly rising from the sea;[105] and   455
the home finally laid claim to and the avenging arrows.

Therefore twin laurels cover the victorious locks of the poet of
Apollo; therefore raised up on twin wings he flees the earth and
thrusts his exalted head among the lofty stars, equal to the gods
and to Jupiter himself, where rebellious Jealousy does not let fly   460
her darts, where the horrid tempest of unjust Envy does not blow;
so he stands out above the world free and unharmed; exulting, he
enjoys the cloudless sky; like the limpid summit of great Olympus
he rises above the rains and the rattling thunder and in perfect se-   465
curity looks down from afar upon the contending winds. With
what tones now shall I rehearse the riches of his noble song? Let
not the Hermus with its full urn compare itself with him, nor
Pactolus gleaming with its golden sands, nor the Tagus nor the
Douro, nor what the daring Dalmatian extracts from hidden cav-
erns, nor what the remote Bessian[106] scours out and the Asturian,   470
nor the molten metal of the Galician ovens, nor what the dark-
skinned Indian finds in the whole region of the Hydaspes, nor the
rain which Rhodes absorbed from the golden clouds, nor what the
blind goddess of the horn of plenty holds in her hand. And as   475
Ocean, the parent of the elements, supplies the springs and rivers
of the great earth, so from these pages every grace flowed down
through the learned mouths of men; from them a fecund opu-
lence, diffused through countless ages, has enriched minds and
flowered in the silent course of history.   480

All things derive from them and in them are all things, whether
you are touched by the beauty of his rich eloquence or the gravity
of the subject. For what a vari-colored warp the weaver's reed sep-
arates at Memphis, what fabrics are embroidered by the painstak-

485 sollicita pinguntur acu, quae tanta colorum
gloria, cum pinnis Zephyri rorantibus adsunt!
Quantus honor vocum, quam multis dives abundat
floribus et claris augescit lingua figuris!
sive libet tenui versum deducere filo,
490 seu medium confine tenet, seu robore toto
fortior assurgit; seu vena paupere fertur
aridius, celeri seu se brevis incitat alveo,
gurgite seu pleno densisque opulentior undat
vorticibus, sive humentes laeto ubere ripas
495 daedala germinibus variat, maiore nec umquam
Sermo potens meminit se maiestate loquentem.
Quod si facta virum victuris condere chartis,
flectere si mavis orando et fingere mentes,
hunc optato ducem. Non causas doctius alter
500 personamque locumque modosque et tempus et arma
remque ipsam expediat, dum nunc iactantior exit,
nunc contorta ruit, nunc se facundia profert
simplicior, varia nunc floret imagine rerum.
Dulcius eloquium nulli nec apertior umquam
505 vis fandi fuit aut quae mentibus acrior instet.
Indole quemque sua pingit, sua cuique decenter
attribuit verba et mores unumque tenorem
semper amat meminitque sui; scit et unde moveri
et quo sit prodire tenus fusumque gubernat
510 arte opus et mediis prima ac postrema revincit.
Nunc teneras vocat ad lacrimas, nunc igneus iram
suscitat; interdum retrahit, probat, arguit, urget;
nunc nova suspendunt avidas miracula mentes
feta bonis, ipsum utiliter celantia verum.
515 Quidquid honorato sapiens canit ore vetustas
doctaque multiiugae post hunc divortia sectae,

ing needle of mighty Babylon, what a great riot of colors along   485
with the zephyrs, their wings dripping with dew, are present in
him! What beauty of words, what rich abundance of colors and
what elegant figures adorn his style! Whether he wishes to spin
his verse with a slender thread or holds to a middle style or rises
more forcefully with full strength; whether he is borne along more   490
unadorned with thinner vein, or more compressed, rushes forward
in swift course, or ripples more sumptuously at full flood and in
swirling eddies, or whether with Daedalian artistry and rich abun-
dance he variegates the moist banks with flowering buds, powerful   495
Eloquence never remembers speaking with greater majesty. But if
you prefer to record the mighty feats of heroes in immortal pages
or to direct and mould men's minds by your oratory, choose him
as your guide. No other can expound more learnedly the causes,
the personalities, the place and the circumstances, the time, the
arms and the action itself, while at one time his eloquence bursts   500
forth more exultantly, now it rushes along with twists and turns,
now it moves forward more simply, now richly ornamented, it
bursts into flower with a multiplicity of images. No one possessed
a sweeter eloquence; to none was ever given a more lucid power of
expression; none could touch the spirit more poignantly; he de-   505
picts each one according to his true character, he attributes words
and conduct proper to each, he loves to maintain an even tenor,
true to himself, and he knows both from whence to begin the nar-
rative and how far to proceed, and he controls the wide scope of
his work artistically and binds the middle together with the begin-
ning and the end. Now he incites to tender tears, now with pas-   510
sion he rouses to anger; at different times he holds back, approves,
rebukes, urges forward; now unheard of marvels, abounding with
good things hold avid minds in suspense, usefully concealing the
inner truth.

Whatever wise antiquity sang with honored voice, whatever   515
distinctions among the multiform philosophical sects were taught

hinc haustum, sive infantis cunabula saecli,
seu conspirantes pugnaci foedere causas
discordemque fidem et genitalia semina rerum,
520 seu potius mundi fines divumque rotatas
contemplere domos atque obluctantia caelo
sidera; quae magnum vis tanta Hyperionis orbem
torqueat, exhaustam reparet quo fonte sororem,
ausam fraternis mediam se opponere flammis
525 et subitis violare diem lucemque tenebris,
conscia fatorum num mens animaverit astra;
unde tremat tellus, trifidane impulsa laboret
cuspide Neptuni, caecis an terga cavernis
subdat atrox Boreas nostrum erupturus in orbem.
530 Ventorum nunc ille vices, nunc fulminis ortus
monstrat et elisis crepitantes nubibus auras;
curque ruunt imbres, subitus cur lumina fulgor
sic ferit ut medium credas discindere caelum.
Esse deum mentem immensam rerumque potentem
535 cunctaque complexum, stabili qui lege gubernet
naturam mundique vices, qui fata solutis
subiuget arbitriis, qui temperet omnia solus;
esse animos leti exsortes, sed corpore claudi
ceu tumulo, quos in varias tamen ire figuras
540 hoc dictante docet tacitae dux ille cohortis,
ante ortus memor usque sui sibique ipse superstes.
Quin et praecelsa rationem sistit in arce
ceu dominam, tristes in pectore concitat iras,
viscera degeneri damnata cupidine passus.
545 Nec tacet unde aeger cruciat dolor, unde rebellem
it furor in rabiem, cur pallent ora timentum,
genua tremunt, stant corda gelu, stant vertice crines;
quae summi sit meta boni, quaeve orbita rectum
signet iter, quo se confundat devius error,

after him, was all derived from him; whether you contemplate the cradle of an infant world, the natural causes conspiring together in an aggressive alliance, discordant accords, and the engendering seeds of things, or instead, the confines of the universe, and the rotating mansions of the gods and the stars that struggle with the heavens; what great force causes the immense disk of Hyperion to turn on its axis, from what source he revives his exhausted sister, who dared to interpose herself to her brother's flames and violate the light of day with sudden darkness; whether a mind conscious of destiny gives life to the stars; what makes the earth tremble, whether it reels from the blow of Neptune's trident or whether cruel Boreas, ready to erupt into our world, hides himself in hidden caverns. Now he expounds the alternations of the winds and the origins of lightning and the crackling of the air from the clashing of the clouds, and why the rains fall, why the sudden lightning strikes the eye in such a way that you would think the sky is split down the middle; that there is a god, an immense intelligence, master of the elements who embraces all things, who governs nature and the revolutions of the universe by a fixed law,[107] who subjects the fates to his free will, who alone moderates all things; that souls are exempt from death but enclosed in the body as in a tomb,[108] which, however, as our poet repeatedly says, the leader of the silent sect teaches can change into various forms, remembering his previous existence and surviving his own death.[109] And furthermore he places reason in the high citadel as a sovereign; he rouses gloomy passions in the heart, leaving the entrails to be subject to ignoble desires;[110] he does not pass over in silence why it is that grievous sorrow torments us and passionate desire turns into uncontrolled madness, why the faces of those in prey to fear become pale, their knees shake, their hearts become rigid with cold, their hair stands on end; he teaches what is the goal of the Highest Good, what track signals the right road, how wandering from the true path confounds itself, the many channels virtue follows,

520

525

530

535

540

545

550   quot virtus fluat in rivos, quo cardine honestum
       vertatur, rebus quantum Fortuna caducis
       praesit, ut humanos toleret mens cruda tumultus;
       quae cives mensura premat, quo robore leges
       firmentur, plus consilio res crescat an armis
555   publica, quas belli tentet dux callidus artes;
       quam vocum sit amica fides, quam magna gregandis
       religio numeris; quantis praesagia signis
       consultes, quantum sucos rimata salubres
       ardua Paeoniae valeat sollertia dextrae.

560   Hinc et magniloquis voces crevere cothurnis,
       hinc lasciva datos riserunt compita soccos,
       hinc hausisse iocos teneri creduntur amores
       quique adstricta brevi claudunt epigrammata nodo.
       Quin et Apellaeos digitis animare colores
565   monstrat; Olympiaco quin is dedit ora Tonanti
       (nec faber ille negat), dum nigris mota laborant
       cuncta superciliis immortalesque sequuntur
       astra iubas, sancta dum maiestate tremendum
       excipiunt magnoque assurgunt numina patri;
570   heroumque idem facies et celsa potentum
       ora deum variisque horrenda animalia formis
       diversasque urbes positusque habitusque locorum
       innumeros sensusque animorum, carmine pulchro,
       naturamque omnem, illa ipsa mirante, figurat.
575   Huic aras, huic templa dedit veneranda vetustas,
       hunc aere, hunc saxo fulvoque colebat in auro,
       hunc unum auctorem teneris praefecerat annis,
       rectoremque vagae moderatoremque iuventae,
       hunc etiam leges vitae agnovere magistrum.
580   Omnis ab hoc doctas sapientia fonte papyros
       irrigat, hunc proprias olim Gangetica tellus
       transtulit in voces, huius natalia septem

on what pivot honor turns, how much power Fortune has over   550
transitory things, how a vigorous mind can tolerate human tur-
moil; what rules should be used to govern the citizen body, what
force can strengthen laws, whether a state prospers more by coun-
sel than by arms, what arts of war a shrewd leader should attempt;
how friendly is the lyre to the voice, what mystical sense there is in   555
the combination of numbers, by how many signs you can interpret
portents, how much efficacy there is in the skillful art of Paean's[111]
right hand, which searches into salubrious potions.

From him also the grandiloquent language of the tragic stage   560
developed; from him the lascivious crossroads roared with laugh-
ter at those who put on the sock of comedy; from him it is be-
lieved tender love affairs derived their sportiveness, and those who
end terse epigrams with a tidy knot. Then he shows how to give
life with your fingers to the colors of Apelles,[112] and it is he[113] who
gave features to the Olympian statue of Jupiter (nor does the   565
sculptor deny it), while all things, moved by a sign from his dark
brow, are set in motion, and the stars follow his immortal locks,
while the gods welcome him, awe-inspiring in his holy majesty,
and rise up before their great father; in his beautiful poem he de-
picts the faces of heroes and the noble countenances of the mighty   570
gods, fearsome animals of various forms, diverse cities, innumera-
ble sites and characteristics of places, emotions and all of nature,
and she herself is filled with wonder. Venerable antiquity erected
altars and temples to him and honored him in bronze, in marble   575
and in yellow gold; it made him the unique model for those of ten-
der years, the one guide and moderator of inconstant youth; even
the laws acknowledged him as the teacher of life. All philosophy
waters its learned pages from this font; the land of the Ganges   580
long ago translated him into their language; seven cities contend in
belligerent rivalry to be his birthplace. Ptolemy,[114] his defender,

quaeque sibi rapiunt studiis pugnacibus urbes,
hunc et Sithonii patientem iura flagelli
585   asseruit patrio vindex Ptolemaeus ab amne.
Hunc quoque captivo gemmatum clausit in auro
rex Macedum, mediis hunc consultabat in armis,
hoc invitabat somnos, hinc crastina bella
concipere, huic partos suetus iactare triumphos.
590   Et nos ergo illi grata pietate dicamus
hanc de Pierio contextam flore coronam,
quam mihi Caianas inter pulcherrima nymphas
Ambra dedit, patriae lectam de gramine ripae,
Ambra, mei Laurentis amor, quam corniger Umbro,
595   Umbro senex genuit, domino gratissimus Arno,
Umbro suo tandem non erupturus ab alveo.
Quem super aeternum staturae culmina villae
erigis haudquaquam muris cessura Cyclopum—
macte opibus, macte ingenio!—mea gloria Laurens,
600   gloria Musarum Laurens; montesque propinquos
perfodis et longo suspensos excipis arcu,
praegelidas ducturus aquas qua prata supinum
lata videt Podium, riguis uberrima lymphis,
aggere tuta novo piscosisque undique saepta
605   limitibus, per quae multo servante Molosso
plena Tarentinis succrescunt ubera vaccis;
atque aliud nigris missum (quis credat?) ab Indis
ruminat ignotas armentum discolor herbas;
at vituli tepidis clausi faenilibus intus
610   expectant tota sugendas nocte parentes.
Interea magnis lac densum bullit aenis,
bracchiaque exsertus senior tunicataque pubes
comprimit et longa siccandum ponit in umbra.
Utque piae pascuntur oves, ita vastus obeso
615   corpore sus Calaber cavea stat clausus olenti

liberated him in the name of his native river when he was suffer-   585
ing the attacks of the Thracian scourge. The King of the Mace-
donians,[115] also, kept his works in a gold case adorned with gems
that he had taken in war, and consulted them in the midst of bat-
tle; with these he invited sleep, and he was wont to devise the next
day's battles from this source and boast to him of triumphs won.

Let us, therefore, dedicate to him with grateful piety this gar-   590
land woven with the flowers of the Muses, which Ambra,[116] most
beautiful among the nymphs of Caiano, gave me, picked from the
grassy banks of the paternal river; Ambra, delight of my dear
Lorenzo, which the horned Ombrone, old Ombrone begot, most
pleasing of streams, to his lord Arno, the Ombrone, which at last   595
will no longer burst forth from its bed. Upon its eternal banks,
Lorenzo, my glory, Lorenzo, glory of the Muses, you are con-
structing the roof-beams of the villa that is going to be built, and
which shall cede in no way to the walls of the Cyclopes (marvel of
riches, marvel of genius!); and you dig a channel through the   600
neighboring mountains and make them rest on a long arching
aqueduct which will bring cool waters to the place where gently
sloping Poggio overlooks the broad meadows, watered by copious
streams, protected by a new embankment and fenced in by canals
rich in fish. Through these meadows, guarded by Molossian
hounds, the udders of the Tarentine cows[117] swell and another   605
herd, of various colors, sent by the dark-skinned Indians,[118] (who
would believe it?) ruminates on strange grasses; but the calves, en-
closed within their warm stalls, await their mothers to suckle all
through the night. In the meantime the dense milk bubbles in the   610
great bronze vats and the old farmer, rolling up his sleeves, and the
young men in tunics press the cheese and deposit it to dry for long
periods in the shade; and as the tender sheep pasture, the huge
Calabrian pig, with its obese body, stays closed in its fetid sty and   615

atque aliam ex alia poscit grunnitibus escam;
Celtiber ecce sibi latebrosa cuniculus antra
perforat, innumerus net serica vellera bombyx;
at vaga floriferos errant dispersa per hortos
620   multiforumque replent operosa examina suber
et genus omne avium captivis instrepit alis;
dumque Antenorei volucris cristata Timavi
parturit et custos Capitoli gramina tondet,
multa lacu se mersat anas subitaque volantes
625   nube diem fuscant Veneris tutela columbae.

with its grunts demands one feeding after another. Look! the
Spanish rabbit burrows subterranean holes; the innumerable silk-
worms spin their silky threads; but the wandering swarms, dis-
persed through the flowery gardens, laboriously fill the cavities of
the cork tree, and all kinds of captive birds make loud noise with   620
their wings; and while the crested fowl from Padua's[119] Timavo
river[120] lays her eggs, and the guardian of the Capitoline[121] crops
the grass, the ducks immerse themselves in the pond and the
doves, the cortege of Venus, taking flight, darken the light of day
with a sudden cloud.   625

NUTRICIA

Sacratissimo Patri Dominoque suo Antoniotto Gentili,
tituli Sanctae Anastasiae Presbytero Cardinali Auriensi,
servulus Angelus Politianus.

Parvum quidem tuo nomini libellum dedico sed, ut spero, nec ina-
nem rerum nec inopem. Multa et remota lectio, multa illum for-
mavit opera. Titulum Nutricia diximus, qua figura et Statius Sote-
ria. Plenior hic enim mihi visus et argumento cohaerentior quam
qui olim placuerat Nutrix. Tu vero electus potissimum in cuius
appareat nomine, non quo rem tantillam tantae virtuti fortu-
naeque convenire arbitrer, aut hoc esse denique putem quod tuis
erga me meritis debeatur; verum cum prodire nollet hic in publi-
cum liber sine patrocinio, tuum praecipue sibi nomen inscripsit, ex
quo tutior foret atque honestior. Quare suscipe, quaeso, quidquid
hoc est mei fetus, qua me quoque ipsum soles humanitate. Dein-
ceps autem plura melioraque forsitan accipies, modo hunc primum
quasi gustum non asperneris. Nec enim vel ignoro vel dissimulo
quantum tua mihi apud Innocentium Pont. Max. suffragata sit
auctoritas; cui quidem et ipsi cottidie a me, si non par gratia, certe
aliqua tamen, pro virili parte, scribendo saltem beneque et sen-
tiendo et eloquendo refertur.

Vale. Florentiae, VI Kal. Iunias, an. salutis MCCCCLXXXXI.

NUTRICIA

To the Most Reverend Father and Lord Antoniotto Gentili,[1]
Cardinal Priest of Orense in the Title of Saint Anastasia,
His Humble Servant Angelo Poliziano.

It is a little book, to be sure, that I dedicate to you but, as I hope, not devoid of subject matter nor jejune. Much recondite reading and much labor produced it. I gave it the title *Nutricia*,[2] using the same figure as Statius for his *Soteria*,[3] for this title seemed fuller to me and more corresponding to the argument than the one I had thought of previously, *Nutrix*. I chose to have it appear under your name, in preference to all others, not that I think that such a slight thing is suitable for such great virtue and high position or, in fine, that this is what is owed to you for your great services to me, but since the book did not want to appear in public without a patron, it inscribed your name in the dedication, from which it could enjoy more protection and honor. Wherefore, accept, I pray, this offspring of mine, whatever its worth, with the usual kindness that you show towards me. In some future time, perhaps, you will receive more and better works, provided that you do not refuse this first foretaste, as it were. I am not unaware nor do I overlook how much favor your authority has gained for me with His Holiness, Pope Innocent,[4] to whom I return thanks daily, as I do to you. Though inadequate, I give thanks to him to the best of my abilities, at least in my writing and by thinking and speaking well of him.

Farewell. Florence, 27 May, in the year of grace 1491.

Angeli Politiani silva cui titulus Nutricia argumentum de poetica et poetis

Stat vetus et nullo lex interitura sub aevo
(divorum atque hominum concors incidit in auro
scilicet hanc Natura parens; dictasse feruntur
fatorum consulta Themis sollersque futuri
5 nondum Caucasea pendens de rupe Prometheus),
quae gratos blandae officio nutricis alumnos
esse iubet longumque pia mercede laborem
pensat et emeritis cumulat compendia curis.
Hinc Italos Phrygio signavit nomine portus,
10 Caietae memor, Aeneas; hinc urbe Quirini
annua cinctutos nudabant festa Lupercos;
hinc pater astrigero Dodonidas intulit axi
Bacchus, Agenoreo facturus cornua tauro;
hinc iubar Olenium ratibus pelagoque pavendum
15 exoritur, siquidem Cretaea fertur in Ida
capra Iovem puerum fidis aluisse papillis.
    Ast ego, cui sacrum pleno dedit ubere nectar,
non olidi coniunx hirci, non rava sub antris
belua, non petulans nymphe, non barbara mater,
20 sed dea Pieridum consors et conscia magnae
Pallados, humanas augusta Poetica mentes
siderei rapiens secum in penetralia caeli.
Quas, rogo, quas referam grates, quae praemia tantae
altrici soluisse queam, nec fulminis auctor
25 nec thyrsi sceptrique potens? Quonam improba ducis
mens avidum? quo me, pietas temeraria, cogis
attonitum? quinam hic animo trepidante tumultus?

A Silva of Angelo Poliziano Entitled Nutricia
Treating of the Poetic Art and of Poets

There is an ancient law, which will never cease to exist in any age.
Nature, the joint parent of gods and men inscribed it in gold; it is
said that Themis, practised in the knowledge of the fates, and Pro-
metheus, skillful in predicting the future, before he hung sus-
pended from the Caucasian rock, dictated it. It is the law that   5
commands nurslings to be grateful for the friendly office of their
gentle nurse and repay her long labor with a dutiful compensation
and load her with gifts for her years of faithful service. For this
reason Aeneas, in memory of Caieta[5] gave a Phrygian name to an
Italian port; for this reason in the city of Quirinus[6] the annual fes-   10
tival made the Luperci[7] strip bare, girded in their loin-cloths; for
this reason father Bacchus raised the nymphs of Dodona[8] to the
starry heavens, destined to become the horns of Taurus,[9] who
bore Agenor's daughter on his back; for this reason the Olenian
star,[10] feared by ships on the high seas, arises, since it is said that a
she-goat on Cretan Mt. Ida nursed Jupiter with her faithful teats.   15

    As for me, it was not the spouse of a foul-smelling goat that
gave me sacred nectar with her full udders, nor a tawny beast in its
cave, nor a wanton nymph, nor a barbarian mother, but a goddess,
sister of the Pierian Muses, who shares the secret knowledge of
Pallas Athena, the august Art of Poetry, that carries off human   20
minds with her to the secret recesses of the starry heavens. What
thanks, I ask, can I render, with what recompenses can I repay
such a nurse, I, who am neither the master of the thunderbolt nor
have the power of the thyrsus[11] or the scepter? Where, presump-
tuous mind, do you lead me in my ardent desire? Where, rash pi-   25
ety, do you constrain me to go, dazed with wonder? What kind of
passion is this in my trembling spirit? Am I in error, or do my in-

Fallor, an ipsa aptum dominae praecordia munus
parturiunt ultro vocemque et verba canoro
30   concipiunt sensim numero inlibataque fundunt
carmina numquam ullis Parcarum obnoxia pensis?
Sic eat. En agedum, qua se furor incitat ardens,
qua mens, qua pietas, qua ducunt vota, sequamur.
    Intulerat terris nuper mundoque recenti
35   cura dei sanctum hoc animal, quod in aethera ferret
sublimes oculos, quod mentis acumine totum
naturae lustraret opus causasque latentes
eliceret rerum et summum deprenderet aevi
artificem nutu terras, maria, astra regentem;
40   quod fretum ratione animi substerneret uni
cuncta sibi ac vindex pecudum domitorque ferarum
posset ab ignavo senium defendere mundo,
neu lento squalere situ sua regna neque aegram
segnitie pateretur iners languescere vitam.
45   Sed longum tamen obscuris immersa tenebris
gens rudis atque inculta virum, sine more, sine ulla
lege propagabant aevum passimque ferino
degebant homines ritu, visque insita cordi
mole obsessa gravi nondum ullos prompserat usus;
50   nil animo, duris agitabant cuncta lacertis.
Nondum religio miseris (si credere fas est),
non pietas, non officium, nec foedera discors
norat amicitiae vulgus; discernere nulli
promptum erat ambiguo susceptam semine prolem;
55   non torus insterni Genio; non crimina plecti
iudicio, nulla in medium consulta referri;
non quaeri commune bonum, sua commoda quisque
metiri, sibi quique valere et vivere sueti.
Et nunc ceu prorsus morientem vespere sero

nermost feelings bring forth of their own a work appropriate for
my mistress, and gradually conceive sounds and words in harmo-
nious rhythm and pour forth flawless songs that shall never be at   30
the mercy of the Fates' spindles. Thus may it go. Come, wherever
ardent frenzy impels me, wherever my mind, my piety, my prayers
lead me, let us follow.

Not long ago on the earth and the new-born world the divine
solicitude introduced this sacred creature[12] which could raise its
eyes towards the sky; which with its acute intelligence could sur-   35
vey the whole work of nature and could call forth the hidden
causes of things and discover the supreme maker of life, who di-
rects the land, the seas and the stars with a nod of his head; a
creature which, relying on the power of reason, could subject all
things to itself alone, and as protector of flocks and lord of wild   40
beasts could save the sluggish universe from decay and would not
inertly allow his kingdoms to lie waste with prolonged neglect or
his life to languish in slothful inactivity. But for a long time the
primitive and crude race of men, sunken in obscure darkness,
leading a life without customs or laws and though human, passed   45
their haphazard existence in the manner of wild beasts; and the
power implanted in their hearts, oppressed by a crushing weight,
had not yet been put to use; they did nothing with their minds,
but everything by brute strength. These unhappy creatures had no   50
religious feelings (if we may believe this), no piety, no sense of
duty; this discordant throng knew nothing of the ties of friend-
ship; it was not possible for anyone to distinguish their own
offspring, conceived of uncertain parentage; the marriage bed was
not dedicated to the family *genius*,[13] crimes were not punished by a
tribunal; no decisions were discussed in common; there was no   55
consideration of the common good; each one looked to his own
advantage, each was accustomed to live and prosper for himself
alone. And at one moment, in their ignorance, they cried at sunset
as if the day were dying; at another time, when light returned,

60 ignari flevere diem; nunc, luce renata,
  gaudebant ceu sole alio, variosque recursus
  astrorum, variam Phoeben sublustris in umbra
  noctis et alternas in se redeuntibus annis
  attoniti stupuere vices; insignia longum
65 spectabant caeli pulchroque a lumine mundi
  pendebant causarum inopes, rationis egentes.
  Donec ab aetherio genitor pertaesus Olympo
  socordes animos, longo marcentia somno
  pectora, te nostrae, divina Poetica, menti
70 aurigam dominamque dedit. Tu flectere habenis
  colla reluctantum, tu lentis addere calcar,
  tu formare rudes, tu prima extundere duro
  abstrusam cordi scintillam, prima fovere
  ausa Prometheae caelestia semina flammae.
75   Nam simul ac pulchro moderatrix unica rerum
  suffulta eloquio dulcem sapientia cantum
  protulit et refugas tantum sonus attigit aures,
  concurrere ferum vulgus, numerosque modosque
  vocis et arcanas mirati in carmine leges,
80 densi humeris, arrecti animis, immota tenebant
  ora catervatim ; donec didicere quid usus
  discrepet a recto, qui fons aut limes honesti,
  quive fide cultus, quid ius aequabile, quid mos,
  quid poscat decor et ratio; quae commoda vitae
85 concilient inter se homines, quae foedera rebus;
  quantum inconsultas ultra sollertia vires
  emineat; quae dein pietas praestanda parenti
  aut patriae, quantum iuncti sibi sanguinis ordo
  vindicet, alternum quae copula servet amorem;
90 quod gerat imperium, fractura Cupidinis arcus
  atque iras domitura truces, vis provida veri,
  vis animae, celsa quae sic speculatur ab arce,

they rejoiced as if it were another sun; they gazed in wonder at the 60
various courses of the stars, the phases of the moon that faintly il-
lumines the shades of night and the alternation of the seasons
with each returning year; they stared for a long time at the heav-
enly constellations and they depended on the beautiful light of the
universe, wanting in knowledge and devoid of understanding, until 65
finally, weary of the stupidity of those obtuse minds and of those
hearts benumbed by a long sleep, the first parent from the heights
of Olympus gave you, O divine Poetry, to be the charioteer and
mistress of our soul. You were the first to dare bend the necks of
the recalcitrant under your bridle, spur on the sluggish, instruct 70
the untaught, extract the spark hidden in our stony hearts and
keep alive the heavenly seeds of Prometheus' flame.

For as soon as Wisdom, sole ruler of the universe, with the 75
support of beautiful Eloquence, put forth sweet song, and the
sound barely touched their timorous ears, the savage crowd rushed
together; and marveling at the rhythms and measures of the voice
and the mysterious laws of poetry, crowding together in bands,
their minds alert, they stood in silence until they learned how cus- 80
tom differs from what is morally right; what is the origin and limit
of the honorable; the observance of the plighted word, what equi-
table justice, custom, propriety and reason demand, what advan-
tages men acquire for their daily existence in their relations with
one another and what compacts they enter into together; how 85
much clever resourcefulness is superior to brute strength; then,
what loyalty is owed to parents and country, what claims are made
by blood ties, what a strong bond preserves mutual love intact;
what power the force of inquiring intellect has, able to break the
arrows of Cupid and subdue savage anger: the force of the spirit, 90
which looks out from its lofty citadel and penetrates even into the

ut vel in astrigeri semet praecordia mundi
insinuet magnique irrumpat claustra Tonantis.
95   Agnorant se quisque feri pudibundaque longum
ora oculos taciti inter se immotique tenebant;
mox cunctos pariter morum vitaeque prioris
pertaesum ritusque ausi damnare ferarum,
protinus exseruere hominem. Tum barbara primum
100   lingua novos subiit cultus arcanaque sensa
mandavere notis, multaque tuenda virum vi
moenia succinctus populis descripsit arator.
Tum licitum vetitumque inter discrimina ferre
et pretium laudi et noxae meditantia poenam
105   vindicibus coeptum tabulis incidere iura;
mox et dictus Hymen et desultoria certis
legibus est adstricta Venus; sic pignora quisque
affectusque habuere suos, bellique togaeque
innumeras commenti artes, etiam aethera curis
110   substravere avidis, etiam famulantibus altum
inseruere apicem stellis animoque rotatos
percurrere globos mundi et sacra templa per orbem
plurima lustrato posuerunt denique caelo.
Sic species terris, vitae sua forma suusque
115   dis honor, ipsa sibi tandem sic reddita mens est.
    An vero ille ferox, ille implacatus et audax
viribus, ille gravi prosternens cuncta lacerto,
trux vitae, praeceps animae, submitteret aequo
colla iugo aut duris pareret sponte lupatis,
120   ni prius indocilem sensum facundia victrix
vimque reluctantem irarum flatusque rebelles
carmine mollisset blando pronisque sequentem
auribus ad pulchri speciem duxisset honesti?
Quippe etiam stantes dulci leo carmine captus
125   submittit cervice iubas roseamque dracones

heart of the star-studded universe and forces itself into the strong-
hold of mighty Jupiter. Each one recognized his barbarity and for
a long time they remained silent and motionless, their eyes cast   95
down. Then of one accord they felt disgust for their previous way
of life; they dared to condemn their bestial mode of behavior and
at once discovered their humanity. Then for the first time their
former barbarous tongue took on new elegance and they commit-
ted secret thoughts to writing, and a ploughman, girding up his   100
clothes with a belt, traced for the populace the perimeter of the
walls that would be defended by force of arms; then they began to
distinguish between what is licit and what is forbidden and to in-
scribe on tablets, where they would remain enshrined, laws assign-
ing reward for merit and punishment for wrongdoing. Next mar-   105
riage was instituted, and love, which formerly was promiscuous,
was now subjected to strict laws; in this way all acknowledged
their own offspring and the objects of their affections; they de-
vised innumerable arts of war and peace and even subjected the
heavens to their avid curiosity and raised their heads to the stars,
now become their servants, and traversed in thought the rotating   110
spheres of the universe, and after surveying the heavens, they built
sacred temples in great numbers throughout the world. Thus
splendor was restored to the earth, beauty to life, and honor to the
gods, as was their due, and at long last the mind was restored to
itself.   115

But would that fierce being, implacable and emboldened by his
strength, laying low all in his path by the force of his arm; would
that being, accustomed to violence and of impetuous spirit, submit
his neck to a just yoke or willingly accede to the harsh bit unless
persuasive Eloquence had first tamed his indocile spirit, the recal-   120
citrant impetus of his anger and his rebellious pride with her
sweet song and led him, who followed with willing ears, to the
beauty of the good? Indeed the lion, captivated by the melodious
song, lowers his bristling mane, and the dragons, rearing up,   125

erecti tendunt cristam et sua sibila ponunt.
Ille quoque umbrarum custos, ille horror Averni,
Cerberus, audita Getici testudine vatis,
latratum posuit triplicem, tria sustulit hiscens
130   ora, novo stupidus cantu qui flexerat atram
Tisiphonen, saevo lacrimas conciverat Orco;
ipsum fama Iovem, cum iam Cyclopea magna
tela manu quatit insurgens tonitruque coruscat
horrisono et caecis miscet cava nubila flammis,
135   ut tamen increpuit nervis et pectine pulcher
Delius alternumque piae cecinere sorores,
placari totumque sua diffundere mundum
laetitia et subito caelum instaurare sereno.
    Nunc age, qui tanto sacer hic furor incitet oestro
140   corda virum, quam multiplices ferat enthea partus
mens alto cognata polo, qui praemia doctae
frontis Apollineas ausi sibi nectere lauros
inclyta perpetuis mandarunt nomina saeclis
expediam. Faveat pulchro nunc Musa labori,
145   Musa, quies hominum divumque aeterna voluptas.
    Iuppiter, ut perhibent, liquidi per et ignea mundi
templa per et stellis radiantibus aethera fixum
aurarumque animas sola terrae et caerula ponti
dissitus, errantes citharae vice temperat orbes
150   ac rapidum imparibus cursum rotat intervallis,
quem rata pars tamen et certum confine diremit.
Hinc nostro maior captu sonus exit, acutas
compensans gravibus septem in discrimina voces;
stellantesque globos sua quaeque innoxia Siren
155   possidet, ambrosio mulcens pia numina cantu.
Nec tamen in nullis hominum simulacra refulgent
mentibus, arcanam caeli testantia Musam
permixtumque Iovem. Nam ceu tralucet imago

stretch their rose-colored crest and cease their hissing; Cerberus, too, the guardian of the shades and terror of Avernus, on hearing the lyre of the Thracian bard, ceased his three-fold barking, and with mouths agape raised his three heads, stupified at the new song that had placated gloomy Tisiphone[14] and wrung tears from cruel Orcus.[15] Jupiter himself,[16] legend has it, when he rose up brandishing Cyclopean weapons in his mighty hand, emitted flashes of lightning with dreadful thunder and filled the hollow clouds with blinding flames, but as soon as the beautiful Delian struck the lyre with his plectrum and the pious sisters sang in chorus, he was appeased, and diffused his joy throughout the universe and immediately restored the clear sky to the heavens.

Come, listen now and I shall expound how this sacred frenzy stirs the hearts of men with sublime inspiration and sing of the countless offspring of the mind possessed by god, akin to the high heavens, and of all those who dared to wreathe their learned brows with Apollo's reward, the laurel, and transmitted their illustrious names to the endless eons of time. May the Muse now show favor to this beautiful undertaking, the Muse, who is the peace of mankind and eternal delight of the gods.

Jupiter, it is said, being dispersed through the fiery regions of the limpid universe and the ether studded with radiant stars, and amid the stirring of the breezes on the earth's surface and the blue of the ocean, guides the wandering spheres with the rhythm of his lyre and causes them to move rapidly, producing unequal musical intervals; yet their motion is differentiated in an exact proportion and within certain fixed limits. From this comes a sound that surpasses our perception, balancing high and low sounds into seven intervals;[17] a benign Siren[18] occupies each starry sphere, charming the pious divinities with her ambrosial song. In some men's minds, however, likenesses gleam that attest to the mystic Muse of heaven and the immanence of Jupiter. For as the image of a star is re-

130

135

140

145

150

155

sideris in speculum, ceu puro condita vitro
160 solis inardescit radio vis limpida fontis,
sic nitidos vatum defaecatosque sonori
informant flammantque animos modulamina caeli.
Is rapit euantem fervor fluctuque furoris
mens prior it pessum. Tum clausus inaestuat alto
165 corde deus, toto lymphatos pectore sensus
exstimulans sociumque hominem indignatus, ad imas
cunctantem absterret latebras; vacua ipse potitus
sede, per obsessos semet tandem egerit artus
inque suos humana ciet praecordia cantus.
170 Non illos cycnaea mele, non daedala chordis
apta fides, non quae duplici geniale resultant
naula citata manu, non vincat dulcior ille
flatus inaequales digitis pulsantibus implens
compresso de folle tubas, pius aemula contra
175 iubila cui referunt chorus alternisque lacessunt.
Agnoscas propere numen. Suspirat anhelo
grandior ore sonus quantusque impleverit antrum
Phoebados aut rupem Euboicam. Nec Martius illum
terrificum clangens rauci canor aeris obumbret
180 nec tonitrus Iovis, aut petulantibus incita flabris
Ossaeo pineta iugo Nilive ruentis
exsurdans vicina fragor. Mirantur et ipsi
saepe (quis hoc credat?) quae nuper cumque, recepto
numine, legitimi cecinere oracula vates;
185 caligatque animus visis nec vindice lingua
defendunt sua dicta sibi, postquam ille quievit
spiritus et pressi tacuit sacer impetus oris.
Ipsaque Niliacis longum mandata papyris
carmina Phoebeos videas afflare furores
190 et caeli spirare fidem; quin sancta legentem
concutiunt parili turbam contagia moto

flected in a mirror, as limpid water poured into a glass gleams in
the sun's rays, so the celestial modulations fashion and enflame the   160
luminous and purified spirits of poets. This ardor carries off the
one who cries "*euoe*"[19] and in a surge of frenzy his mind is first
overwhelmed; then the god, shut up in the depths of his heart,
seethes, arousing frenzied feelings in his breast. Resenting associa-   165
tion with man, he frightens him and drives him into the deepest
recesses against his will; the god himself takes possession of the
empty place, occupies and pervades his limbs, and instills his song
in the human heart. Its sweetness is not surpassed by the song
of the swan or the skillful lyre fitted with strings or the festive mel-   170
odies played with both hands on the psaltery; or the music made
by the air escaping from the compressed bellows that fill the un-
even pipes when the fingers touch the keys, to which the sacred
chorus in emulation responds with joyful antiphonal singing. One   175
can quickly discern the presence of the divinity. A greater sound
issues from the breathless mouth, large enough to fill the cave of
the Sibyl of Apollo or the Euboean rock.[20] Neither the terrifying
blare of the hoarse clarion could overshadow its sound nor the
thunder of Jupiter nor the pine groves of Mt. Ossa,[21] shaken by
the boisterous winds, nor the deafening roar of the cascading   180
Nile.[22] Even true prophets themselves (who would believe it?)
wonder at the oracles they have just pronounced after being pos-
sessed by the god; their mind is clouded by the visions they have
seen and they do not defend the truth of what they said af-   185
ter that spirit has quietened and the sacred impulse on their
muted lips has become silent. You could see that the poems them-
selves, committed long ago to the Nile's papyruses, transmitted the
Apollonian inspiration and breathed the music of the celestial lyre;
indeed a sacred contagion excites the throng of readers with a like   190

deque aliis alios idem proseminat ardor
pectoris instinctu vates, ceu ferreus olim
anulus, arcana quem vi Magnesia cautes
195   sustulerit, longam nexu pendente catenam
implicat et caecis inter se conserit hamis.
Inde sacros Musarum amnes, Heliconia tempe,
multisoni celebrant numeroso gutture cycni.
    Prima tamen dubias fuderunt carmina sortes.
200   Quippe etiam ante Iovem sagis instincta resolvit
ora sonis Nereus, Nereus quem prisca marinum
dictat fama senem; tuque, o consulte Prometheu,
qui tenuem liquidis ignem furatus ab astris
mirantem frustra satyrum captumque decoro
205   lumine, ne flammae daret oscula blanda monebas.
Mox quoque Phocaico verum mugivit ab antro
alma Themis, qua rupe pares utrimque volatus
armigerae posuere Iovis. Tum Iuppiter ipse
fatidico movit cantu Dodonida quercum
210   praesciaque in Libycis concussit cornua lucis,
moxque Lycaonias Pan carmine terruit umbras.
Carmen Apollinei tripodes laurusque locutae
quaeque coronatum sonuere Philesia Branchum,
pastorem Branchum, tribuit cui gratus amorum
215   sortilegas voces admissus ad oscula Paean,
et sua per carmen ducibus responsa latinis
noctivagus cecinit, calcato vellere, Faunus.
Vos quoque per carmen, triplices, oracula, Parcae,
vestra datis; quin et veteres prompsere Sibyllae
220   carmen, Amalthea, et fati Marpesia dives,
Herophileque Idaea genus praedoctaque Sabbe,
Demoque Phygoque, et veri gnara Phaennis
et Carmenta parens et Manto et pythia longos
Phemonoe commenta pedes et filia Glauci

enthusiasm and the same ardor passes from one poet to engender inspiration in the heart of others, like the iron ring lifted up by the hidden force of a Magnesian stone[23] that attaches to itself a long chain in a pendant bond and fastens them together with invisible hooks. Thus the polyphonous swans celebrate with rhythmical voice the sacred streams[24] of the Muses and Heliconian Tempe.   195

Nonetheless the first poetry spread obscure oracles abroad. For even before Jupiter, Nereus loosened his lips, inspired with prophetic words, Nereus who antique legend says was an old man of the sea, and you also, wise Prometheus, who stole the subtle flame from the bright stars, warned the satyr,[25] who was admiring it in vain, enthralled by its captivating light, not to kiss the flame. Soon also kindly Themis[26] bellowed out true utterances from the Phocaean cave, on the mountain where the eagles of Jupiter[27] ended their equi-distant flight from opposite ends of the earth; then Jupiter himself stirred the Dodonian oaks[28] with prophetic song and caused the prescient horns in the Libyan groves[29] to vibrate. Next Pan[30] terrifed the Lycaonian shades with his song; the tripods and the laurel trees of Apollo[31] spoke their prophecies; and the Philesian temple,[32] too, echoed with Branchus' prophecies—the shepherd Branchus from whom, grateful for his love, Apollo accepted a kiss and to whom he gave the gift of prophecy; and Faunus,[33] roaming by night, sang his responses in verse to the Latin chieftains, who stretched themselves out on animal skins. You also, threefold Fates, give your oracles through song; and the ancient Sibyls[34] likewise uttered their prophetic song, Amalthea, and Marpessa, rich in oracles, and Herophile of Ida's race, and clairvoyant Sabbe, and Demo, and Phygo and Phaennis, acquainted with the truth, and mother Carmenta, and Manto and the Pythian Phemonoe, who invented the hexameter, the longlived Deiphobe, daughter of Glaucus; and the Marcian brothers[35]   200 205 210 215 220

225   Deiphobe nimium vivax; et Marcia fratrum
nomina lymphatusque Bacis subterque triones
natus Hyperboreos Ollen inque Atthide terra
clarus honore Lichas Dodoniadesque columbae.
Nam quid ego innumeras variantem Protea formas,
230   sed dubio risus vultu lacrimasque perosum?
Quidve loquar te, Glauce senex? plenumque parente
Idmona, fulminei prostratum dentibus apri?
Ampycidenque pium, Libycis quem fudit harenis
vipera fatifero fauces accensa veneno?
235   Quid te, cui volucrum linguae patuere, Melampu?
Quid cui post visos nudatae Pallados artus
cernere nil licitum? Quid quem impia prodidit uxor
hosticaque hausit humus? Quique alto in melle necatum
restituit luci, quo nuper vixerat anguis
240   gramine, Minoum Dictaeo carcere Glaucum?
Aut qui mille rates peritura ad Pergama duxit,
Thestoriden? Aut qui magica fera murmura lingua
ingeminans, liquido deduxit ab aethere fulmen
in caput ipse suum propugnarique bidental
245   iussit Achaemenium servantia busta tiaram?
     An memorem Solymos, praelustria nomina, vates?
psallentemque deo regem, qui turbine fundae
icta Philistaeo secuit puer ora giganti?
Teque Palaestini laqueantem culmina templi,
250   mentis opumque potens, Salomon, nec odora tacentem
oscula sollicito languentis amore puellae?
Pars hymnos fudere Deo. Sic maximus ille
nondum clara sacris radiatus tempora Moses
ignibus, ut rubras sicco pede transiit undas,
255   demerso insignem cecinit Pharaone triumphum;
tuque puer, modo dicte mihi, Iessaee, vicissim
dulcia terribili mutans psalteria bello,

and the possessed Bacis[36] and Olenus,[37] born under the sign of the   225
Hyperborean oxen, and Lichas,[38] honored and revered in the land
of Attica, and the Dodonian doves.[39] Why mention Proteus, who
changed into innumerable forms, who with ambiguous expression
shunned laughter and tears? Why should I speak of you, aged   230
Glaucus?[40] And Idmon, filled with the spirit of his father, pros-
trated by the teeth of the lightning-swift boar? And the pious
Ampycides,[41] who fell victim to the venomous mortal bite of a vi-
per in the Libyan desert? Why mention you, Melampus,[42] who
knew the secret of the language of birds? and him who having   235
seen the naked limbs of Pallas Athena could see no longer?[43] him
who was betrayed by his faithless wife and was swallowed up by an
enemy land?[44] And of him[45] who with an herb that had previously
resuscitated a serpent brought Glaucus, son of Minos, back to life
in a Cretan cave, after he had been drowned in a jar of honey. Or   240
of Calchas, son of Thestor, who led a thousand ships to Troy to
destroy it? Or of him[46] who, repeating barbarous formulas in a
magic language, invoked a lightning bolt from the clear sky upon
his own head and ordered that a temple[47] containing his remains
be built where the lightning struck, which would protect the sov-
ereign of Persia?   245

Or shall I mention the illustrious names of the Hebrew proph-
ets, the king who sang psalms to God and who cut off the head of
the Philistine giant after striking it with his whirling sling? And
you, Solomon, rich in wisdom and resources, who adorned the
ceilings of the temple of Jerusalem and did not wish to conceal   250
the perfumed kisses of a young girl languishing with a passion-
ate love?[48] Some of them offered hymns to God; so Moses, their
greatest leader, before the sacred flames radiated around his
locks,[49] after crossing dry-foot the waves of the Red Sea, sang a
hymn of triumph[50] over the drowned Pharaoh; and you, son of   255
Jesse, whom I just mentioned, alternating the sweet psaltery with
horrid warfare, placate God with your voice; like those who were

voce Deum placas; ut quos Babylone rebelli
lambit in horrisonis non noxia flamma caminis
260   quosque alios, veteris gens servantissima ritus,
retrorsum Iudaea legit.
                    Sed enim aethera magnum
custodesque alii genios, ita iusserat error
publicus, innumerosque lares functosque sepulchris
mille deos variisque animatum partibus orbem,
265   heu! frustra coluere pii veniamque rogantes,
qualiacumque suo placabant numina cantu.
Mox chaos et teneri prima incunabula mundi
et divum genus atque hominum et Titania saecla
non humili dixere tuba, quoque edita partu
270   gramina frondiferumque nemus gentesque ferarum,
quidve parens Natura agitet, quosve aurea ducant
astra choros; ut se fraternis Delia flammis
induat et radiis eadem mox depleat haustis;
quae caelo portenta volent, quemve ille tumultum
275   misceat aut quantis varietur ab ignibus aer;
quo saliat quassante solum, qui torqueat error
oceani refluas undas molemque natantem.
Inde sacrosanctas modulati carmine leges,
multisonum fecere nomon; nec vulnera tantum
280   saeva, sed et caecos vincebant carmine morbos
sacrifici quondam, nec dis ignara poetae
nomina; quin magicas arcano murmure linguas
in varios duxere modos.
                  Nec fabula mendax
Parrhasio lapides movisse Amphiona plectro,
285   Orpheos atque lyram curva de valle secutas
in caput isse retro liquido pede fluminis undas,
cumque suis spelaea feris, cum rupibus ipsis
dulcia Pierias properasse ad carmina fagos,

not harmed by the flames in the roaring furnace during the revolt
in Babylon,[51] and the others of whom the Jewish race, observant of
their ancient ceremonials, read from right to left.[52]   260

But alas! Pious men of old worshipped the great upper air in
vain, and tutelary personal spirits (so erroneous official religion
had ordained), innumerable household gods, a thousand gods bur-
ied in their tombs and a universe endowed with spirit in its vari-
ous parts; seeking pardon they placated any deity whatever with   265
their song. Then in no humble style they sang of chaos and the
pristine beginnings of the young universe, and the race of gods
and of men, and the centuries of the Titans, and how plants were
brought forth, and the leafy forest and the races of wild beasts;
what part Mother Nature plays or what are the courses of the   270
golden stars; how Delia puts on the flaming clothes of her brother
and then, after using up its rays, divests herself of them;[53] what
signs fly through the heavens or what tempests the air stirs up or
with how many stars it is adorned; what it is that causes the earth   275
to tremble, what devious motion diverts the course of receding
tides of ocean and the mass of water. Then, having versified the
sacrosanct laws, they created oft repeated melodies; as at one time
priests overcame not only cruel wounds but obscure maladies by
incantation and the names poets used were not unknown to the   280
gods; in fact they adapted magic languages with their strange
sounds into rhythmic measures.

It is no lying fable that Amphion moved stones with Mercury's
lyre; and that, following the lyre of Orpheus from a winding val-
ley, the waves of a river[54] turned back on liquid foot to their   285
source; and that caves with the wild beasts inhabiting them and
Pierian beech trees together with the rocky cliffs hastened to hear
his sweet song; and the bird, hovering on its wings in the beaten

quaeque avis applauso libraret in aere pinnas,
290   paene intercepto vix se tenuisse volatu.
Illius argutis etiam patuere querelis
Tartara, terrificis illum villosa colubris
tergemini stupuere canis latrantia monstra.
Tum primum et lacrimas, invita per ora cadentes
295   Eumenidum, Stygii coniunx mirata tyranni
indulsit vati Eurydicen; sed muneris usum
perdidit, heu durae nimia inclementia legis!
At iuvenem postquam Thressarum iniuria matrum,
frustra suave melos, frustra pia verba moventem,
300   dispersit totis lacerum furialiter agris,
cum lyra divulsum caput a cervice cruenta
heu! medium veheret resonans lugubre per Hebrum,
reliquias animae iam deficientis amatam
movit in Eurydicen tamen, illam frigidus unam
305   spiritus, illam unam moriens quoque lingua vocabat.
Lesboum stupuit vulgus cum flere natantes
sponte fides atque os domini vectare cruentum
vidit et heu! lassis velut aspirare querelis.
Improbus hanc stulte chelyn affectare Neanthus
310   ausus, Apollinea pendentem sustulit aede,
quem tamen, indocto ferientem pollice chordas,
vindice discerpsit rictu nocturna canum vis.
Illa recepta polo, ceu quondam saxa nemusque,
sic nunc stelliferis agit aurea cornibus astra.
315   Quin et Pellaei quondam praesaga triumphi
delicuit sudore sacro Libethris imago.
Tantus honor Getico fuit, et post funera, vati!
    At tu, qui merito dulcem Cratera magistro
obtuleras, volucri penetrans in saecula fama,
320   cantando trahis Elysios, Musaee, minores.
Contra autem indocilem nimis exsecratur alumnum

air, could scarce maintain itself aloft, nearly stopping in mid-flight. At Orpheus' tuneful plaints Tartarus threw open its gates, the 290 barking monstrous apparition of the three-headed dog, shaggy with terrifying snakes, stood in amazement. Then the spouse of the Stygian tyrant, marveling at the tears shed by the Furies for the first time, against their will, conceded Eurydice to the poet; but he was not able to enjoy his gift: ah! excessive severity of a 295 harsh law! But afterwards because of the injury done to them the Thracian women in a fury scattered the mangled body of the young poet over the fields, as in vain he attempted to move them 300 by his sweet melodies and his pious words, while the lyre transported his head, severed from his blood-stained neck, down the Hebrus river with doleful sound. Still he turned the remaining forces of his dying spirit to his beloved Eurydice; her alone his icy breath, her alone his tongue even in death invoked. The people of 305 Lesbos were astonished when they saw the lyre floating by itself on the water, emitting a plaintive sound and carrying the bloody head of its master and alas! seeming to utter weary cries of lament. With impudence Neanthus[55] stupidly dared to take possession of the lyre and stole it from where it was hanging in Apollo's shrine, 310 but one night as he was attempting to strike the chords with inexpert fingers, he was torn apart by the avenging jaws of a band of dogs. Received into the heavens, it now leads the golden heavenly bodies with its star-studded tips, as it once did the rocks and woods. And one day, presaging the triumph of the hero of Pella,[56] the statue of the poet in Libethra melted in a sacred sweat. So 315 great was the honor of the Thracian poet, even after his death.

But you, Musaeus,[57] who offered to your deserving master a sweet *Mixing Bowl*, penetrating into the centuries with winged fame, by your song win over the less important dwellers in Elysium. By contrast, Linus curses his indocile student and calls the 320

immemoremque Linus vocat ingratumque laborum
Amphitryoniaden, qui quondam triste perosus
doctoris magni imperium, veneranda rebelli
325   contudit ora lyra et clamantem plurima frustra
tendentemque manus obtestantemque peremit,
heu! non ista piae meritum sibi praemia linguae!
Iam Methymnaeum vatem delphine revectum,
iam Thamyran cantu doctas anteire sorores
330   fretum, mox citharae damnatum et luminis orbum
quis nescit? Princeps idem (ni vana vetustas)
ad faciles Venerem inlicitam convertit ephebos
insignemque sacro tulerat certamine palmam
tertius: hoc etenim Cirrhaeus honore Philammon
335   claruit ante pater, sed Cres praevenerat ambos
Chrysothemis. Nam Demodoci vivacior aevo
fama Meletaeis gaudet iuvenescere chartis,
et tua Neritias invito pectine mensas
qui celebras.
              Etenim ut stellas fugere undique caelo,
340   aurea cum radios Hyperionis exseruit fax,
cernimus et tenuem velut evanescere lunam,
sic veterum illustres flagranti obscurat honores
lampade Maeonides; unum quem dia canentem
facta virum et saevas aequantem pectine pugnas,
345   obstupuit prorsusque parem confessus Apollo est.
Proximus huic autem vel, ni veneranda senectus
obstiterit, fortasse prior, canit arma virumque
Vergilius, cui rure sacro, cui gramine pastor
Ascraeus Siculusque simul cessere volentes,
350   quem non tabifico mordax attingere livor
dente queat, livor tandem et sandalion ausus
carpere, cum dominam asseruit sua forma Dionen.
Excipiunt gemini procul hos longeque sequuntur

son of Amphitryon[58] forgetful and ungrateful for his efforts, but one day, with loathing for the severe discipline of his great teacher, Hercules broke his venerable head with his rebellious lyre and killed him as he in vain cried aloud and stretched out his hands in supplication. Alas! his pious words did not merit such a recompense! Who does not know of the poet of Methymna,[59] carried to shore by a dolphin, or Thamyris,[60] confident of surpassing the learned sisters in song, who was then deprived of his lyre and his sight. He was the first (if tradition does not lie) to convert complaisant young men to illicit love and was the third to carry off the glorious victory in the sacred contest. His father, Cirrhaean Philammon,[61] won this honor before him but the Cretan Chrysothemis anticipated them both. The name of Demodocus,[62] which outlives time, rejoices in regaining his youth in the poetry of Homer, as does your fame, you who celebrate the banquets of Ithaca with unwilling plectrum.[63]

For just as we see the stars fleeing from the heavens on every side when the golden torch of the sun unveils its rays, and the pale moon vanish, so the poet of Maeonia eclipses the luminous honors of the ancient writers with his blazing lamp; he alone, singing the divine exploits of heroes and matching the savage battles with his song, struck Apollo dumb and led him to confess that he was altogether his equal. Closest to him or perhaps even superior (if his venerable age did not prevent it), Virgil sings of "arms and the man"; to him the Ascrean and the Sicilian shepherd alike gladly cede, in the sphere of the sacred countryside and the meadows. Carping jealousy dare not touch him with her putrifying tooth, the livid jealousy that dared to criticize Venus' sandal,[64] although she was vindicated by her own beauty. Two poets come next, following at a great distance, who summon the seven kings to the

qui septem Cadmaea vocent ad moenia reges:
355 hunc Phoebea Claros, Cumaea Neapolis illum
protulit; hic elegis etiam tua funera, Lyde,
flet pius, herois ille audax versibus effert
magnanimum quoque Peliden; hic denique magni
instar habet populi pendentem ad verba Platonem,
360 ille etiam *Silvis* partum sibi praedicat aurum.
Ecce alii primo tentatum remige pontum
Palladiamque ratem tabulasque dedere loquaces,
quorum Threicio personam primus ab Orpheo
accepit, genitus Miscelli gente salubri;
365 alter Alexandri Nilotidas abnegat arces
exosus natale solum tumidamque colosso
solis et irriguam pluvio Rhodon expetit auro.
Huius in Ausonio vestigia pulvere Varro
pone legit, linguae haud opulens, ut barbara Narbo,
370 ut quem parvus Atax Latiae transcripserat urbi;
atque idem imparibus proprios exponit amores
Leucadiamque suam numeris, succedere magno
Auruncae quondam frustra conatus alumno.
Nam te, Flacce, sinu sulcantem caerula pleno,
375 heu! iuvenem cursu excussit mors saeva priusquam
Aesonides Pagasas patriamque revectus Iolcon.
  At tibi Daedaleos monitus, Heliconie vates,
qui sequeris neque ventosis in nubibus alas
expandis neque serpis humi, sed praepete lapsu
380 ceu medium confine teris, quo carmine dignas
addiderim tandem, quove ore aut pectore laudes?
Scilicet huic, patriis pecudes in vallibus olim
servanti, cunctae se se indulsere videndas
Aonides laurumque viro vocemque dedere,
385 qua superum caneret stirpem praeceptaque morum,
descriptosque dies operum clypeumque tremendi

walls of Cadmus:[65] the one born in Claros,[66] sacred to Apollo, the
other in Cumaean Naples.[67] The first also piously mourns your   355
death, Lyde, in elegiac verse; the other daringly exalts magnani-
mous Achilles in heroic verse,[68] the one considered Plato's rapt at-
tention to his words[69] the equivalent of a huge public; the other
proclaimed that he received gold for his *Silvae*.[70] Behold others   360
sang of the sea first essayed by the oarsman and the ship built by
Pallas Athena and the talking planks.[71] The first of these, born
from the healthy race of Croton,[72] narrated the story in the person
of Thracian Orpheus; the other,[73] detesting his native land, re-
nounces the citadels of Alexandria on the Nile and seeks out   365
Rhodes, proud of its colossus of the sun and watered by a golden
rain. Varro[74] follows in his footstep in the Ausonian dust, not rich
in eloquence, to whom barbarous Narbonne and tiny Atax gave
citizenship in the Latin city. He sang of his love affairs and of his   370
Leucadia in elegiac meter and once tried in vain to succeed the cel-
ebrated son of Aurunca.[75] And you, Flaccus,[76] as you cut through
the blue waters with full sail, alas! were thrown from the ship by
cruel death when you were still young, before Jason had returned   375
to Pagasae and his native Iolcus.

But with what verses, with what tongue and with what senti-
ments could I add praise worthy of your name, O Heliconian
poet,[77] who follow the counsel of Daedalus by neither spread-
ing your wings in the wind-swept clouds or crawling along the
ground,[78] but with rapid flight, treading a middle ground?[79] To   380
this poet, as is well known, one day as he watched over his flocks
in his native valley, the entire company of the Muses conceded
their presence, and they gave him the gift of the laurel and elo-
quence with which to sing of the race of the gods,[80] moral pre-
cepts, the days prescribed for various tasks, the shield of awe-   385
inspiring Hercules and the ancient heroines of divine race. There-

Herculis et veteres divum genus heroinas.
Ergo et Chalcidico vatum certamine quondam
rettulit auritum tripoda, et (si vera minores
390   audimus) cantu magnum quoque vicit Homerum.
Moxque dolo extinctum mersumque ad litora tristes
delphinum vexere chorus, nec defuit index
turba canum medioque darent qui corpora sontum
mersa mari et meritam placarent mortibus umbram;
395   ossaque fatali tellus Minyaea sepulchro
nunc habet, annosae conspectu inventa volucris.
Nec quae magnanimum nodosae robore clavae
instruit Alciden, nullum nomenque decusque
conciliat sterili Pisandria Musa Camiro.
400   Nec qui bissenos iterum memorare labores
audet et a primo vatum figmenta priorum
usque chao repetit, non saltem laudibus aequet
Ascraeum Clariumque senes. Neque Chalcis alumnum
Euphoriona tacet, vario qui personat ore
405   Mopsopiam, neque Tyrtaei Lacedaemona cantu
victricem se ferre pudet, licet impare gressu
tenderet. Adde novis mutantem corpora formis
Parthenium pictique notantem lumina mundi
(namque hoc praecipue se carmine iactat) Aratum,
410   cui cor ab intonsi fax ore accensa Philini
urebat miserum, quem terra Cilissa recepit
et portentoso celebrem dedit esse sepulchro.
Nec te, quem Colophon tulerit, Nicandre, tacebo,
Paeoniis celebrem studiis, qui nigra venena
415   prodis et emissas serpentum fauce salivas;
tum medicam subiungis opem, praedicere finem
morborum et tacitas gnarus deprendere causas;
atque idem pia rura sonas, dulcissima miscens
austero figmenta operi. Sed lustra ferarum

fore, once at a poetic competition in Chalcis[81] he won a two-han-
dled tripod and (if we who come after know the truth) he even de-
feated great Homer in song.[82] Later he was treacherously killed   390
and thrown into the sea, and a sad group of dolphins carried him
to shore; but a pack of dogs revealed the crime with the result that
the bodies of the murderers were thrown into the sea and by their
death the shade received the appeasement that was his due. The
land of the Minyans now holds his bones in the tomb reserved for
him by fate, which were found when an aged raven came into view.   395
Nor does the Muse of Pisander,[83] which first equipped great-
souled Hercules with the might of the knotty club, fail to win re-
nown and glory for sterile Camirus. The same is true of him[84]
who dares in his turn to narrate the twelve labors and retraces the   400
fables of the ancient poets from primordial chaos, but cannot be
compared to the old poets of Ascra and Claros. Nor does Chalcis
keep silent about its offspring, Euphorion,[85] who sings the
Mopsopsia in varied registers. Lacedaemon is not ashamed to de-
clare itself victorous, thanks to the poetry of Tyrtaeus,[86] although   405
he walked with a limp. Add to these Parthenius,[87] who changed
bodies into new shapes; and Aratus,[88] who described the luminar-
ies of the painted sky (for it is of this poem that he is most
proud), whose heart, poor wretch, was inflamed with love like a
torch, enkindled by the beauty of beardless Philinus: the land of   410
Cilicia received his body and rendered him famous by a sumptu-
ous tomb. Nor shall I pass you over in silence, Nicander,[89] whom
Colophon bore, celebrated for Paean's science. You reveal the black
poisons and the salivas produced in the jaws of serpents; then you   415
give the name of their remedies, having the knowledge to predict
the end of maladies and to discover their hidden causes; and you
also sing of the hallowed countryside, inserting pleasant fiction in
the austere subject matter. Oppianus[90] explores the dens of wild

420   scrutatur, captat volucres prolemque natantum,
          mox dat habere Pio gratissimus Antonino
          Oppianus, docti praedives honore laboris.
          Pingit et exiguus totum Dionysius orbem
          terrarum in tabulis, sed non et proelia Bacchi
425   Nonnus in exigua potuit contexere tela.
          Battiades Hecalen sonat et Marathonia gesta
          celsior assueto causasque aetate latentes
          prodit et undeno molles pede cantat amores;
          et nunc ingratum tenebrosus devovet Ibin,
430   nunc superos celebrat, nunc tristibus ardet iambis,
          nunc humili premitur socco, nunc ille cothurno
          altior assurgit, centumque poemata pangens,
          dissipat in varios Heliconia flumina rivos.
             Sed Tiberim, dominum rerum mundique potentem,
435   ambigitur riguine tener Sulmonis alumnus
          nobilitet magis an vero tibi, Roma, pudori
          sit potius, Getica sic semisepultus harena
          (proh dolor!) exsul, inops, nimium quia forsan amico
          lumine Caesareae spectaverit ora puellae.
440   Ille novas primo facies transformat ab aevo;
          ille cupidineas versu canit impare flammas
          involvitque novum dubiis ambagibus Ibin,
          vel dat amatricum dictatas ore tabellas,
          vel miser exilium cycnaeo gutture deflet;
445   temporaque et causas Romani digerit anni,
          vel memorat pisces et adhuc ignara Latinis
          nomina, vel caelo labentia computat astra
          et replet adstrictas diverso epigrammate chartas;
          consutum quoque syrma trahit; suspendit et unca
450   nare malos, quorum nunc omnia plena, poetas,
          indulgens tamen usque sibi. Nam praeditus acri
          nimirum ingenio, faciem putat esse decoram

beasts, captures birds and fish. Soon, as a token of his great grati-   420
tude, he will present it to Antoninus Pius, who will reward him
richly for his learned work. Dionysius[91] describes the whole world
in his miniature depictions; but Nonnus[92] was not able to weave
the battles of Bacchus on a small loom. Callimachus[93] sings of   425
Hecale and the heroic deeds of Marathon in verse more elevated
than his usual style, and he reveals causes hidden in time and sings
of tender loves in elegiac distichs; and now in obscure language he
curses the ungrateful Ibis; now he celebrates the gods above, now
he is enraged in bitter iambs, now he sinks to the level of the lowly   430
sock,[94] now he rises to the tragic cothurnus. Composing hundreds
of poems, he disperses the Heliconian streams into a multitude of
rivulets.

It is uncertain whether the dear scion of well-watered
Sulmona[95] lends more nobility to the Tiber, master and ruler of   435
the world, or whether he is rather a source of shame to you,
Rome, half-buried as he was on the Getan shore, alas! an impover-
ished exile, perhaps because he cast too fond a glance at Caesar's
young daughter. He it is who transforms the appearance of things
from the beginning of time; he sings of the flames of desire in ele-   440
giac verses and involves a new Ibis in enigmatic toils, or publishes
a book of letters dictated by amorous heroines, or miserably
mourns his exile in a swan song; he classifies the periods of the
Roman year and their origins, or writes of fish and rehearses their   445
names previously unknown to the Latins, or calculates the courses
of the stars in the heavens, and he fills a condensed little book
with diverse epigrams; he also composes a tragedy sewed together
with borrowed material; he sneers at bad poets (of whom there is
now a great abundance), but is a bit too self-complacent:[96] for   450
though undoubtedly gifted with a sharp-witted genius, he consid-
ers the appearance of the poem more appealing if some mole,

carminis, inspersus maculet quam denique naevus.
Iam senior triplici vates qui corde superbit,
455   Maeonides Italis, ni fallunt visa, secundus,
bella horrenda tonat Romanorumque triumphos
inque vicem nexos per carmina digerit annos;
arte rudis sed mente potens, parcissimus oris,
pauper opum, fidens animi morumque probatus
460   contentusque suo nec bello ignarus et armis.
Quem Rudiis ortum rigidi quaestura Catonis
ad septemgeminas iuvenem deduxerat arces;
mox comes armorum Fulvi, qui sanguine partas
scilicet haud dubitat Latiis sacrare Camenis
465   exuvias, dedit Aetolis hostilia campis
corpora multa neci; longe gratissimus idem,
Scipio magne, tibi et Calabris vicinus in hortis
virute emeritis, cuius gentile sepulchrum
mox tenuit, nullo patiens sua funera fletu
470   produci laetusque virum volitare per ora.
Praeterea tragico boat ampullosus hiatu,
comica lascivo proscenia laxat iambo,
exponit satyros Latioque Euhemeron infert.
Et modo reprensi deflorans carmina Naevi,
475   carmina quae quondam fauni vatesque canebant,
mox gemet ipse suo natas in litore conchas
praecultum purgare fimo et sibi ferre Maronem.
Sed quamquam in primis docto Verona Catullo
gaudet, vulnificos elegis qui miscet iambos
480   et sub adoptivum redigit te, Clodia, nomen,
parturit et fortem forti quoque carmine Achillem
atque urbis proceres multo sale defricat audax
Caesareaeque notas et inurit stigmata fronti.
Non nihil Aemilium tamen haec quoque iactat alumnum
485   texentem tenui Macrum subtegmina filo,

added as a final touch, disfigure it.[97] Then that ancient poet who
took pride in his three hearts,[98] a second Homer for the Italians (if
visions do not deceive),[99] intones terrible wars and Roman tri-   455
umphs and orders the succession of years in his poem,[100] crude in
his art but powerful in thought,[101] very sparing in his words, poor
in possessions, assured in spirit, irreproachable in morals, content
with his lot, and not unacquainted with war and arms. Born in   460
Rudiae,[102] he was brought to the city of the seven hills as a young
man when stern Cato was quaestor; soon after he was the com-
panion in arms of Fulvius,[103] who, as we know, did not hesitate to
offer the spoils of war to the Latian Camenae, and killed many en-
emy troops on the fields of Aetolia; he was the apple of your eye,   465
great Scipio, and he was your neighbor in your Calabrian retreat,
which he merited by his bravery, and later was buried in your fam-
ily tomb,[104] he did not wish his death to be mourned, happy
to "fly about on the lips of men."[105] Furthermore he declaims   470
in the bombastic diction of tragedy,[106] he delights the comic stage
with his mischievous iambs; he wrote satires and introduced
Euhemerus to Latium. And although he borrowed from the po-
ems of Naevius, whom he criticized,[107] "poems that once fauns
and poets sang,"[108] later he will complain that the refined Virgil   475
cleansed of filth the pearls found on his shores and appropriated
them for himself.[109] But while Verona takes pride principally in
the learned Catullus, who alternates injurious iambs with elegiacs,
and hides you under a fictitious name, Clodia,[110] and heralds the   480
birth of the powerful Achilles in an equally powerful poem,[111] and
audaciously rubs down the elite of the city with a good dose of
salt,[112] and sears the brand of infamy on Caesar's brow, it also can
boast somewhat of another son, Aemilius Macer,[113] who weaves
his weft with a thin thread as he describes birds, plants and snakes   485

dum volucres numeris, dum gramina pingit et angues.
Nec qui philtra bibit nimioque insanus amore
mox ferro incubuit, sic mentem amiserat omnem
ut non sublimi caneret Lucretius ore
490 arcanas mundi causas elementaque rerum,
doctus et Arpino tamen exploratus ab ungui.
Scilicet et veteres naturam pandere Grai
carmine tentarunt celebri, ceu maximus ille,
aerisonas pedibus qui quondam inductus amyclas,
495 insiluit Siculi rapidum cratera camini,
et cui de vocum tenebris cognomina flenti
addita quosque alios studio sapientia dulci
implicuit cecinitque diu memoranda vetustas.
    Emicat Hesperio trifidum ceu fulmen ab orbe
500 qui, vix puber adhuc rudibusque tenerrimus annis,
Haemonios iterat currus auroque repensum
Hectora Tartareasque domos dirumque Neronem
Orpheaque et meritae peragit praeconia Pollae
lascivitque iocis; ac torrens voce soluta
505 Dulichias aequare nives et fulmina tendit
quanta Pericleo lepor intorquebat ab ore.
Mox tonat ardenti Pharsalica proelia cantu
Aegyptique nefas, primo vix flore genarum
conspicuus, torvo quem protinus ore secundum
510 respexit, captae vix ausus fidere palmae,
Vergilius. Sed iniqua bonis Rhamnusia tantis
heu, decus hoc orbi invidit, ne vindice ferro
assereret miseras incesto a principe terras.
Tu felix tamen, o iuvenis (nam conscia poenam
515 corda levant), felix, inquam, licet ille cruentum
rugiat et truncas desiccet sanguine venas,
fronte minax, diraeque instinctus verbere matris.

in verse. And Lucretius,[114] the poet who drank the philter and crazed by an excessive love, threw himself upon his sword, had not lost his mind to such an extent that he could not sing in sublime language of the secret origins of the universe and the first elements of things. Learned he was, but he did not escape the exacting scru-   490
tiny of Cicero.[115] Of course, the ancient Greeks also attempted to make known the secrets of nature in celebrated verse, as, for exam-ple, that very great poet,[116] who one day, putting bronze boots on his feet, jumped into the red-hot crater of the Sicilian volcano. There was also the weeping poet[117] who was given the name "the   495
shadowy one" from the obscurity of his language, and the others whom wisdom involved in pleasant study and whom memorable antiquity has celebrated.

　Flashing forth from the Western part of the world like a three-pronged lightning bolt comes the poet,[118] who, barely arrived at the age of adulthood, still immature and without experience, re-   500
counts again the Thessalian chariot and the ransom of Hector with gold and the dwellings of Tartarus, and cruel Nero, and Or-pheus, and the encomium of the virtuous Polla, and risqué epi-grams; and rushing headlong in the medium of prose, he tries to match the words of Ulysses, that fell like snow-flakes on a winter's day, and the lightning that charming persuasion hurled from the   505
mouth of Pericles. Then in impassioned verse, an unknown, fresh-cheeked lad, he makes the battles of Pharsalus[119] and the crime of Egypt[120] reverberate. Virgil, as if in doubt about whether he had gained the palm of victory, looked back at him, a close second, with a fierce glance.[121] But the Rhamnusian goddess,[122] prejudiced   510
against such great fortune, alas! jealously deprived the world of this ornament so that he could not liberate the unhappy world from this incestuous tyrant with avenging sword. Yet you are fortunate, O youth, (for awareness of innocence alleviates the pain) — fortunate, I say, despite the bloodthirsty bellowings of the menacing tyrant[123] and his draining the blood from your severed   515

Macte animo! Non te, o vates, Parnasside lauru
nequiquam deus et cithara dignatus honora est.
520 Post hunc Sidoniae damnat periuria gentis
emeritosque foro Musis tandem asserit annos
Silius, Ausonio qui quondam fulgidus ostro
expulit horribilem vitaque aulaque tyrannum;
ipse obiit plenusque aevi natoque superstes
525 aspera congenito fixus vestigia clavo.
An taceam Bassum gravido tua dona ferentem,
Vespasiane, sinu? et fantem Sicula arma Severum?
aut te Sidonias repetentem, Pontice, Thebas?
aut Pelusiaci missum de plebe Canobi,
530 pulchra suum quem nunc Florentia iactat alumnum,
gaudentem Stygio dominam iunxisse marito
magnanimique vagos ducis ostentare labores?
Aut te, Niliaca relegentem sidera cura,
bis vates, Manli, et Babylonia signa sequentem?
535 Quosque sibi aequaevos puro vocalior ore,
nequa laboranti incumbant oblivia famae,
Naso refert, queruli tangens confinia Ponti?
    Et qui Smyrnaeis poterat contendere plectris
Valgius, ut tersi memorat pia Musa Tibulli,
540 Musa sibi primos quae iure adsciscat honores
imparibus numeris, ni blanda Propertius ora
solvat et ambiguam faciat certamine palmam.
Plania materiam teneri dat et Hostia cantus,
nomine supposito, ceu Galli mima Citheris
545 personam falsae lasciva Lycoridos affert
in scenam et docto clausam se iactat amanti,
dum miser ipse suo fodiat praecordia ferro.
At non exigui tenuis quoque pagina Calvi
dissimulat pulchram, sed acerbo funere raptam
550 Quintiliam. Nec Cous ad haec non sacra Philetes,

veins, driven on by the verbal lashing of his cruel mother. Blessings on you for your courage! Not in vain did the god deem you worthy of the laurel of Parnassus and the honored cithara. After him Silius[124] condemns the perfidy of the Sidonian people[125] and after retiring from the forum dedicates himself to the Muses, who when he was garbed in the brilliant purple of the Ausonian land,[126] drove the monstrous tyrant from life and from the court; he himself died at an advanced age, outliving his son, immobilized by a painful tumor he had from birth. Shall I pass over in silence Bassus,[127] who carried your generous gifts, Vespasian, in the folds of his garment? And, Severus,[128] who sang of Sicilian arms? Or you, Ponticus,[129] who went back again to Sidonian Thebes? Or the poet, native of Egyptian Canopus,[130] whom beautiful Florence now boasts as its son,[131] he who was pleased to have given Proserpina as spouse to her Stygian husband[132] and to make known the far-flung conquests of the courageous chieftain. Or you, Manlius,[133] twice a poet, retracing the stars with Egyptian science and following Babylonian astrology? Or those contemporaries whom Naso, he a poet of more limpid eloquence, in his last lamenting elegy from Pontus,[134] mentions lest oblivion weigh upon their struggling fame?

And Valgius,[135] who could contend with the Smyrnean plectrum, as the pious Muse of polished Tibullus relates,[136] a Muse that would rightly claim primacy for itself in elegiac poetry if Propertius did not give free rein to his seductive verse and cast doubt on who should win the prize. Plania and Hostia[137] supply the subject matter of their love poems, under fictitious names, just as the mime, Cytheris, the mistress of Gallus,[138] wantonly assumed the false personage of Lycoris on stage and boasts that she is untouched by the feelings of her learned lover while he, pitifully, pierces his heart with his own sword. But the refined page of diminutive Calvus[139] does not conceal the name of the beautiful Quintilia, but she was carried off by a premature death. Nor is

520

525

530

535

540

545

quamquam est aeger, adest, quamquam vestigia lento
fulta gravat plumbo; nec qui sine amore iocisque
iucundum nihil esse putat.
                              Quid rustica dicam
iubila pastorum silvis meditata sub altis?
555 Ut patrias Moschus non inficietur avenas
externasque Bion? Ut opaca Tityron umbra
provocet Ausonio Calpurni fistula cantu?
      Aerios procul in tractus et nubila supra
Pindarus it, Dircaeus olor, cui nectare blandae
560 os tenerum libastis, apes, dum fessa levaret
membra quiete puer mollem spirantia somnum.
Sed Tanagraea suo mox iure poetria risit,
irrita qui toto sereret figmenta canistro;
tum certare auso palmam intercepit opimam,
565 Aeoliis praelata modis atque illice forma.
Ille Agathoclea subnisus voce coronas
dixit Olympiacas et qua victoribus Isthmos
fronde comam Delphique tegant Nemeaeaque tesqua
lunigenam mentita feram. Tum numina divum
570 virtutesque virosque undanti pectore torrens
provexit sparsitque pios ad funera questus.
Frugibus hunc libisque virum Cirrhaeus ab ara
Phoebus et accubitu mensae dignatus honoro est;
Panaque pastores solis videre sub antris
575 Pindarico tacitas mulcentem carmine silvas.
Inde senem puer gremio cervice reposta
infusum et dulci laxantem corda sopore
protinus ad manes et odoro germine pictum
Elysium tacita rapuit Proserpina dextra.
580 Quin etiam hostiles longo post tempore flammae,
quae septemgeminas populabant undique Thebas,
expavere domum tanti tamen urere vatis

146

Philetas of Cos[140] absent from these sacred rites, although he is   550
infirm and must support himself with a leaden weight when he
walks; nor is he absent who deems that there is no happiness
without love's diversions.[141]

What shall I say of the rustic songs of the shepherds, which
they compose in the thick forest? How Moschus[142] does not refuse
his native city, nor Bion[143] those foreign to him? How the shep-   555
herd pipe of Calpurnius[144] challenges Tityrus in the dense shade
with Italian song?

Far in the distance, high into the expanses of the sky and above
the clouds, Pindar[145] flies, the swan of Dirce, whose tender lips,
kindly bees, you touched with nectar while the young boy rested   560
his tired limbs immersed in soft sleep. But soon the poetess of
Tanagra[146] rightfully laughed at him for stringing together empty
fictions by the basketful; then when he challenged her to a contest,
she took first prize, winning the preference by her Aeolian meters
and alluring beauty. Encouraged by the words of Agathocles,[147] he   565
sang of Olympic crowns[148] and the wreaths with which Isthmus,
Delphi and the wooded land of Nemea, which invented the legend
of a lion born on the moon, crown the locks of the victors; then in
a flood of eloquence, overflowing with emotion, he exalted the
majesty of the gods, virtues and heroes and offered pious regrets   570
to the dead. Phoebus, god of Cirrha,[149] considered this man wor-
thy of the fruits and sacrificial cakes of his altar and of the honor
of sitting at his table; shepherds saw Pan in lonely caves charming
the silent forests with the verses of Pindar. Finally, when he was an   575
old man, lying down and resting his head in the lap of a boy and
relaxing his mind in sweet slumber, Proserpina, seizing him by the
hand, silently carried him off with her right hand to the spirits of
the dead without a sound and took him to Elysium adorned with
fragrant flowers.[150] A long time afterwards enemy flames that   580
completely destroyed Thebes of the seven gates were afraid to

et sua posteritas medios quoque tuta per enses
sensit inexhausta cinerem iuvenescere fama.
585   Non ego te, longo praesignis, Anacreon, aevo
transierim bicolore caput redimite racemo,
cui citharae cordi, cui nigri pocula Bacchi
semper et ancipiti stimulans Amathusia cura.
Nam modo Threicii crinem miraris ephebi,
590   nunc Samium celebras (iubet Adrastea) Bathyllum,
nunc teneram Eurpylen tenerumque Megisthea laudas;
tandem acino passae cadis interceptus ab uvae.
Ipse Lyci nigros oculos nigrumque capillum
quamque vides digito nativam inolescere gemmam
595   exactosque canis, pugnax Alcaee, tyrannos,
Aeolium docto pertentans barbyton auro;
arma sed Actaeae tua fles suspensa Minervae.
Sustinet heroi valida testudine pondus
carminis et damnans Helenen laudansque vicissim,
600   amittit recipitque oculos tuus, Himera, civis
Stesichorus, quem trux Phalaris veneratus et hostem est;
cuius et in labris sedit puerilibus olim
Daulias et vestrum, Musae, cantavit alumnum.
Sed vocat ad lacrimas Cei pia naenia vatis;
605   unum Mnemosyne quondam praeque omnibus unum
quem coluit, saevae quem subtraxere ruinae
Ledaei iuvenes; vacuam cui tristis ad arcam
Gratia flet, laniata comas nudata lacertos,
quique sui vindex fuit et post fata sepulchri.
610   Ipsi etiam patria pressi brevitate Lacones
ascitum largo tamen ore Alcmana recensent,
quem tulit auriferos ostentans Lydia fontes,
nunc gemit heu! tineis artus et tabe peresum.
At te cui numeros dictat dea Suada canoros,
615   Ibyce, quique marem tantum meditaris amorem,

burn the house of so great a poet, and his descendants, secure
even in the face of swords, saw that his ashes were imperishable
because of his unquenchable fame.[151] I shall not omit your name,
Anacreon,[152] conspicuous for your long life, your head garlanded   585
with grapes of two colors, whose great love was ever the cithara,
cups of red wine and the goddess of Amaltha,[153] who roused your
passions for both sexes: for at one time you admire the tresses of a
Thracian youth,[154] and now you celebrate the Samian, Bathyllus
(so Adrastea commands), and now you praise the tender Eurypyle   590
and the tender Megistheus; in the end you die suffocated by the
stone of a dried grape.[155] And you, aggressive Alcaeus,[156] you sing
of the dark eyes and black hair of Lycus and the birthmark grow-
ing on his finger, and you sing of the expulsion of tyrants, strum-   595
ming the Aeolian cithara[157] with a golden plectrum; but you weep
over your arms hanging up in the temple of Attic Minerva.[158]
Himera, your citizen, Stesichorus,[159] sustains the weight of heroic
song on a strong lyre, and condemning and praising Helen by
turns, he loses and then recovers his sight; the cruel Phalaris hon-   600
ored him, though he was an enemy. Once when he was a boy, a
nightingale alighted upon his lips and in its song declared him
your offspring, O Muses. But the pious dirge of the Cean poet[160]
moves us to tears. Mnemosyne once honored him above all others,
when the sons of Leda saved him from a terrible disaster.[161] One   605
of the Graces sadly weeps before her empty chest,[162] tearing her
hair out and with her arms bared, and even after his death he laid
claim to his own tomb.[163] Even the Laconians, so restrained in the
brevity of their speech, mention Alcman,[164] to whom they gave   610
citizenship, with prolix eloquence; he whom Lydia, proud of her
gold-bearing rivers, bore, now makes loud lament, his body con-
sumed by lice and putrefaction. But you, Ibycus,[165] to whom the
goddess Persuasion dictates melodious measures and who sings

nec superi nec avis Pygmaea reliquit inultum,
et nunc Rheginis tua sedibus ossa quiescunt.
Nec vulgare canit dulcis ab Iulide Siren,
Bacchylides.
　　　　　　　Sed enim lyricis iam nona poetis
620　Aeolis accedit Sappho, quae flumina propter
Pierias legit ungue rosas unde implicet audax
serta Cupido sibi; niveam quae pectine blando
Gyrinnem Megaramque simul cumque Atthide pulchram
cantat Anactorien et crinigeram Telesippen.
625　Et te conspicuum recidivo flore iuventae
miratur revocatque, Phaon, seu munera vectae
puppe tua Veneris, seu sic facit herba potentem.
Sed tandem Ambracias temeraria saltat in undas
quae totiens Gorgo, totiens incesserat atrox
630　famosam Andromeden patriaque libidine turpem.
Non illi Praxilla suos praedoctaque Nossis
contulerint Myrtisque modos, non dulcis Agacles,
non Anyte, non quae versus Erinna trecentos
Castalio ceu melle rigat, non candida Myro,
635　nec Telesilla ferox, non quae canit aegida saevae
Pallados effusum crinem vittata Corinna.
Illam etiam decimo cunctae accepere sedili
Pierides sertumque novem de floribus auro
contextum nitidis laetae imposuere capillis.
640　　　Hinc Venusina favos dulci iucunda susurro
carpsit apis, sed acu ferit irritata cruento
haec eadem rigidis Auruncae in vepribus errans,
quas Persi manus et bilem succensus Aquinas
mox legere sibi. Neque enim his metuendus iambo
645　certet echidnaeo, licet acrem effusus in iram
ore Lycambiadas rabioso occiderit ambas
Archilochus, medio licet illum in Marte peremptum

only of masculine love, neither the gods nor the Pygmean bird   615
left unavenged; and now your bones rest in the land of Reggio
Calabria. And it is no common song that Bacchylides[166] the sweet
Siren from Iulis, sings.

But now Aeolian Sappho approaches, ninth among the lyric
poets, who gathers the roses of Pieria along the rivers with her   620
own hand, with which bold Cupid may twine a garland for him-
self; with her melodious plectrum[167] she sings of Gyrinne, white
as snow, and Megara and the beautiful Anactoria together with
Atthis, and Telesippe with her long hair; and you, Phaon,[168] she
admires and calls upon to return, so striking in appearance, with
the renascent bloom of youth, whether you received this as a gift   625
for giving passage to Venus in your bark or whether an herb gave
you this power. But at the end, recklessly, she leaps into the
Ambracian waves,[169] she who so often ferociously attacked Gorgo
and infamous Andromeda,[170] guilty of lusting after her father.
Neither Praxilla[171] nor the learned Nossis nor Myrtis could match   630
her verses, nor sweet Agacles, nor Anyte, nor Erinna, who bathes
her three hundred verses with the honey of the Muses, as it were,
nor fair-skinned Myro, nor fierce Telesilla, nor Corinna, who with
her flowing hair crowned with fillets, sings of the aegis of cruel   635
Pallas Athena.[172] It was she whom the Muses welcomed unani-
mously to dwell among them as the tenth Muse, and with joy they
placed upon her shining hair a garland made up of nine flowers,
interwoven with gold.

From her the Venusian bee[173] culled the honeycombs, joyfully,   640
with gentle buzzing; but when irritated this same bee strikes
with its cruel sting,[174] wandering among the rough brambles of
Aurunca, which the hand of Persius[175] and the poet from
Aquinum,[176] incensed with bile, later picked for themselves. Nor
can the formidable Archilochus[177] vie with them with his viperous
iambs, although, roused to bitter anger, he caused the death of   645
both daughters of Lycambe by his rabid verse, and although the

vindicet et nigro sit Pythia dura Calondae;
nec ferus Hipponax, atro qui felle cruentus
650   Bupalon et stratum morsu laniavit Athenin;
nec Batius spinisque Bibaculus asper acutis.
    Multi, Bacche, tuo proculcavere cothurno
fortunas regum ambiguas et sceptra tyrannis
extorsere feris totumque tremore metuque
655   horribiles totum luctu opplevere theatrum.
Pluraque Palladiae quondam impendistis, Athenae,
dum scena Oedipoden pavidumque agitatis Oresten
Atreaque et medica percussum Telephon hasta
Oenidaeque facem Furiisque Alcmaeona pulsum
660   quosque alios olidum cantor produxit ob hircum,
quam cum barbarico Marathonia sanguine tellus
incaluit multoque obstructae funere Xerxen
Thermopylae tarda refugum videre carina.
Auctorem perhibent Thespin, quem iusta Solonis
665   cura cothurnatis iussit descendere plaustris.
Tres porro insignem sibi defendere coronam:
Aeschylus, aeriae casu testudinis ictus,
quemque senem meritae rapuerunt gaudia palmae,
quemque tegit rabidis lacerum pia Pella Molossis.
670   Invasere locum Plias septena secundum.
Quippe alios, quos nec centum sit dicere linguis,
fortunae nunc quemque suae famaeque relinquam,
ni Latium Varius tamen obiectare Thyesten
ambiat atque suum iactet mihi Corduba vatem,
675   cuius ad Herculeum tremefacta orchestra furorem est.
Ecce et grandiloquo semet quoque suggerit ore
Accius et magna conturbat voce canentem
Pacuvius nitidumque ostentat Musa Secundum.
    Adde et mordaci quatientes pulpita risu:
680   Eupolin, in medium quem mendax fabula pontum

Pythian oracle avenged his death on the battlefield, showing her-
self pitiless to raven-black Calondas.[178] Nor can ruthless Hip-
ponax[179] rival them, who cruelly savaged with his black venom
Bupalos and Athenis, who was laid low by his bite; nor Bassus[180]   650
nor Bibaculus[181] with his sharp thorns.

Many were those, Bacchus, who, wearing your cothurnus,[182]
trampled over the uncertain fortunes of kings and wrested the
scepter from cruel tyrants and by their terrifying appearance filled
the whole theater with fear and trembling and grief. At one time,   655
Athens, city of Pallas, you expended more effort staging Oedipus
and the terrified Orestes[183] and Atreus[184] and Telephus,[185] who
was stricken by the healing spear, and the torch of the son of
Oeneus;[186] and Alcmaeon[187] pursued by the Furies, and other per-
sonages that the poet brought on stage for the sake of a stinking
goat,[188] than the time when the soil of Marathon grew hot with   660
barbarian blood, and Thermopylae, choked with corpses, saw Xer-
xes fleeing away on his slow ship.[189] They say that Thespis[190] was
the originator of the tragic theatre, whom with just reason Solon
ordered to descend from the tragic wagons.[191] Later three poets   665
contended for the glorious prize: Aeschylus, who was struck by a
turtle falling from the sky, the other who in his old age was carried
off by his exultation in winning the prize,[192] and the one who was
torn apart by rabid Molossian dogs and lies buried in holy Pella.[193]
The seven poets of the Pleiad[194] occupied second place. As for the   670
others, whom I could not name if I had a hundred tongues, I
would leave each to his fame and fortune, if Varius[195] were not
anxious that I cite his Latin *Thyestes* and Córdoba did not boast of
her poet[196] to me, who made the audience tremble with his *Hercu-
les furens*. And behold Accius[197] also presents himself in grandilo-   675
quent style, and as he sings in a loud voice Pacuvius disconcerts
him; and the Muse makes show of elegant Secundus.[198]

Add also those that shake the platforms with mordant laughter:
Eupolis,[199] who a false report says was thrown into the sea from   680

Cliniadae manibus puppi deturbat ab alta;
quique leves Nebulas Actaeae effuderat urbi,
salsus Aristophanes compotoremque Cratinum.
Adde novos etiam soccos exemplaque morum
685 et variae specimen vitae: iam grata Menandro
posteritas ipsoque volente Philemone palmam
restituit; longe sequitur quem plurima turba
haud nostro referenda sono, sed pagina docti
reddit Athenaei tamen insinuatque futuris.
690 Claudicat hic Latium vixque ipsam attingimus umbram
Cecropiae laudis; gravitas Romana repugnat
scilicet. Et quamvis veterum sit multus in ore
Caecilius, quamvis iucundi scripta Terenti
Scipio dissimulet, quamvis Plautina Camenis
695 lingua Opicis placeat, scenam tamen ipsa suorum
Aeneadum fugit alma Venus tantumque togatis
interdum Afrani grato se indulget honore.
Hos tamen atque alios Volcatius ordine sistit
Sedigitus. Mimos sed enim scripsere protervos
700 implicitusque Sophron risuque Philistio tandem
perditus; hinc Laberi lascivia multaque Publi
claruit Ausonio sententia dicta theatro.

     Pars quoque sotadicos ceu prostituere cinaedos,
pars tenues sparsere sales epigrammate multo,
705 sed Latio celebres: quem misit Iberia Marcum
Romuleumque suis exornans fascibus annum
Ausonius. Mitto Hortensi doctique Catonis,
qui solus legit quondam fecitque poetas;
mitto et Cornifici lusus Ticidaeque Perillam
710 et Cinnam obscurum teque, ore protervior, Anser.
Pammetron hic cecinit; sillos dedit ille licentes;
ille Menippeae ioca miscellanea perae
infersit; satyros alius nudavit agrestes

the high poop deck at the hands of the son of Clinias; and witty
Aristophanes, who spread light clouds[200] over the city of Athens,
and his drinking companion, Cratinus.[201] Add New Comedy[202]
also with its moral examples and specimens of various manners of
life; grateful posterity, with the approval of Philemon[203] himself,
restored the palm to Menander;[204] he is followed at a great dis-   685
tance by a great throng of writers whom I cannot mention here,
but whom the learned page of Athenaeus[205] describes and makes
known to future generations. Here Latium limps,[206] and we barely
attain to a shadow of Cecropian[207] glory; obviously Roman *gravitas*   690
stands in the way. And although Caecilius[208] is often spoken of
by the ancient writers, although Scipio denies authorship of the
writings of the agreeable Terence,[209] although the language of
Plautus[210] pleases the Italic Muses, kindly Venus shuns the theatre   695
of her descendants of Aeneas and only occasionally shows some
sign of favor to the *fabula togata* of Afranius.[211] Volcacius Sedigi-
tus[212] ranks both these writers and others in his list. Impudent
mimes were also written by the subtle Sophron[213] and Philistio,[214]
who in the end died of laughter; in their train the licentiousness of   700
Laberius[215] and the many wise sayings of Publius[216] won fame in
the Latin theatre.

   Certain authors also prostituted, so to speak, sotadic obsceni-
ties,[217] others sprinkled witticisms into their numerous epigrams,
which were popular in Italy: Marcus,[218] who came from Spain;
Ausonius,[219] who adorned the Roman year with the consular fas-   705
ces. I omit the poems of Hortensius[220] and the learned Cato,[221]
who at one time single-handedly selected and created poets; I omit
also the trifles of Cornificius[222] and Ticidas'[223] Perilla, and the ob-
scure Cinna,[224] and you, Anser,[225] more shameless than the rest.
One composed a *Pammetron*,[226] another the libertine *silloi*;[227] one[228]   710
stuffed Menippus' satchel with a melange of humorous verse;

et patuere novae per mille poemata curae.
715 Quas ego, si Pyliae duplicentur tempora vitae
iam mihi, si cunctas nostra in praecordia voces
fama ferat rigidoque sonent haec pectora ferro,
non amplecti ausim numero, non ore profari
evaleam tantaeve situm indagare senectae.
720 Nec tamen Aligerum fraudarim hoc munere Dantem,
per Styga, per stellas mediique per ardua montis,
pulchra Beatricis sub virginis ora volantem;
quique cupidineum repetit Petrarcha triumphum
et qui bisquinis centum argumenta diebus
725 pingit; et obscuri qui semina monstrat amoris,
unde tibi immensae veniunt praeconia laudis,
ingeniis opibusque potens, Florentia mater.
Tu vero aeternam per avi vestigia Cosmi
perque patris (quis enim pietate insignior illo?)
730 ad famam eluctans, cuius securus ad umbram
fulmina bellorum ridens procul aspicit Arnus,
Maeoniae caput, o Laurens, quem plena senatu
curia quemque gravi populus stupet ore loquentem,
si fas est, tua nunc humili patere otia cantu
735 secessusque sacros avidas me ferre sub auras.
Namque importunas mulcentem pectine curas
umbrosae recolo te quondam vallis in antrum
monticolam traxisse deam. Vidi ipse corollas
nexantem numerosque tuos prona aure bibentem;
740 viderunt socii pariter, seu grata Dianae
nympha fuit, quamquam nullae sonuere pharetrae,
seu soror Aonidum et nostrae tunc hospita silvae.
Illa tibi lauruque tua semperque recenti
flore comam cingens pulchrum inspiravit amorem.
745 Mox et Apollineis audentem opponere nervis
Pana leves calamos nemoris sub rupe Pherei

another[229] introduced naked satyrs on stage, and new literary experiments found expression in a thousand poems, which I would not dare to pass in review, nor would I be capable of giving voice to   715
them or investigating the mouldering records of antiquity if I lived twice as long as Nestor, if the goddess Fame brought all her voices into my breast and I had lungs of steel.

Nevertheless, I would not wish to defraud Dante Alighieri[230] of this tribute, who flies across the Styx, through the stars and under   720
the beautiful gaze of the virgin Beatrice through the steep places of the mountain[231] that separates the two realms; nor Petrarch, who sings of the triumph of love,[232] and him who relates a hundred tales in ten days,[233] and him who reveals the origins of arcane   725
love,[234] whence come to you, mother Florence, endowed with genius and riches, proclamations of immense praise. And you Lorenzo, leader of Tuscany, striving towards eternal fame in the footsteps of your grandfather, Cosimo, and your father[235] (who   730
was more renowned for his piety than he?), you in whose shade the Arno, the capital of Tuscany, free from care, looks at the thunderbolts of war in the distance and laughs,[236] you whose grave eloquence the court,[237] crowded with senators, and the people listen to in awe, permit me now in my humble song (if it be fitting) to hold up to eager fame the poetic fruits of your leisure hours and holy retreats. For I remember once when you were soothing your   735
oppressive cares with the lyre, you attracted a mountain nymph[238] into a grotto of Vallombrosa, and I myself saw her plait a garland, listening attentively and drinking in the rhythm of your verses. Your companions also saw her, whether she was a nymph favored by Diana, although she bore no sounding quiver, or a sister of the   740
Muses, a guest in our woodland. Wreathing your locks with your laurel and flowers that did not lose their freshness, she inspired a beautiful love in you. Then, while you were celebrating in song Pan's attempt to oppose his humble pipes to the cords of Apollo[239] under a rock in the woods of Pherae, the same virgin came to your   745

carmine dum celebras, eadem tibi virgo vocanti
astitit et sanctos nec opina afflavit honores
Ergo et nocticanum per te Galatea Corinthum
750   iam non dura videt. Nam quis flagrantia nescit
vota cupidineoque ardentes igne querelas?
Seu tibi Phoebeis audax concurrere flammis
claro stella die, seu lutea flore sequaci
infelix Clytie, seu mentem semper oberrans
755   forma subit dominae; seu pulchrae gaudia mortis
atque pium tacto iurantem pectore Amorem
atque oculos canis atque manus niveisque capillos
infusos humeris, et verba et lene sonantis
murmur aquae violaeque comas blandumque soporem,
760   laetaque quam dulcis suspiria fundat amaror
quantum addat formae pietas, quam saepe decenter
palleat utque tuum foveat cor pectore nymphe.
Non vacat argutosque sales satyraque bibaces
descriptos memorare senes; non carmina festis
765   excipienda choris, querulasve animantia chordas.
Idem etiam tacitae referens pastoria vitae
otia et urbanos, thyrso exstimulante, labores,
mox fugis in caelum, non ceu per lubrica nisus,
extremamque boni gaudes contingere metam.
770   Quodque alii studiumque vocant durumque laborem,
hic tibi ludus erit: fessus civilibus actis,
huc is, emeritas acuens ad carmina vires.
Felix ingenio, felix, cui pectore tantas
instaurare vices, cui fas tam magna capaci
775   alternare animo et varias ita nectere curas!
     Quod ni blanda meum lactant praesagia sensum,
ni pietas, ni longus amor, ni vana magistros
aura suo nimios iubet indulgere favores
quemque operi, ni me tacita experientia fallit,

side when you called upon her and without your expecting it breathed divine beauty into your song. Therefore, thanks to you, now Galatea does not look harshly at Corinthus,[240] the nocturnal singer. For who does not know of the intense desires and the ardent plaints enkindled by Cupid's fire?[241] Whether it is the star in the bright light of day that dares to rival Phoebus' flames, or whether it be the pale flower,[242] unhappy Clizia, or whether it is the form of your lady, always hovering before your eyes, that suggests itself to you; whether you sing of the joys of a beautiful death and pious Love swearing fidelity, touching your breast, or sing of eyes and hands and tresses streaming down upon snow-white shoulders, and words and the soft murmur of flowing water, the blooms of the violet and sweet slumber and how sweet bitterness brings forth happy sighs, how piety adds to beauty, how often the nymph grows becomingly pale, how she cherishes your heart in her own. There is no time to mention the clever witticisms and the bibulous old men you describe in your satire[243] or the songs to be sung by festive choruses or those that give life to plaintive strings.[244] Recounting the pastoral leisures of a quiet life and the hardships of the city, goaded on by poetic inspiration, soon you will take flight into the heavens, not struggling on a slippery path, and you will rejoice to reach the ultimate goal of the Highest Good.[245] What others call study and hard labor for you will be a diversion; wearied by civic duties you come hither to sharpen your proven poetic powers. You are fortunate to possess such talent, fortunate that your temper permits you to make such a change repeatedly, and to alternate in your soul such great undertakings and in this way interweave such varied tasks.

And if pleasant presentiments do not delude my understanding, if neither devotion nor long love nor vain opinion incline teachers to look too favorably upon their own work, if my silent

780 ibit in exemplum natus, mea maxima cura;
ibit in acta patris, sese tanta indole dignum
praestabit. Lustris nondum tribus ecce peractis,
iam tamen in Latium Graiae monimenta senectae
evocat et dulci detornat carmina plectro;
785 meque per Aoniae sequitur compendia silvae
ereptans avide montem iamque instat anhelo
it iam paene prior. Sic, o sic pergat et ipsum
me superet maiore gradu longeque relinquat
protinus, et dulci potius plaudatur alumno
790 bisque mei victore illo celebrentur honores!

Absoluta est in Faesulano, VIII Idus Octobris MCCCCLXXXVI

experience does not deceive me, your son,[246] my greatest care, will
follow your example; he will follow the achievements of his father,   780
he will show himself worthy of such great talent. Behold, he has
not yet completed fifteen years yet he summons the masterpieces
of Greek antiquity into Latium and moulds poems on his sweet
lyre and follows me through the bypaths of the Aonian wood,
clambering eagerly up the slope, and already he is at my heels,   785
though I am out of breath, and already he is almost passing me.
So may he continue, and may he surpass me with a longer stride
and soon leave me far behind, and may there be louder applause
for my dear pupil, and in his victory may my glory be celebrated
twice over.   790

Completed on the hill of Fiesole, 6 October 1486

Note on the Text

The texts in this volume are based on the excellent critical edition of the *Silvae* (Florence: Olschki, 1996) by Francesco Bausi. For the first three poems, *Manto, Rusticus, Ambra,* he relied mainly on the editions published during Poliziano's lifetime by the Bolognese printer, Francesco Platone de' Benedetti. These reprints incorporated some, but not all variants introduced into the earliest editions and also added new variants. This circumstance suggests that Poliziano himself may have overseen the de' Benedetti editions. The de' Benedetti editions in turn were the basis of the Aldine *Opera omnia* of 1498, edited after Poliziano's death by Pietro Crinito and Alessandro Sarti. Poliziano met Sarti during a visit he made to Bologna, from 4 to 9 June 1491, in the company of Pico della Mirandola, when they stopped there during a trip to visit the libraries of Northern Italy. It is possible that Sarti persuaded de' Benedetti on that occasion to reprint the *Nutricia* since it appeared two weeks later, 21 June 1491, less than a month after the *editio princeps* printed by Miscomini in Florence, on 26 May 1491. In 1492 de' Benedetti reprinted the first three *Silvae* in quick succession: 9 June, 15 June and 22 June, and from that time on became Poliziano's chief printer. In the case of the *Nutricia* Bausi follows the Aldine edition since it has four important corrections, vv. 364, 592, 692–3, 772, which originated in an *errata corrige* included at the end of de' Benedetti's edition of the *Ambra,* all of them involving errors in prosody. These must be attributed either directly to Poliziano or to Sarti at the direction of Poliziano.

I have preferred readings differing from Bausi's in the following verses, where I have reverted to the early editions:

Manto 43: hinc *editio princeps (Firenze: Miscomini, 1482),* Aldus: hic Bausi

Rusticus 310: Veneris *editio princeps (Firenze: Miscomini, 1483):* Venerisque *Aldus,* Bausi

Ambra 255: pro *editio princeps (Firenze: di Lorenzo, 1485):* o Bausi

Nutricia 310: sustulit *editio princeps (Firenze: Miscomini, 1491)*: substulit *Aldus, Bausi*

I have given the original titles as printed in the first editions rather than the abbreviated forms used in Bausi's edition. The marginal annotations in the two editions of the *Nutricia*, which Bausi believes may have been inserted by the author or the editor, have been omitted. The punctuation is much more sparse than that of the critical edition and in some instances supports a different interpretation of the text. A modern spelling has been adopted in order not to distract the reader with the anomalies and oscillations of Renaissance orthography. The confusion in the spelling of proper Greek names has also been alleviated. I have followed Bausi in the use of the spellings *Vergilius* and *Silvae* in the titles for the reasons which he gives, viz., that Poliziano introduced the spelling *Vergilius* in all his writings beginning in 1485, and the spelling *Silvae* appears in the second, corrected editions of the first three poems and in the first edition of the *Nutricia*.

Notes to the Translation

MANTO

1. Lorenzo di Pierfrancesco de' Medici (1462–1507) was the second cousin of Lorenzo the Magnificent. He later sided with the anti-Medici oligarchy.

2. Winged insects of the genus *Ephemera*. Cf. Aristotle, *History of Animals* 5.19.552b.

3. Potted plants that bloomed but for a few days, dedicated to Adonis by worshippers in honor of his brief life.

4. The Argonaut expedition departed from the Thessalian port of Pagasae.

5. Descendants of Minyas, king of Thessaly. Another name for the Argonauts.

6. A centaur, tutor of Achilles.

7. A favorite of Achilles who was later abducted by nymphs.

8. Cognomen of the poet Virgil.

9. Greek goddess of retribution.

10. Aonia was that part of Boeotia in which Mt. Helicon, home of the Muses, was situated.

11. Nestor, king of Pylos, counselor of the Greeks at Troy, famed for his eloquence.

12. Ennius (239–169 BC), often called the father of Roman poetry. He sang of war in his epic poem, the *Annales*.

13. Theocritus (*fl.* early third century BC), Hellenistic pastoral poet, born in Syracuse.

14. The Sirens, who were said to inhabit an island off the shore of Sicily.

15. With reference to Orpheus.

16. Wooded mountain range in Phrygia, center of the worship of Cybele.

17. Muse of epic poetry.

18. Procne and Philomela, the daughters of Pandion, were transformed into a swallow and a nightingale, respectively. Here the reference is probably only to nightingales.

19. A plant with aromatic root said to ward off the evil eye.

20. Prophetess, daughter of Teiresias, who, coupling with the river-god Tiber, gave birth to Ocnus, who founded the city of Mantua. Cf. *Aeneid* 10.198–200.

21. One of the three ancient mythical singers, whose genealogy is variously given. Here he is identified as the son of the first Argive king.

22. Amphion built the walls of Thebes with the sound of his lyre. Tyrian is used for Theban since Cadmus, founder of Thebes, came from the land of Phoenicia.

23. These three cites were the birthplaces of Hesiod, Theocritus (Arethusa is a spring in Syracuse) and Homer, respectively.

24. Most of the poems mentioned here, the so-called *Appendix Vergiliana*, once ascribed to Virgil, are now considered spurious. Poliziano follows the canonical list given in the *Vita Vergili* of Donatus: *Dirae, Culex, Priapea, Catalepton, Aetna, Ciris*.

25. Another name for Priapus, worshipped in Lampsacus in Asia Minor. Poliziano attributes the *Priapea* to Ovid in the *Miscellanea* 1.59.

26. The Cyclopes, smiths of Vulcan. With the plural patronymic *Acmonidas* ("sons of the anvil") Poliziano seems to refer to the other two Cyclopes, Pyracmon and Steropes.

27. Old Greek name for Sicily.

28. A monster who attempted to ascend to heaven. He was struck down by a lightning-bolt of Jupiter and buried under Mt. Etna.

29. Daughter of Nisus, king of Megara, who for love of Minos killed her father by pulling out the purple hair that rendered him invincible. She was turned into a marine bird, the *ciris*, title of the poem in question.

30. Virgil's wealthy patron, C. Cilnius Maecenas. Verse 100 is a clear echo of Horace, *Odes*, 1.1.1, *Maecenas, atavis edite regibus*.

31. Octavian, the future emperor Augustus.

32. Cremona was confiscated by the soldiers of Octavian.

33. A river that empties into the sea near Tarentum, here signified by the Latin adjective *Phalanteus*, i.e., of Phalantus, a Spartan leader under whom the city rose to power.

34. These two paragraphs allude to the main themes of Virgil's *Eclogues*.

35. Poliziano accepts the Christian interpretation of the poem as a prophecy of Christ.

36. A country in the south of Palestine, here standing for Judea.

37. An elderly drunken wood-spirit, the tutor of Bacchus.

38. The river of Mantua.

39. A sea-nymph loved by the Cyclops, Polyphemus.

40. Cornelius Gallus was an elegiac love-poet whose poems are not extant, though several pseudo-Gallan poems were attributed to him in the Renaissance. He was a friend of Virgil and his love themes are the subject of *Eclogue* X. Lycoris was the pseudonym of his beloved Cytheris, a mime-dancer.

41. Poliziano now passes to Virgil's poem on agriculture, the *Georgics*. The new farmers are the veterans of the civil wars to whom land was given in the region of the Po.

42. A young man of Eleusis beloved of Demeter. She gave him a chariot drawn by dragons, in which he flew over the land and gave men the arts of agriculture.

43. A Greek river-god. Hercules tore off one of his horns, which naiads filled with an abundance of flowers and fruit; this was identified in some versions of the myth with the cornucopia.

44. It was believed that at the time of the winter solstice the leaves of the olive tree turned over.

45. The Cinyps was a river in Libya. The surrounding region was famous for its herds of goats.

46. It was an ancient belief that bees were generated from the putrified carcass of an ox (*bougonia*). The story is told in *Georgics* 4.281–314.

47. Reference to the birthplace of Hesiod, who wrote *Works and Days*, a didactic poem on agriculture.

48. These same seven cities, in that order, appear in a poem of Antipater of Sidon in the Planudean Appendix, 296. *Greek Anthology* V, tr. W. R. Paton (New York: Heineman, 1918), p. 337. They all claimed to be the birthplace of Homer.

49. He is identified by Servius (commentary on *Aeneid* 10.198) with Ocnus, founder of Mantua.

50. Mythical king of Troy, father of king Priam.

51. The Greek who tricked the Trojans with his false tale into taking the wooden horse into Troy. Cf. *Aeneid* 2.77–104.

52. Citadel of Troy.

53. Juno, here designated by the patronymic, *Saturnia*, daughter of Saturn, an ancient Roman god, perhaps of Etruscan origin.

54. The *pronuba* was a married woman who conducted the bride to the nuptial chamber.

55. God of marriage.

56. Son of Aeneas.

57. Another name for Italy.

58. Goddess of the rainbow, here depicted with the upside-down horns of a bull, which absorbed the waters of the earth into the clouds.

59. Aeolus, god of the winds.

60. Zancle was the ancient name for Messina.

61. A king of Sicily.

62. Palinurus, having fallen asleep, fell into the sea and drowned.

63. Cumae, home of the Sibyl, founded by Greek colonists from the island of Euboea.

64. The lake of Avernus near Cumae was regarded as the entrance to the underworld.

65. A river of the underworld whose waters conferred oblivion on those who drank of it.

66. A spring on Mt. Parnassus sacred to the Muses.

67. One of the Furies.

68. The temple of Janus, whose doors were open in time of war and closed in time of peace.

69. Aeneas, son of Venus, who was worshipped on the island of Cythera, south of the Peloponnesus.

70. Turnus, leader of the Rutulians, an indigenous people of Latium, whose capital was Ardea.

71. Etruscan chieftain, ally of Turnus. His son Lausus was killed by Aeneas.

72. Camilla, a legendary heroine who fought against Aeneas.

73. The young warrior, Pallas, was killed by Turnus, who is in turn killed by Aeneas in their final duel when Aeneas sees that he is wearing Pallas' baldric.

74. The mythical founder of Pallanteum, later the Palatine hill of Rome. He was the father of Pallas.

75. In a theater in which some verses of Virgil were read the audience rose to its feet and bestowed on the poet, who was present, honors equal to those reserved for the Emperor. The anecdote is told in Tacitus, *Dialogus de oratoribus* 13.2.

76. The embroidered robe placed on the statue of Athena at the Panathenaic festival celebrated every five years at Athens.

77. The hanging gardens of Queen Semiramis in Babylon.

78. The horn altar in the temple of Apollo at Delos was supposed to have been built by the child Apollo with the horns of goats killed by his sister Diana.

79. A mythical rain of gold watered Rhodes, signifying the extraordinary fertility of its soil.

80. The tomb of Mausolus, satrap of Caria, erected by his wife Artemisia at Halicarnassus.

81. The chryselephantine statue of Zeus at Olympia executed by the famous sculptor, Phidias.

82. A city and an island in the western mouth of the Nile.

83. An ancient Roman divinity of high places. The name became an epithet of Jupiter.

84. Caurus was the name of the northwest wind.

85. A sea-goddess, wife of Oceanus; by metonymy the sea.

THE COUNTRYMAN

1. Jacopo di Giovanni Salviati pursued a brilliant political career, becoming counselor to the Medici popes, Leo X and Clement VII. He was the fiancé of Lorenzo's daughter, Lucrezia, whom he would later marry, in 1488.

2. A pastoral figure who appears in the first line of the *Eclogues*, here standing for Virgil himself.

3. This refers to Hesiod's *Works and Days*. Virgil uses the phrase *Ascraeum carmen* at *Georgics* 2.176. The scene represents the solemn investiture of the poet as singer of the countryside.

4. A fabulous mountain range in the extreme north, later identified with the mountains of Scythia.

5. A region of the Arabian peninsula.

6. An old name for Attica.

7. Darius, successor of Achaemenes, founder of the Persian dynasty.

8. Referring to the ancient oaks of Dodona in Chaonia, a region of Epirus in western Greece, where there was an oracle of Zeus.

9. The brightest star of the constellation Boötes.

10. The swallow. Daulis was a city in Phocis, a region of central Greece. Procne, the spouse of the Thracian king Tereus, was turned into a swallow to escape his wrath.

11. A geometrical pattern resembling the five points on the dice cube.

12. Aurora was considered variously as the cousin, sister or daughter of the Titan Pallas.

13. The west wind.

14. Tithonus, the spouse of Aurora.

15. From the city of Idalium on the island of Cyprus, sacred to Venus. In running to aid her beloved Adonis, who was being pursued by Mars, Venus pricked her foot on the thorns of a rose, which from being white took on the color red. Poliziano tells this story at length in the *Miscellanea* I.II. He derived the story from Aphthonius' *Progymnasmata* 2.22.

16. Ajax, son of Telamon, king of Salamis. The hyacinth seemed to have the letters "ai" inscribed on its petals from the first two letters of Ajax, from whose blood the flower originally sprung.

17. The city of Corycus in Cilicia was famed for its saffron.

18. The city of Tyre in Phoenicia was famous for its crimson dye obtained from the murex shellfish.

19. Daughters of Jupiter and Themis, goddess of order and justice, they represent peace and justice.

20. From the union of Eunomia and Jupiter the three Graces were born.

21. Daughter of Ceres, she was abducted by Pluto, god of the underworld, but returned to earth in spring and summer.

22. The goddess of flowers and her husband, Zephyrus. Poliziano re-evoked this same scene in famous verses of the *Stanze per la giostra*: "ove tutto lascivo, drieto a Flora / Zefiro vola e la verde erba infiora," 1.68.7–8.

23. The naiads are nymphs of springs, fountains and rivers, oreads of mountains, Napaean maidens and dryads of woodlands and valleys.

24. A goddess who presides over childbirth, usually identified with Juno or Diana.

25. This description derives from a famous passage of Lucretius, 2.355–366, with admixtures of Virgil.

26. The Corybantes were priests of Cybele who clashed their cymbals in a mad religious frenzy.

27. Precious black marble from caves near the promontory of Taenarus at the southernmost tip of the Peloponnesus.

28. Mauretania was a region of northwest Africa.

29. Celebrated Greek sculptor of the fifth century BC.

30. Prized wool from Miletus, a city of Caria on the southwestern coast of Anatolia.

31. Poliziano relates a myth taken from Pollux's *Onomasticon,* in which Hercules is credited with discovering the original Tyrian purple dye in order to satisfy a young girl who desired this color. See *Miscellanea* 1.12, where he cites this verse.

32. Pergamum, a city in northwestern Asia Minor, which reached the height of its fortunes under the Attalid dynasty. It was famous for it gold-inwoven cloth.

33. A city in Lower Egypt.

34. A Spartan hunting dog.

35. A breed of hunting dog originally from Epirus in western Greece.

36. A Roman god associated with the forest and uncultivated land, usually adorned with a cypress tree in remembrance of his love for Cyparissus.

37. Lecherous old satyrs in the train of Bacchus.

38. Also called Ithyphalluses, well-endowed rustic gods of fecundity.

39. An ancient Italian goddess of flocks and pastures.

40. A city in Thessaly where Apollo grazed the flocks of Admetus as part of a divine punishment.

41. The oil-press.

42. Caria was a country in the southwestern part of Asia Minor, famous for its figs.

43. This fruit has a large cup-shaped "eye" that forms a disk resembling a king's crown.

44. Sicyon was a city in the Peloponnesus near Corinth that was rich in olive trees.

45. Helios was the son of the Titan Hyperion and the Titaness Teia.

46. Amalthea, the goat that suckled Jupiter at his birth, was transformed into the constellation of Capricorn, which brought storms.

47. A poet and singer from Methymnia in Lesbos who was rescued from drowning by a dolphin.

48. Daughters of Atlas and Pleione, transformed into a constellation, whose rising presages rainy weather.

49. A group of five stars in the constellation of Taurus, also believed to bring rainy weather.

50. This passage draws its inspiration from *Georgics* 2.276–286, and Hesiod, *Works and Days* 765–821.

51. A warm, humid wind from the south.

52. The Aeolian Islands off Sicily where Aeolus, the god of winds, dwelt.

53. Iris, the rainbow.

54. The Two Asses, stars on either side of the nebula Praesepe.

55. From the observation of the formations in the flight of cranes he fashioned new letters for the alphabet.

56. The Medici villa on the hill of Fiesole.

57. Florence, so-called from its Etruscan origins. The Etruscans were thought to have come from Lydia, once called Maeonia, in Asia Minor.

58. Greek, Latin and Tuscan.

AMBRA

1. Son of Giovanni Tornabuoni, cousin of Lorenzo de' Medici, a favorite pupil of Poliziano together with Piero de' Medici. After the overthrow of the Medici in 1494 he fought for their return and for this reason was arrested, tried and condemned to death in 1497.

2. The old name of the Medici villa at Poggio a Caiano. Lorenzo had sung of it in his poem of the same name.

3. I.e., Bacchus, who received this epithet from the Greek word for thunder, *bromos*, since at his birth his mother Semele was struck by Jupiter's thunderbolt. Pales is a tutelary deity of Xocks and birds.

4. Homer was said to have been born in Smyrna, a city of Maeonia, or Lydia, in Asia Minor.

5. The magnet or lodestone was discovered in Magnesia and Heraclea, named after Hercules, in Lydia. Plato in the *Ion* (533D-E) said that good poets were drawn by a divine frenzy, and just as the stone at Magnesia attracted iron rings and they in turn attracted others, forming one long chain, so the Muse inspires poets and this inspiration is transferred from one poet to another.

6. Ganymede, cup-bearer of Jupiter, who gave the gods nectar to drink.

7. Muse of history.

8. They were regarded as a pious and devout people who offered rich sacrifices to the gods.

9. One of the most ancient of the gods, born of heaven and earth.

10. Sister and spouse of Oceanus, symbol of the fertility of the sea.

11. The Bistonians were a war-like people of Thrace.

12. Therapne was a village of Laconia near the river Eurotas, where Jupiter transformed himself into a swan to unite with Leda.

13. The goddess Diana, born on the island of Delos.

14. Mercury, born in Arcadia.

15. Cupid. The epithet refers to the promontory on Cyprus where there was a famous temple of Venus.

16. Hercules, descendant of Alceus.

17. The lion of Nemea, a valley in the Argolid near Corinth. Hercules killed him as one of his labors and wore his skin from then on.

18. Pallas Athena wore the helmet of Pluto, which rendered her invisible.

19. One of the Gorgons, who turned all who looked upon her into stone. When Perseus had decapitated her, he gave her head to Athena, who changed the Medusa's hair into serpents and wore Medusa's head on her breast.

20. The twins, Castor and Pollux, transformed into twin stars.

21. Janus as the guardian of the gates of heaven is represented as carrying keys.

22. Ancient Roman god who was represented with woolen bands around his feet, which were loosed during the feast of the Saturnalia. Cf. Erasmus, *Adagia* 1.10.82.

23. Poliziano uses the epithet Mulciber for the god Vulcan. He walked slowly because he was lame.

24. A demigod who stole fire from heaven and gave it to man. Zeus chained him to a rock in the Caucasus.

25. Spouse of Neptune.

26. Sea-nymphs born of Nereus and Doris.

27. Supernatural marine beings usually depicted holding conch-trumpets.

28. Ancient marine deity, born of Gaia and Pontus, father of the Medusa.

29. An old fisherman of Boeotia who became immortal by eating a magic herb, but becoming weary of his old age, jumped into the sea and became a sea-god.

30. Ino, daughter of Cadmus, fleeing from her maddened husband Athamas, plunged into the sea with her son Melicertes and both became marine deities, Leucothea and Palemon.

31. A sea-god able to change shape at will. This aspect of the myth, according to which Proteus neither laughed nor smiled, refers to his sorrow after his two sons were killed by Hercules since they were brigands. Poliziano got this story from Lycophron's *Alexandra* and the scholiast, Joannes Tzetzes, as he mentions in his *Commentario a Stazio,* p. 230.

32. Leader of the Nereids, wife of a mortal, Peleus, and mother of Achilles.

33. A monster who lived in a cave on Mt. Corycus in Cilicia, where his mother, Gaia, had hidden Jupiter's thunderbolt. Poliziano derived this material from the late Greek writer, Nonnus, who dedicated a great part of the first two books of his *Dionysiaca* to the myth of Typhoeus. Thetis took Jupiter's side in the uprising of the giants.

34. Since Fate had predicted that Thetis would give birth to a son mightier than his father, Jupiter renounced marrying her and gave her in marriage to Peleus.

35. Apollo. Virgil recounts at *Aeneid* 6.56–58 that Apollo aided Paris in treacherously killing Achilles. This murder is only vaguely prophesied by Hector in the *Iliad* 22.359.

36. Mountain in Lydia where Niobe turned to stone in her grief after her seven sons and seven daughters were slaughtered by the arrows of Apollo and Diana, and her tears continued to flow.

37. Patroclus, boon companion of Achilles, was born in the city of Opus in Boeotia.

38. Sarpedon, son of Jupiter and Laodamia.

39. Son of Aurora, sister of Pallas Athena. He was slain by Achilles.

40. The three-headed dog that guarded the entrance to the underworld.

41. The Furies.

42. The abode of the blessed after death.

43. The sorceress, Medea, who came from Colchis, a country on the southeast of the Black Sea.

44. A city in Cyprus where Venus was worshipped.

45. Helen, although the offspring of Jupiter and Leda, is often referred to as the putative daughter of Tyndarus. Like her brothers, Castor and Pollux, she was transformed into a star.

46. Achilles, grandson of Aeacus. According to one legend Achilles married Helen on the island of Leuke in the Black Sea.

47. An Ethiopian people who lived near the sources of the Nile.

48. This refers to the constellation of Ursa Major, since the Hypoboreans were thought to inhabit the regions of the far north.

49. Legendary queen of Assyria, said to have founded Babylon.

50. Legend had it that Alexander visited the tomb of Achilles at Sigeum, promontory of Troy, and declared him fortunate to have had a poet like Homer sing of his exploits.

51. A river of India, now the Jhelum, that was rich in precious stones.

52. Goddess of childbirth.

53. Smyrna, situated on the Hermean Gulf. Of the seven cities that claimed to be the birth place of Homer, Poliziano here chooses Smyrna, following the opinion of Aristotle. Cf. *Manto* n. 48.

54. Theseus was a hero of Attic legend, but is here associated with Thessaly (Poliziano uses the adjective *Boibeius* from the name of a lake in Thessaly) probably because of his battles there with centaurs and Amazons.

55. River near Smyrna along whose banks Homer was said to have been born.

56. A maiden from the nearby island of Chios who in her union with a daimon from the chorus of the Muses brought forth Homer. Poliziano credits this rather esoteric information to Aristotle in his *Oratio in expositione Homeri*.

57. The Graces. Eteocles, king of Orchomenos in Boeotia, was the first to establish their cult.

58. A legendary king of Athens.

59. From Hybla, a town on the southern slopes of Mt. Etna.

60. A river of Lydia.

61. The river that empties into the Hermean Gulf near Smyrna.

62. A river in Phrygia famous for its winding course.

63. Calamus, son of the river-god Meander, loved the beautiful boy Carpos, who drowned as they were swimming in the river. Calamus then drowned himself out of desperation. Carpos was turned into a fruit tree and Calamus into a reed. Once again Poliziano derived this little known tale from Nonnus.

64. With particular reference to Orpheus.

65. According to a story recounted by Hermias Alexandrinus in his scholia on Plato's *Phaedrus*, Homer became blind when he contemplated the shade of Achilles, which he invoked at a visit to his tomb in the Troad.

66. This epithet signifies his inspiration by the Muses of Mt.Helicon.

67. Calchas, chief seer of the Greeks at Troy, demands that Agamemnon surrender his prize, Chryseis, daughter of the priest of Apollo.

68. Ulysses silences the wicked tongue of the impertinent Thersites.

69. The eight fledglings plus the mother were interpreted by the priest Calchas as meaning nine years of war and the taking of the city in the tenth year.

70. Menelaus, Helen's husband, and her lover, Paris. In a solemn pact the two armies decided to entrust the outcome of the war to a duel between the two. As Paris was about to succumb, Venus rescued him and carried him off in a cloud.

71. He was king of Argos and one of the Greek heroes in the siege of Troy.

72. Hector and Sarpedon, respectively.

73. When Diomedes faces the Lycian commander, Glaucus, in battle and recognizes that their fathers were bound by ties of hospitality, the two put down their spears and exchange armor, Diomedes receiving the golden armor of Glaucus in exchange for bronze. *Iliad* 6.212–236.

74. Hecuba, wife of King Priam, together with the Trojan women, offers the peplum to Athena in supplication.

75. Andromache, wife of Hector,

76. Astyanax, son of Hector, whose fate was the subject of a short epic by the neo-Latin poet Maffeo Vegio (1406–1458).

77. Ajax, son of Telamon.

78. A Trojan spy killed by Ulysses.

79. Rhesus, king of Thrace, killed in his sleep by Ulysses and Diomedes. This action takes place in Book Ten of the *Iliad* and Virgil also recounts the episode in the *Aeneid* 1.469–472.

80. Literally, those from Argos, but used as the collective designation of the Greeks in the Trojan war.

81. Euphorbus, who was the first to wound Patroclus, asked for his body, but was struck down by Diomedes.

82. Actually the father of Helios but often used by the poets to mean simply the sun.

83. Poseidon confronted Apollo on the battlefield but then withdrew, not daring to fight his father's brother.

84. Diana, daughter of Latona.

85. A spring in Corinth associated with Pegasus and the Muses.

86. A spring in Pieria in the southwest of Macedonia sacred to the Muses.

87. A hunter, son of Poseidon, placed in the heavens together with his dog as a constellation.

88. In later myths Telegonus, the son of Ulysses by Circe, went in search of his father and in his wanderings landed at Ithaca. There, starving, he raided the shepherds, whom Ulysses came to help. Not recognizing his father, Telegonus transfixed him with a javelin armed with the poison of the sting-ray. The story is told in Apollodorus and Hyginus.

89. After the death of Achilles there was a contest between Ajax and Ulysses to have his armor and it was awarded to Ulysses.

90. Inside the wooden horse the Greeks could hear Helen's voice. Anticlon was about to shout out to her but Ulysses closed his mouth with his fist.

91. Pallas Athena destroyed the fleet of Ajax, son of Oileus, and impaled him on a jagged crag because on the night of Troy's fall he assaulted Cassandra, who had sought sanctuary in her temple.

92. A promontory on the island of Euboea, scene of the shipwreck of the Greek fleet.

93. People of southern Thrace, friends of the Trojans, whose city Ulysses sacked.

94. They lived on the coast of North Africa.

95. Aeolus, god of the winds, gave the bag of winds to the companions of Ulysses, but they opened it, letting loose a great storm.

96. King of the giant Laestrigonians, who hurled huge stones down on the Greeks.

97. The goblets contained a magic filter which turned Ulysses' men into pigs.

98. They lived in utter darkness.

99. Tiresias.

100. Spirits of the dead to whom Ulysses made sacrifice in order to descend to the underworld.

101. Two half-human sea monsters who guarded the Straits of Messina.

102. Daughter of Helios. She complained to her father that her herds of cows had been slaughtered.

103. The name given to Ino (see above, note 30) on becoming a sea-goddess. She showed kindness to Ulysses.

104. Island of the Phaeacians. Homer called it Scheria but it soon came to be identified with Corcyra, the modern Corfú.

105. Alcinoos, king of the Phaeacians, had Ulysses returned to Ithaca in one of his own ships, which on its return was changed into a mountain.

106. The Bessians were a people of Thrace. All of these places were famous for the extraction of precious metals, gold and silver.

107. The 'engendering seeds' of line 519 and the 'immense intelligence' controlling the elements, as well as other elements of this Homeric cosmology, are possibly allusions to the doctrine of Anaxagoras (c. 500–c. 428 BC), which Poliziano would have known from Diogenes Laertius.

108. The immortality of the soul was a Pythagorean and Platonic concept central to the philosophy of Poliziano's colleague Marsilio Ficino. Here Poliziano alludes to the proverbial similarity between the two Greek words *soma*, body, and *sema*, tomb.

109. Followers of Pythagoras, who imposed five years of silence upon his disciples. The Pythagoreans believed in reincarnation and the ability to recollect one's previous lives, doctrines alluded to here.

110. Poliziano alludes to the doctrine of the tripartite soul, found in Plato's *Republic* and later philosophers, according to which the rational faculty is located in the head, the passions in the breast, and the appetites in the lower organs.

111. God of healing.

112. Famous Greek painter of the fourth century BC.

113. Phidias, famous Athenian sculptor of the fifth century BC.

114. King Ptolemy II Philadelphus of Egypt, a great admirer of Homer, punished with death the rhetor Zoilus, a native of Thrace, nicknamed *Homeromastix* ("scourge of Homer") for having dared to critize the Homeric poems.

115. Alexander the Great.

116. Name of a stream that flowed near the property of the villa of Poggio a Caiano. Lorenzo de' Medici in his poem of the same name converted the stream into the nymph, Ambra, with whom the river-god Ombrone falls in love. She flees his embraces and is turned into a rock by Diana, the origin of the hill on which the villa was perched. Poliziano makes Ambra the daughter of the Ombrone.

117. Virgil speaks of the excellence of various herds of animals in Tarentum, *Georgics* 2.195–197.

118. It is not known to what animals Poliziano is referring. Lorenzo received a gift of exotic animals from the sultan of Egypt in 1487, thus later than the publication of this poem.

119. Poliziano uses the adjectival form of the name of Antenor, a Trojan prince, reputed founder of Padua.

120. The Timavo is a tiny river of Venezia Giulia that empties into the Gulf of Trieste, but was often used to indicate Padua.

121. The sacred geese of Juno in her temple on the Capitoline warned the Romans by their cackling of the Gauls' attack on the city in 390 BC.

NUTRICIA

1. Antoniotto Gentili (1441–1507) was created bishop of Ventimiglia by Sixtus IV, was a datary cardinal of Orense in Spain, and in general an influential person at the papal court. He did not seem especially pleased with the dedication of the book to him, as we learn in a letter of his to Poliziano of 30 June 1491.

2. *Nutricia* were the fees prescribed by law to be made to wet-nurses. In this case Poliziano acknowledges his debt to poetry, which nurtured him.

3. A poem of Statius, *Silvae* 1.4, in thanksgiving for the recuperation of Rutilius Gallus. *Soteria* means "deliverance" in Greek.

4. Poliziano had ambitions to succeed Giovanni Lorenzi as librarian of the Vatican. He dedicated an ode and the translation of Herodian to the pontiff Innocent VIII.

5. The nurse of Aeneas. The Roman hero named the port of Caieta, now the city of Gaeta, after her. See *Aeneid* 7.1–4.

6. Ancient Roman deity, often identified with Romulus, worshipped on the Quirinal hill in Rome.

7. Priests who took part in the feast of Lupercalia, February 15th, in honor of the she-wolf who nourished Romulus and Remus.

8. The Hyades, nymphs of Dodona in Epirus, who were nurses of Bacchus. They were transformed by him into the constellation that bears their name.

9. The constellation of Taurus recalled the abduction of Europa, daughter of Agenor, by Jupiter in the guise of a bull.

10. The she-goat who nourished Jupiter on Mt. Ida belonged to the nymph Amalthea, native of Olenus in Aetolia. In other versions Amalthea is the name of the goat herself (see *Rusticus*, note 46).

11. A staff tipped with a pine cone or ivy carried by Bacchus and his followers.

12. This section on the primitive life of man and the civilizing force of poetry owes much to the fifth book of Lucretius' poem *On the Nature of Things* and also to Cicero's *De inventione* 1.2.

13. The male spirit of a *gens* existing in the head of the family and subsequently the tutelary or attendant spirit allotted to every person at his birth.

14. One of the Furies.

15. The god of the underworld, another name for Pluto or Dis.

16. This scene is described in Hesiod's *Theogony* 36–53.

17. This description of the harmony of the heavenly bodies depends once more on Lucretius and various Platonic and Neoplatonic texts, including *Epistola* 1.6 of Marsilio Ficino entitled *De divino furore*, and in particular Cicero's *Dream of Scipio* 18–19.

18. This detail comes from Macrobius' *Commentary on the Dream of Scipio* 2.3.1.

19. Cry of the Bacchantes, symbolic of the ecstatic frenzy.

20. Site of the Sibyl at Cumae, a city near Naples founded by colonists from Chalcis, chief city of Euboea.

21. Situated in Thessaly.

22. The first cataract at Assuan.

23. See *Ambra* note 5.

24. The spring of Hippocrene and the river Permessus on Mt. Helicon, sacred to the Muses. For the phrase *Heliconia Tempe* see Ovid, *Amores* 1.1.15.

25. This story about the satyr is told in an essay of Plutarch, "How to Profit from One's Enemies," *Moralia* 86E-F.

26. Her oracle was on Mt. Parnassus.

27. Jupiter sent two eagles from east and west to the center of the earth and they met at Delphi. Cf. Plutarch, *On the Delphic Oracle* 1.

28. Dodona in Epirus was the seat of an oracle of Jupiter. The prophetic responses were given through the rustling of the leaves of the ancient oaks.

29. There was a famous oracle at Ammon in the Libyan desert, where there was a statue of an Egyptian god with ram's horns, which was identified with Jupiter.

30. There was an oracle of Pan in Arcadia, whose ancient mythical king was called Lycaon.

31. Referring to Delphi.

32. So-called because of the kiss Branchus was permitted to give to Apollo (hence Philesian, from the Greek word to kiss). The temple was located in Didyme near Miletus in Asia Minor.

33. The Latin god Faunus pronounced his oracles at night in the woods of Latium to the Latin chieftains, who lay on the skins of the animals they had sacrificed to him. Virgil recounts the custom in the *Aeneid* 7.81–103.

34. Poliziano lists eleven Sibyls, relying on various sources, including Pausanias, Plutarch, Clement of Alexandria and the Suda among others. To mention a few of the undisputed ones: Sabbe is identified as a Hebrew Sibyl; Carmenta was the mother of king Evander and her oracles are recorded in the *Aeneid* 8.339–341; Manto exercised the art of divination at Delphi; Phemonoe, daughter of Apollo, was the first Pythian prophetess; Deiphobe is identified by Poliziano as the Cumaean Sibyl, following *Aeneid* 6.35–36.

35. The Marcian brothers are mentioned by Livy 25.12.2, and Cicero, *De divinatione* 1.89. Servius, commenting on *Aeneid* 6.70, says that their oracles were preserved with the Sibylline books.

36. A certain Bacis of Boeotia is mentioned by Pausanias 10.12.11 and Cicero, *De divinatione* 1.34 as being divinely possessed.

37. The first priest of Apollo at Delphi according to Pausanias 10.5.7–8.

38. The most probable candidate for this figure seems to be a personage mentioned by Pausanias just before Bacis in the same passage quoted above, although the name there is Lyco, not Lichas. There is mention of a Lichas in Herodotus 1.67–68, but he is a Spartan, not an Athenian. He found the bones of Orestes at Tegea through the help of the Pythian priestess.

39. Two black doves from Egypt endowed with human voices indicated the location of the oracles of Jupiter at Ammon and Dodona.

40. A seer of Argos, son of Apollo, who took part in the expedition of the Argonauts.

41. Mopsus, a famous diviner who also accompanied the Argonauts. The two, Idmon and Mopsus, are often mentioned together in Valerius Flaccus' poem, *Argonautica*, with which Poliziano was very familiar.

42. Another famous soothsayer and healer who understood the language of birds. He figures in Statius' *Thebaid*.

43. Tiresias, the blind prophet of Thebes.

44. The seer referred to in this allusion is Amphiaraus, who did not want to participate in the expedition of the Seven against Thebes, foreseeing his death. His wife, Eryphile, bribed by the gift of a necklace, persuaded him to do so. In the course of the battle he was struck by a thunderbolt and disappeared into a hole that opened up in the earth

45. Polyidus, descendant of Melampus, saved the child Glaucus.

46. Zoroaster. Poliziano probably got this information from the *Suda*, an historical encyclopaedia compiled about the end of the tenth century.

47. The Latin word *bidental* signifies a place struck by lightning, which became a *templum*, or sacred enclosure. The word comes from *bidens*, an animal, usually a sheep, with two permanent teeth, which was sacrificed in the place where lightning struck.

48. With reference to the *Canticle of Canticles*.

49. When Moses came down from Mt. Sinai with the two tablets of the covenant, his face shone because he had been talking to God. *Exodus* 34:29–35.

50. The song of Moses is in *Exodus* 15:1–18.

51. The story of the three young men in the fiery furnace, Shadrach, Mischach and Abednego, who refused to worship the golden statue that king Nebuchadnezzar had set up. They sang a hymn to God and escaped unharmed. *Daniel* 3:1–97

52. I.e., other musical prophets mentioned in the Hebrew Bible.

53. I.e., they sang of the phases of the Moon. Delia is Diana, the goddess identified with the moon.

54. The chief river of Thrace, now called the Maritza.

55. This story is told in Lucian, *Against the Ignorant Book-Collector*, 12, in *Lucian*, vol. 3 (Cambridge: Harvard University Press, 1960), p. 191.

56. Plutarch relates in his *Life of Alexander* 14.5 that as he was setting out on his expedition to Persia, the statue of Orpheus at Libethra in Thracia sweat profusely.

57. A mythical poet, disciple of Orpheus.

58. Hercules is given this patronymic from his natural father although he was born of Jupiter.

59. Arion, from the city of Methymna in Lesbos. He was captured by sailors and thrown into the sea but saved through the intervention of Apollo by a dolphin that carried him safely to shore.

60. A Thracian bard who was deprived of his musical ability and his sight by the Muses for boasting that he could excel them.

61. A legendary musician, son of Apollo (hence the adjective *Cirrhaeus*, from a town near Delphi). He came in second to Chrysothemis in a competition in honor of Apollo.

62. Bard of the *Odyssey*, who lived in the town but was often summoned to sing for the Phaeacian rulers.

63. "You" is Phemius, the court poet of Ithaca, mentioned in the Odyssey.

64. This refers to Momus, a legendary arch-critic who, since he could find nothing else to criticize in Venus, complained that her sandals squeaked when she walked. See the eponymus novel of Leon Battista Alberti, in this series (ITRL vol. 8, ed. Sarah Knight and Virginia Brown, Cambridge, Mass., 2003).

65. Referring to the city of Thebes, founded by Cadmus.

66. Antimachus (*fl.* 400 BC), wrote a *Thebais* in thirty-four books, of which almost nothing remains, and a narrative elegy in two books composed after the death of Lyde, either his wife or mistress.

67. The poet Publius Papinius Statius (born *ca.* AD 45, died before 96).

68. The *Achilleid*, which remained incomplete.

69. According to an anecdote narrated by Cicero, *Brutus* 51.191, all the listeners departed from his recitation except Plato.

70. Statius tells us in *Silvae* 4.2.66–67 that he was awarded a golden crown by the emperor Domitian.

71. When Pallas Athena built the Argo she incorporated into the center of the keel planks made from the oaks of Dodona so that the ship was endowed with the voice of prophecy. Cf. Apollonius of Rhodes, *Argonautica* 1.524–527.

72. Myscelus, an obscure poet, called the Croton Orpheus, after the city he founded, according to Ovid, *Metamorphoses* 15.12–59. He wrote an *Argonautica*.

73. Apollonius of Rhodes (third century BC), a poet of major importance, was born in Alexandria but transferred to Rhodes after the cool reception given to his poem and because of the enmity of Callimachus.

74. Terentius Varro Atacinus (born *ca.* 80 BC), from Gallia Narbonensis near the river Atax, tributary of the Aude. He wrote an *Argonautica* in imitation of Apollonius.

75. Lucilius (180–102 BC), an early Roman satirist.

76. Valerius Flaccus (died *ca.* AD 92), composed an *Argonautica* in eight books, left incomplete probably because of his early death.

77. Hesiod, born in Ascra on the slopes of Mt. Helicon.

78. Daedalus gave this advice to his son Icarus in Ovid, *Metamorphoses* 8.203–204.

79. Quintilian, *Institutiones oratoriae* 10.1.52, described Hesiod as an example of the middle style. The investiture by the Muses is narrated by the poet himself in *Theogony* 22–34.

80. His works are listed in this order: *Theogony, The Teachings of Chiron, Works and Days, The Shield of Heracles, The Catalogue of Women.*

81. Hesiod mentions the poetic contest at Chalcis in *Works and Days* 654–659. In The *Contest of Homer and Hesiod*, a text of about twelve pages dating from the age of Hadrian, each poet recites beautiful passages from his works. Homer receives the applause of the crowd for his battle scenes but the prize is awarded to Hesiod as a poet more useful to society. The account of his death is contained in this poem while the other details are found in Plutarch and Pausanias.

82. An ancient marginal note to Hesiod says that he defeated Homer in this contest.

83. Pisander (seventh or sixth century BC) was born in the town of Camirus on the island of Rhodes. He was the first to organize the exploits of the hero.

84. Panyassis of Halicarnassus (fifth century BC) wrote a poem on the twelve labors of Hercules. There is no record of his having written a poem on primal chaos.

85. Euphorion (third century BC) of Chalcis wrote about the myths and ancient traditions of Attica, once called Mopsopsia.

86. Spartan poet of the mid-seventh century BC who wrote elegies and martial songs.

87. Parthenius of Nicaea, born in the first century BC, taken to Rome as a prisoner and subsequently freed, was a friend of the elegiac poet Cornelius Gallus and of Virgil. His *Erotika pathemata*, a collection of prose summaries of esoteric love stories, survives.

88. Aratus of Soli in Cilicia (*ca.* 315–240 BC) wrote the astronomical poem, *Phaenomena*. It was very popular in antiquity and was translated by Cicero.

89. Nicander wrote a poem on serpent-bites, the *Theriaca*, and one on the antidotes to poisons, the *Alexipharmaca*, another on predicting the progress of maladies, the *Prognostica*, based on Hippocrates, and a poem on farming, the *Georgica*. Paean's (or Apollo's) science is medicine.

90. Oppian of Cilicia (late second century BC) wrote a poem on hunting, *Cynegetica*; on fowling, *Ixeutica*; and on fishing, *Halieutica*. According to a life of Oppian prefixed to his works, the emperor Antoninus Pius paid him a gold coin for every verse he wrote. Perhaps hoping for a similar reward, the *Halieutica* was translated by Poliziano's contemporary, Lorenzo Lippi da Colle, who dedicated the work to Lorenzo de'Medici.

91. Dionysius Periegetes (second century AD) wrote a poem on the geographical description of the inhabited world in 1185 hexameters.

92. Nonnus of Panopolis (fifth century AD) was the author of the *Dionysiaca*, a huge epic poem of 25,000 verses on the life and exploits of the god Bacchus. Poliziano had access to this work in MS Plut. XXXII 16 in the Medici library and, as Alessandro Perosa observes, was responsible for its re-discovery and diffusion in the Renaissance.

93. Poliziano here refers to Callimachus by his patronymic Battiades, descendant of Battus, mythical founder of Cyrene, where he was born. He

was court poet under Ptolemy II of Alexandria (*fl.* 285–246 BC) and literary arbiter of the Hellenistic period. He is credited in the ancient sources with more than 800 books. Poliziano lists his major works: the short epic, *Hecale*, named after Theseus' nurse and narrating the hero's combat with the bull of Marathon, and the *Aitia*, a learned poem on the etiology of myths.

94. I.e., comedy.

95. The poet of Sulmona, a city in the modern region of Abruzzi, is Publius Ovidius Naso (43BC-AD 17). He died in exile in Tomi on the Black Sea among the Getans, a Thracian tribe. Ovid was suspected of having been amorously involved with Julia, daughter of the emperor Augustus. Poliziano briefly enumerates his works in this order: the *Metamorphoses*, *Amores*, *Ars amandi*, *Remedia amoris*, *Ibis*, *Heroides*, *Tristia* and the *Epistulae ex Ponto*, *Fasti*, *Halieutica* (probably not by Ovid); a lost poem entitled *Phaenomena*; a book of epigrams no longer extant; *Medea*, a tragedy, also lost; and short compositions against bad poets, not extant.

96. Quintilian, 10.1.88, says of him that he was too much in love with his own genius (*nimis amator ingenii sui*).

97. This judgment was made of him by Seneca the Elder, *Controversiae* 2.2.12.

98. Ennius is credited with saying this of himself in Gellius, *Attic Nights* 17.17.1, which he attributes to the fact that he spoke three languages: Greek, Latin and Oscan.

99. At the beginning of the *Annales* Ennius narrates that the soul of Homer transmigrated into his body.

100. The *Annales*, in which he narrates the history of early Rome.

101. Poliziano repeats here the judgment expressed by Ovid: "Ennius ingenio maximus, arte rudis," *Tristia* 2.424.

102. A town near the modern city of Lecce in what is now called Apulia, corresponding to the ancient Calabria. Ennius took part in the second Punic War, fighting in Sardinia in 204 BC, whence he was called to Rome by Cato the Elder.

103. In 189 Ennius fought in the war with Aetolia under the command of Marcus Fulvius Nobilior, who wanted him to sing of his conquest of Ambracia.

104. There is no record of Ennius possessing an estate in Calabria (present-day Apulia). Poliziano is here paraphrasing a distich of Ovid (*Ars amatoria* 3,409–410), which in the manuscripts and incunabula read: "*Ennius emeruit Calabris in montibus hortos / contiguos paene, Scipio, magne, tuis,*" and so they are cited by Poliziano in his commentary on Statius. The humanist, Aulo Giano Parrasio, made a brilliant emendation of these lines, accepted in all modern editions, substituting "*ortus*" for "*hortos,*" and *contiguus poni*" for "*contiguos paene,*" which then gives complete sense, that from his humble origins in Calabria Ennius merited to be buried near the tomb of the Scipios. Rather than for his bravery perhaps it was for his panegyric poem *Scipio* that he was given this honor.

105. According to tradition Ennius was buried in the tomb of the Scipios, the remains of which can still be seen on the Via Appia. Cf. Cicero, *Pro Archia* 9.22. 101. This was Ennius' own epitaph, as quoted in Cicero, *Tusculan Disputations* 1.15.34 and 1.49.17.

106. Of Ennius' tragedies we possess twenty titles and some fragments, of his comedies only two titles. Ancient sources speak of four or six books of satires and the *Euhemerus,* a prose work on the origins of the gods modeled on the Greek work of Euhemerus of Messene.

107. Cf. Cicero, *Brutus* 19. 75–76.

108. Ibid., 18.71, lines of Ennius which Poliziano understands as referring to Naevius.

109. Donatus Auctus, *Vita Vergilii* 71.

110. Usually believed to be the wife of Caecilius Metellus, whom she is said to have poisoned. Catullus uses the pseudonym Lesbia for her in his love lyrics.

111. *Carmen LXIV* of Catullus is a learned short epic on the wedding of Peleus and Thetis, in which the Fates prophesy the birth of Achilles.

112. The expression is taken from Horace, *Satires* 1.10.3–4, who thus describes the satiric poet, Lucilius.

113. Like Catullus a native of Verona, Aemilius Macer (d. 16 BC) wrote brief didactic poems on birds, serpents and herbs.

114. Titus Lucretius Carus (d. 55 BC), author of the *De rerum natura*, an epic poem on the Epicurean view of the universe. The story of the love philter and his suicide is told by Jerome in his *Chronicon*.

115. Cicero referred to Lucretius but once, remarking to his brother Quintus in a letter that his poems contained many flashes of genius, but also the signs of great literary art, *Ad Quintum fratrem* 2.9.3. In the passage cited above Jerome says that Cicero emended the poem.

116. Empedocles (*ca.* 492–432 BC), a philosopher from Acragas (now Agrigento), wrote a poem *On Nature*. The bronze boots were called *amyclae* from the city of that name in Laconia, where they were made.

117. The philosopher Heraclitus (*fl. ca.*500 BC) was wont to weep over the foibles of mankind and was given the nickname *skoteinos,* "shadowy."

118. This is the poet Lucan (AD 39–65), born in Córdoba. Poliziano lists early works of Lucan, no longer extant, as given in the *Vita Lucani* of Vacca and mentioned also in Statius' *Genethliacon Lucani* (*Silvae* 2.7): the *Iliacon*, on the death of Hector; the *Catachthonion*, a poem on the descent to the underworld; a poem in honor of Nero and one on Orpheus; a poem in praise of his wife, Polla Argentaria, epigrams, and declamations.

119. The *Pharsalia*, an epic poem in ten books on the civil war between Caesar and Pompey.

120. The cruel assassination of Pompey, who had fled to Egypt after his defeat at Pharsalus, but was stabbed to death by the henchmen of king Ptolemy XII as soon as he landed.

121. This anecdote is told by Statius, *Silvae* 5.3.63, and by Poliziano in his Latin epigram XXXVII.15.

122. The goddess Nemesis, worshipped in the deme of Rhamnus in Attica, where there was a famous cult statue of her. Lucan was accused of plotting against Nero and was condemned to death.

123. Suetonius, *Life of Nero* 34, tells us that after killing his mother Agrippina, Nero was tormented by her ghost.

124. Silius Italicus (*ca.* AD 26–102) wrote an epic poem, the *Punica*, in seventeen books, on the Second Punic War.

125. The Carthaginians, originally from Sidon in Phoenicia. Livy gave currency to their perfidy in a phrase he used to describe Hannibal, *perfidia plus quam Punica*, "a more than Punic perfidy."

126. Silius wore the purple-bordered toga as consul in AD 68, the year of Nero's death.

127. Caesius Bassus, a friend of the satirist Persius.

128. Cornelius Severus, a friend of Ovid and author of a *Bellum Siculum* on the war in Sicily between Octavian and Sextus Pompeius.

129. Ponticus, a friend of Ovid and Propertius, author of a *Thebaid*.

130. Claudius Claudianus (*ca.* AD 370–404). Canopus is a town in the mouth of the Nile.

131. It was generally believed in the Middle Ages and the Renaissance that Claudian was a Florentine. Filippo Villani in his *Liber de civitatis Florentiae famosis civibus* conjectures that he was either born in Egypt of Florentine parents or born in Florence and moved to Egypt with his father, a merchant. The error no doubt arose from the false interpretation of the proper name Florentinus, a prefect of Milan, to whom Claudian addressed the second book of the *De raptu Proserpinae*. Poliziano merely reports the story without giving credence to it.

132. Claudian's most famous work is the *De raptu Proserpinae*, on the carrying off of Proserina to the underworld by Pluto. The subject of the second work alluded to is his panegyric on the consulship of Stilicho, who was regent for the Emperor Honorius from 395 to 408.

133. Poliziano uses this spelling of his name although the usual spelling is Manilius. He wrote his famous didactic poem, the *Astronomica*, a Stoic hymn to the universe, during the reign of Augustus. He refers to himself as twice a poet, i.e., poet and astronomer, in verses 20 and 22 of his poem.

134. Ovid gives a long list of minor poets in the last of the *Epistulae ex Ponto* 4.16.

135. Valgius Rufus is compared to Homer in the *Panegyricus Messalae*, preserved in the Tibullan corpus but now no longer thought to have been written by Tibullus.

136. Quintilian 10.1.93 described Tibullus as *tersus atque elegans*, but added that there were some who preferred Propertius.

137. Their pseudonyms in the elegies of the two poets were Delia and Cynthia.

138. Cornelius Gallus (born *ca.* 69, died 26 BC), author of four books of love elegies, of which only a few lines remain, although in the Renaissance a number of forgeries circulated under his name. He committed suicide not out of love, but to save himself from ignominy.

139. Licinius Calvus (82–47 BC), orator and poet, author of a grief-filled epicedion over the death of his wife, Quintilia. Several of his fellow poets allude to his smallness of stature. *Tenuis*, here translated as "refined," might also be rendered "unornamented" or even "exiguous," referring to the slightness of his known oeuvre.

140. A poet and scholar born *ca.* 340 BC. His poetry was admired for its learning and high polish. It was said of him that he was so emaciated by his studies of philosophy that he had to put lead weights in his shoes in order not to be blown away.

141. Mimnermus of Smyrna (*fl.* 630 BC), a love poet credited as being the founder of the genre. "What life is there, what pleasure without golden Aphrodite?" is the opening of his most famous poem.

142. Moschus was a native of Syracuse who flourished around the middle of the second century BC and wrote elegant bucolic poetry. Poliziano translated his poem "Runaway Love" into Latin, *Amor fugitivus*.

143. A bucolic poet of the third century BC from Smyrna.

144. Calpurnius Siculus, a poet who flourished during the reign of Nero, composed seven eclogues in the style of Virgil. In Poliziano's time eleven eclogues were attributed to Calpurnius but in 1492 the scholar Taddeo Ugoletti of Parma identified the last four as belonging to Nemesianus, a poet of the third century AD born in Carthage. This explains the absence of Nemesianus in the enumeration.

145. Pindar, born in Thebes in 518 BC, was regarded in antiquity as the greatest of the nine lyric poets of Greece. Poliziano adheres to this canonical listing, but adds Corinna. Pindar is called the swan of Dirce after the fountain of that name near Thebes.

146. The poetess Corinna from Tanagra in Boeotia, perhaps an older contemporary of Pindar. The story of the poetic competition is told by Pausanias 9.22.3 and is recounted by Poliziano in his commentary on Statius, p. 681.

147. Agathocles was Pindar's teacher.

148. Poliziano refers to the four books of epinician odes: *Olympian, Isthmian, Pythian and Nemean*. The source for the story about the Nemean lion being born on the moon is told by Achilles Grammaticus in his commentary on Aratus' *Phaenomena*, which was available to Poliziano in the Medici library.

149. Cirrha is the port of Delphi. The story of this honor bestowed on the poet comes from Pausanias 9.23.3.

150. Concerning the death of Pindar Poliziano combines traditions found in Valerius Maximus 9.12.ext.7, and again in Pausanias 9.23.3.

151. These details are taken from an anonymous *Vita metrica* of the poet. In other sources Alexander the Great spared Pindar's house in his conquest of Thebes, as the Spartans had done before him.

152. Anacreon of Teos, born perhaps about 575 BC, was the original proponent of wine, women and song, although he himself was more attracted to young boys. He lived to the age of 80.

153. Amathus was a city in Cyprus where there was a famous sanctuary of Aphrodite.

154. Poliziano takes the names of these boys from various epigrams of Anacreon in the *Palatine Anthology*. Poliziano seems to have confused Bathyllus with another young boy, Cleoboulus, whom Anacreon insulted one day; but Adrastea, the goddess of revenge, punished him later on by making him fall in love with the boy. The story is in Maximus of Tyre, *Dialexeis* 21.2.

155. The story of Anacreon's death is narrated by Valerius Maximus 9.12.ext.8.

156. Alcaeus of Mytilene (VII-VI century BC), poet of love and war. The name of Lycus comes from a poem of Horace on Alcaeus, *Odes* 1.32.11, but is not found in the fragments of Alcaeus. Cicero mentions the story of the birthmark in *De natura deorum* 1.28.79.

157. Alcaeus, like Sappho, wrote in the Aeolic dialect.

158. Alcaeus took part in the war between the Lesbians and the Athenians for the possession of the promontory of Sigeum in the Troad. During the combat he lost his armor and the Athenians hung it up in the temple of Athena.

159. Greek lyric poet from Himera in Sicily, active *ca.* 600–550 BC, who wrote choral odes on mythical themes in the Doric dialect, interspersed with Homeric diction. He was blinded by Castor and Pollux for having written a poem defaming their sister, Helen, and was restored his sight when he wrote a palinode. His admiration for the tyrant Phalaris is attested in the *Epistles of Phalaris*, now considered apocryphal.

160. Simonides of Ceos (born *ca.*556 BC) is famous for his dirges or threnodies but he wrote in a great variety of genres.

161. Simonides was saved by Castor and Pollux from a building that collapsed by being called away just before the disaster. Cicero tells this story in the *De oratore* 2.352–353.

162. To a man who promised only thanks for a poem he wished to commission Simonides responded that he had two chests, one for thanks, which was always empty, and another for money, which was always full.

163. Phoenix, tyrant of Agrigento, during a war against the Syracusans, had a tower built with stones taken from the tomb of Simonides near Syracuse. From that tower he captured the city.

164. Alcman (seventh century BC) was born in Lydia and taken as a slave to Sparta, where he was later granted citizenship. He died of phtheriasis, infestation of the body with lice.

165. A poet born in Reggio Calabria (sixth century BC) who sang of pederastic love. The story is told that as he was about to be killed by

brigands he foretold that he would be avenged by a crane (*ibyx* in Greek), a bird thought to be the enemy of the pygmies. One of the brigands gave himself away exclaiming "Behold the avengers of Ibycus" when he saw a group of cranes.

166. Bacchylides (sixth-fifth century BC) was born in Iulis on the island of Ceos. He is called the melodious Siren in a poem of the *Palatine Anthology* 9.184.1.

167. Sappho is credited with the invention of the plectrum in the ancient sources.

168. In a story told by Lucian, *Dialogues of the Dead* 19.2, Phaon was made young again for ferrying Venus from the island of Chios to the mainland.

169. Ambracia is a region of southern Epirus opposite the island of Leukas. For love of Phaon Sappho leaped into the sea from the promontory on this island.

170. Two rival schools of poetry, headed by Gorgo and Andromeda, competed with Sappho according to Maximus of Tyre 18.9.

171. Praxilla of Sicyon, Nossis of Locri, Myrtis of Anthedon (who according to tradition was the teacher of both Pindar and Sappho), Anyte of Tegea, Erinna of Telos, who wrote a poem of 300 hexameters entitled *The Distaff*, Myro of Byzantium, Telesilla of Argos (called "fierce" because she fought the Spartans when they attacked her city), Corinna of Tanagra.

172. All the poetesses mentioned here are listed in a poem of the *Palatine Anthology* 9.26, save for Agacles, which seems to be a curious error of Poliziano, who mistook the accusative of the adjective *agaklēs*, meaning "renowned," for a proper noun.

173. Horace (65–8 BC) was born in Venusia (Venosa) in the present-day province of Apulia. He calls himself a bee of Matina, which is a spur of Monte Gargano not far from his birthplace.

174. With reference to Horace's *Satires*, in which he speaks of his predecessor, Lucilius of Sessa Aurunca in Campania, who wrote pungent satires.

175. Persius (AD 34–62) from Volterra, of whom we possess only six notoriously difficult satires.

176. Juvenal (AD *ca.* 50–127) wrote a book of sixteen satires.

177. Archilochus (seventh century BC), born on the island of Paros, was renowned for his mordant satire written in iambic verse. He repeatedly attacked a certain Lycambes, who had renegued on his promise to give one of his daughters in marriage to him. In revenge he wrote scathing verse against the two daughters, both of whom, according to the legend, hanged themselves for shame.

178. A soldier named Calondas, nicknamed "the crow," hence the adjective *nigro*, killed Archilochus in battle, but when he went to Delphi he was expelled from the temple by the priestess of Apollo for having killed such a great poet.

179. Hipponax of Ephesus (sixth century BC) wrote violent poems against the sculptors Bupalus and Athenis, who produced crude statues of him.

180. Bassus, an iambic poet mentioned in Ovid's list, *Tristia* 4.10.47, perhaps identical with Caesius Bassus mentioned above (cf. note 123).

181. Furius Bibaculus from Cremona is recorded by Tacitus as having written lampoons against "the Caesars."

182. The cothurnus or buskin is a kind of thick-soled boot worn by tragic actors on the Greek stage. Tragedies were performed in Athens during the feast of the Dionysia in honor of Dionysus, or Bacchus.

183. Orestes was hounded by the Furies after killing his mother, Clytemnestra. The theme is treated in Aeschylus' *Eumenides*.

184. Atreus was the father of Agamemnon and Menelaus. Sophocles wrote a tragedy of that name, which is not extant.

185. Telephus was wounded by the spear of Achilles and the wound would not heal until Achilles applied some of the rust from his spear to the wound. Both Aeschylus and Euripides wrote tragedies of that name, which are no longer extant.

186. At the birth of Meleager, son of Oeneus and Althea, the Fates predicted that he would live until a log on the hearth was consumed. Althea took it off the fire and extinguished it.

187. Alcmaeon, like Orestes, was pursued by the Furies for having killed his mother, Eriphyle.

188. In the first competitions among the tragic poets the prize was a goat, hence the name tragedy, derived from *tragos*, goat.

189. After the battle of Salamis, two months after the encounter at Thermopylae, Xerxes' fleet was impeded in its flight by the wreckage and cadavers strewn over the sea.

190. Thespis (sixth century BC), the legendary founder of tragedy, was the first to introduce an actor in the performance of the dithyramb.

191. It was a tradition that during the Dionysiac festival in Athens people would hurl abusive jokes from a wagon. Cf. Horace, *Ars poetica* 257. Solon considered the fictions of the poets to be deleterious to the populace.

192. Sophocles' is said to have died of joy upon learning that he had won a poetic contest.

193. Euripides spent the end of his life as guest of king Archelaus in Macedonia. One night, returning home from a banquet, he was attacked and killed by rabid dogs. He was buried in Pella, capital of Macedonia.

194. A group of seven or more Alexandrian tragic poets at the court of Ptolemy II Philadelphus.

195. Varius Rufus, a friend of Virgil and Horace, author of the play *Thyestes*, highly praised by Quintilian 10.1.98.

196. Seneca (AD 4–65), of whom nine tragedies, famous for their macabre qualities, are extant. In the Renaissance it was commonly believed that Seneca the tragedian and Seneca the philosopher were different persons.

197. Accius and Pacuvius are usually paired together as representative of the Roman tragic stage. Pacuvius was born in 220 BC and flourished during the Scipionic age; Accius, known for his linguistic experimentation, was born about fifty years later. Poliziano refers here to a story re-

Key Terms

lated by Aulus Gellius 13.2, according to which, as Accius was reciting his *Atreus* to the elderly Pacuvius, the latter remarked that his style was grand but rather harsh.

198. Pomponius Secundus was a dramatist in the time of Claudius. Besides writing tragedies on Greek subjects he wrote a *fabula praetexta* (a play on a Roman historical subject) about Aeneas.

199. Eupolis, a writer of Old Comedy towards the end of the fifth century. The story of his being thrown into the sea by Alcibiades (son of Clinias), the famous Athenian statesman, for having attacked him in a play, was branded as false by Cicero in a letter to Atticus 6.1.18.

200. Reference to Aristophanes' *The Clouds*, which makes fun of Socrates and the Sophists.

201. He is the third of the writers of Old Comedy mentioned by Horace in *Satires* 1.4.1–2.

202. Greek New Comedy is often described as a comedy of manners. Poliziano describes this genre at length in his commentary on Terence's *Andria*.

203. Philemon (*ca.* 360–263 BC), a writer of New Comedy, is said to have written 97 comedies in his long lifetime.

204. Menander (342-*ca.*-292 BC) is acknowledged as the greatest writer of New Comedy. One complete play, the *Dyscolos*, and many sizeable fragments of his plays were found in papyri during the twentieth century.

205. Athenaeus of Naucratis (*fl.*AD 200) preserved many fragments of these writers in his *Deipnosophistae*, a collection of learned conversations at a series of banquets.

206. Poliziano reports the judgment of Quintilian 10.1.99.

207. I.e., relating to Attica or Athens, given this epithet from Cecrops, first king of Attica.

208. Caecilius Statius (*ca.* 230–168 BC) was the chief Roman dramatist of his day, coming at a point of time between Plautus and Terence.

209. Terence (*ca.* 185–159 BC) wrote six comedies, preserved in their entirety. His plays are marked by a refinement of language and study of

character in contrast to the exuberance of Plautus. His enemies made the accusation that his plays were really written by Hellenizing friends of his, Scipio Aemilianus and Laelius.

210. Plautus (*ca.* 250–184 BC), a native of Sarsina in the modern region of Romagna, was an extremely prolific writer. 130 titles of his plays are recorded. The grammarian Varro remarked that if the Muses wanted to speak Latin it would be in the language of Plautus. *Opici* is Greek for Oscan, an Italic tongue.

211. Afranius (*ca.*160–120 BC) wrote comedies with Roman or Italian settings. A *fabula togata* is a Latin play written on a Roman theme and presented in Roman dress, as opposed to the *fabula palliata*, a play in Greek dress adapted from Greek comedy and translated from the Greek.

212. Volcacius Sedigitus, early first century BC, wrote a history of poets, of which the section on comedies survives. He ranks Caecilius first, Plautus second, and Terence only sixth.

213. Sophron of Syracuse (fifth century BC) wrote mimes in some kind of rhythmic prose, thus Poliziano places him among the poets.

214. Philistio of Nicaea, active at Rome in the first century AD, was supposed to have died from laughter, according to his epitaph in the *Palatine Anthology* 7.155.4.

215. Decimus Laberius (*ca.* 105–43 BC), almost an exact contemporary of Cicero, wrote mimes in imitation of real life that were often crude and grotesque.

216. Publilius Syrus, contemporary and rival of Laberius, was not of free birth, as his cognomen indicates. A selection of *sententiae* or wise sayings was taken from his works as early as the first century AD. There is frequent confusion in the spelling of his name.

217. Sotadic verse was named after the Cretan Sotades of Maronea (fourth-third century BC), author of licentious and satiric poems. Poliziano probably intends a *double entendre* on the word *cinaedus*, which in Greek can mean both "obscene poetry" and "effeminate youth."

218. Marcus Valerius Martialis (Martial) (*ca.* AD 34–104), a native of Bilbilis in Spain, author of twelve books of witty epigrams.

219. Ausonius (*ca.* AD 310–394) was born in Bordeaux and became professor of rhetoric there. He was summoned to teach the emperor Gratian and became consul in the year 379. He is the most famous of the learned poets active in the second half of the fourth century.

220. Hortensius was a famous orator, rival of Cicero. He tried his hand at poetry without notable success.

221. Valerius Cato, born before 90 BC, was the acknowledged head of an avant-garde school of poetry, the neoteric poets, as they styled themselves.

222. Quintus Cornificius, orator and poet, friend of Catullus and Cicero.

223. Aulus Ticidas, contemporary of Catullus, wrote erotic verse, including poems to Perilla.

224. Helvius Cinna, a native of Brescia, friend of Catullus, who gave high praise to his short epic, *Smyrna*, on the incestuous love of Myrrha for her father, Cinyras.

225. Anser is mentioned in the list of erotic poets given by Ovid in the *Tristia* 2.4.35.

226. Diogenes Laertius (third century AD), famous for his *Lives of the Philosophers*, was also the author of a collection of funeral epigrams in various meters, the *Pammetron*.

227. The Greek genre, *silloi*, derived from an adjective meaning squint-eyed, were lampoons directed against philosophers. The most famous collection was that of Timon of Phlius (third century BC).

228. Marcus Terentius Varro (116–27 BC) was the most learned of the Romans according to Quintilian. Among his many writings were Menippean satires, a mixture of prose and verse, on the model of Menippus of Gadara (III century BC).

229. Pratinas of Phlius (a town southwest of Corinth) was the first to introduce wild satyrs on to the stage naked. Cf. Horace, *Ars poetica* 220.

230. Poliziano Latinizes Dante's name into *Aligerum*, i.e., "winged one," and puns on his flying across the Styx.

231. The mountain of Purgatorio in the *Commedia*.

232. *Trionfo dell'Amore*.

233. Boccaccio and his *Decameron*

234. The reference is to Guido Cavalcanti's philosophical *canzoni*, especially the famous *Donna me prega*.

235. Cosimo il Vecchio (1389–1464) and Piero di Cosimo (1416–1469).

236. Probably alluding to the peace concluded on August 11, 1486, through Lorenzo's intervention, between the Pope and the Kingdom of Naples. Poliziano alludes to the phrase *sub umbra Lauri*, "under the shade of the Laurel" (i.e. Lorenzo), commonly used by Lorenzo's clients to refer to his patronage and protection.

237. The so-called *Consiglio dei Cento* in Florence.

238. With reference to the nymph who inspired Lorenzo's bucolic poetry in his retreat in Vallombrosa. He sings to her in his *Apollo e Pan* 100–120.

239. The *Apollo e Pan*, which recounts a poetic contest between the two deities in Pherae, a city in Thessaly.

240. Corinthus is a shepherd, protagonist of Lorenzo's eclogues of that name, who sang of his love for Galatea.

241. The following verses recall the various love themes of Lorenzo's *Comento*.

242. Ovid tells the story of Clytie in *Metamorphoses* 4.256–270. She becomes passionately in love with the Sun but he ignores her love. She turns into a heliotrope and continues to turn lovingly towards him.

243. *I Beoni*. Beone is a colloquial word for "boozer."

244. The *Canzoni a ballo* and *Canti carnascialeschi* of Lorenzo, which were intended to be sung to music.

245. Referring to Lorenzo's poem *De summo bono*, also known as *L'Altercazione*, in which he argues with the shepherd Alfeo, exalting the life of the city over that of the country in the first capitolo, then, with the guidance of the philosopher Marsilio Ficino, ascends to the Highest Good in the remaining five.

246. Piero de' Medici had been Poliziano's pupil from the age of three. The only composition of Piero's remaining to us is his Latin translation of Leonardo Bruni's brief *Constitution of the Florentines,* written in Greek for the Greek visitors to the council of Florence in 1439. It is a very creditable effort for a young boy. No doubt his teacher lent some help.

Bibliography

꧁꧂

Bettinzoli, Attilio. *Daedaleum iter. Studi sulla poesia e la poetica di Angelo Poliziano*. Florence: Olschki, 1995.

Branca, Vittore. *Poliziano e l'umanesimo della parola*. Turin: Einaudi, 1983.

Cesarini Martinelli, Lucia. "De poesi et poetis": Uno schedario sconosciuto di Angelo Poliziano." In R. Cardini, E. Garin, L. Cesarini Martinelli, G. Pascucci, *Tradizione classica e letteratura umanistica: Per Alessandro Perosa*. Rome: Bulzoni, 1985.

Garin, Eugenio. *Prosatori latini del Quattrocento*. Naples-Milan: Ricciardi, 1952.

Godman, Peter. *From Poliziano to Machiavelli*. Princeton: Princeton University Press, 1998.

——. "Poliziano's Poetics and Literary History." *Interpres* 13 (1993) 110–209.

Maïer, Ida. *Ange Politien. La formation d'un poète humaniste (1464–1480)*. Geneva : Droz, 1966.

McLaughlin, Martin. *Literary Imitation in the Italian Renaissance*. Oxford: Clarendon Press, 1995.

Perosa, Alessandro. *Mostra del Poliziano nella Biblioteca Medicea Laurenziana*. Florence: Sansoni, 1955.

——. *Un commento inedito all'Ambra del Poliziano*. Rome: Bulzoni, 1994.

——. *Studi di filologia umanistica / Alessandro Perosa*, a cura di Paolo Viti. Rome: Edizioni di storia e letteratura, 2000.

Poliziano, Angelo. *Commento inedito alle Selve di Stazio*, a cura di Lucia Cesarini Martinelli. Florence: Sansoni, 1978.

——. *Le selve e la strega: prolusioni nello studio fiorentino*, a cura di Isidoro del Lungo. Florence, Sansoni, 1925.

——. *Les silves. Texte traduit et commenté* par Perrine Galand. Paris : Les Belles Lettres, 1987.

——. *Silvae*, a cura di Francesco Bausi. Florence: Olschki, 1996.

Wesseling, A. "Poliziano and Ancient Rhetoric." *Rinascimento* 30 (1990): 191–204.

Index

References are by work and line number: A = *Ambra*; C = *The Country-man*; M = *Manto*; N = *Nutricia*; Pr. = Preface to *Manto*. Ded. = dedicatory letter.

Publication of this volume has been made possible by

The Myron and Sheila Gilmore Publication Fund at I Tatti
The Robert Lehman Endowment Fund
The Jean-François Malle Scholarly Programs and Publications Fund
The Andrew W. Mellon Scholarly Publications Fund
The Craig and Barbara Smyth Fund
for Scholarly Programs and Publications
The Lila Wallace–Reader's Digest Endowment Fund
The Malcolm Wiener Fund for Scholarly Programs and Publications